COMMUNITY, EDUCATIONAL, AND SOCIAL IMPACT PERSPECTIVES

Edited by

Donna Hager Schoeny
Larry E. Decker

UNIVERSITY
PRESS OF
AMERICA

LANHAM • NEW YORK • LONDON

Acknowledgements

Many people put many hours into the preparation of this publication. Julie Estes, project assistant, was especially helpful throughout the project. She was involved from the first project activities to the final preparation of the manuscripts and her competence and editing skills enhanced the quality of the product. Mary Richardson Boo cannot be thanked or praised enough for her advice and the outstanding technical editing she provided. Virginia Decker contributed invaluable editorial assistance and deserves special thanks for her professional judgment and support throughout the project. Edith K. Mosher shared her incomparable experiences, wisdom, and editing skills.

The continuing cooperation and support of the U.S. Department of Education Community Education Program staff, Ron Castaldi, Gene Wilhoit, and Laura Karl were especially helpful in accomplishing the project goals. Ginny Fisher and Pat Roupe put in many patient hours typing, re-typing, and assisting in the proofreading of the drafts of the manuscripts.

A final thank you is extended to all the contributors for their cooperation and enthusiasm for the project.

D. H. S.
L. E. D.

This project was made possible through a Federal grant No. G008104713 from the United States Department of Education. However, the opinions expressed herein do not necessarily reflect the position or policy of the United States Department of Education, and no official endorsement by the United States Department of Education should be inferred.

About the Book

The Mid-Atlantic Center for Community Education at the University of Virginia was awarded a grant from the U. S. Department of Education, Community Education Program, in 1981-82 for a project entitled "The Impacts of Community Education on National Educational and Community Social Issues." The project used an interdisciplinary approach to address the intent of the federal community education legislation, "to further the concept of community education nationally," and "to explore ways community education can ultimately improve education in the nation."

The first project activity was to survey leading educators and policy makers throughout the nation for a rating of community education's actual and potential impact on issues affecting education and to solicit nominations of accomplished writers with expertise in each area. The issue areas addressed were: (1) cost effectiveness/efficiency; (2) educational program of students (examples: achievement, attitudes, vandalism, alternative education); (3) social issues (examples: taxpayer unrest, technology, multicultural concerns, aging population, leisure time); (4) school closings and shifting populations; (5) political processes and citizens participation; and (6) coordination of human services delivery.

The survey identified the writers and reactors and indicated the perceptions of respondents about the extent to which community education has impacted the six major issue areas and its potential for impacting them. Respondents consistently felt that community education has great potential for impact but has not yet realized it. Community education programs were judged to have been most successful to date in addressing use of increased leisure time, use of facilities, and decreasing school vandalism. Respondents identified citizen participation in decision-making, governance, and confidence in schools; human services delivery; and multicultural concerns as the community education areas with the least realized potential.

Primary papers by outside experts were commissioned in each of the major issue areas. For most of the primary papers, two reaction papers were commissioned from writers both inside and outside the field of community education. The major writers and reactors attended a writers' conference in Washington, D.C., on June 9-11, 1982. The interchange at this conference was a stimulating and productive experience. Selected education and general interest press representatives were also invited to attend. The papers presented at the conference were edited and are included in this volume. Additional products from this project include: an executive summary brochure and a 50-minute videotape of the excerpts from the Writers' Conference.

Preface

by
Richard M. Brandt, Dean
School of Education, University of Virginia

What the National Community Education Impact Project produced was not an ordinary conference. It had an ambitious agenda and was intended to serve several purposes. It brought together scholars from a variety of disciplines to focus on the impact of community education on major social and educational issues. We wanted to track the roots and relationships as broadly as we could across the various disciplines. It also was an information-sharing conference, designed to disseminate community education concepts and to suggest actions to a broad constituency of professionals and lay people across the country.

Many of the concepts associated with community education have been around for a long time: citizen involvement, shared facilities, cooperative partnerships on behalf of children, etc. What has been missing is the sharing of these concepts across various disciplines, including education.

This is a time when the support bases for education, for public education in particular, are eroding. According to the fall 1981 Gallup Polls, public schools have indeed lost credibility in the public eye. The barrage of criticism heaped on public education in the last few years has obviously taken its toll. Despite a loss of credibility, however, education is still more highly regarded by lay people than are most other government and many non-government institutions.

Educators are challenged today, as perhaps never before, to restore lost public confidence and to salvage what certainly is the most far reaching, if not the greatest, public education system in the world. In my opinion, community education has a major role to play in restoring that faith and preserving that status. The issues of the conference were indeed critical ones. They must be addressed and resolved satisfactorily. It was the hope of the project staff that the products and outcomes of the National Community Education Impact Project could help move us at least a step toward satisfactory resolution of the social and educational issues that confront us.

CONTENTS

CONTENTS 7

PRINCIPAL AUTHORS

William S. DeJong is the assistant executive director of the Council of Educational Facility Planners, International. He is formerly director of the Center for Community Education Facility Planning, Columbus, Ohio; assistant director of Community Education of the Grand Rapids, Michigan Public Schools; and a community school director and community education teacher coordinator. He is active in many civic and professional organizations. He has published several articles related to planning in education, uses of surplus schools, and energy use in community schools. He received his Ph.D. from the University of Michigan in 1978 with an emphasis in Educational Leadership, Planning, and Community Education.

Philip L. Doughty chairs the program for Instructional Design, Development, and Evaluation at Syracuse University, where he has been a member of the faculty since 1972. His recent projects include design of cost analysis models for educational radio and television, for teacher education, and for military courses; design of a computer-based test development program; development of a training evaluation system for the New York State Department of Education; and evaluation of Special Education Regional Resource Center services for the Department of Education. His consultancies related to community education include the West Virginia College of Graduate Studies, the University of Mid-America, the British Open University, and the Indonesian National Center of Educational Communications and Technology. Dr. Doughty has published numerous reports and articles on the topic of cost-effectiveness analysis.

Amitai Etzioni is the first University Professor of The George Washington University. He was guest scholar at the Brookings Institution in 1978-79 and served as Senior Advisor in the White House in 1979-80. From 1958 to 1978 he was a professor of sociology at Columbia University; during part of that time he was Chairman of the department. He founded the Center for Policy Research, a not-for-profit corporation dedicated to public policy, in 1968 and has been its director since its inception. Dr. Etzioni has consulted for, or provided presentations to, Allied Corporation, Aetna, AT&T, Bethlehem Steel, Bristol-Myers, Quaker Oats, Pfizer, and Prudential. He has consulted widely for government agencies, including the Departments of Health and Human Services, Labor, Commerce, and the Treasury; for the National Science Foundation, the President's Commission on the Causes and Prevention of Violence, and several White House administrations. He is the author of 12 books, including *A Comparative Analysis of Complex Organizations*, *Modern Organizations*, *Political Unification*, *The Active Society*, *Genetic Fix* (nominated for the 1973 National Book Award), *Social Problems*, and, most recently, *An Immodest Agenda* (in press). He has published more than 100 articles in journals and newspapers. Dr. Etzioni's achievements in the social sciences have been acknowledged by several fellowships, including those of the Social Science Research Council (1960-61), The Center for Advanced Study in the Behavioral Sciences (1965-66), and the Guggenheim Foundation (1968-69). Dr. Etzioni's voice is frequently heard in the popular press, including *The New York Times*, *The Washington Post*, and *Psychology Today*, and on network television.

Mario D. Fantini has taught students of all age levels, from elementary to college, including the mentally retarded and the emotionally disturbed. He has served the Ford Foundation in various capacities. He was a professor and dean of the Faculty of Education of the State University of New York at New Paltz, and is currently professor and dean of the School of Education at the University of Massachusetts, Amherst. His consultancies include the United States Office of Education Bureau of Educational Personnel Development, the Institute for Advancement of Urban Education, the Metropolitan Applied Research Corporation, and Select Committee on Equal Opportunities, and the National Committee for Citizens in Education. Dr. Fantini is the author of many articles dealing with various aspects of school reform, parent and student participation, professional development, teaching methods, alternative education, and humanistic education. Among his most important books are *Public Schools of Choice: A Plan for the Reform of American Education* and *Alternative Education: A Source Book for Parents, Teachers, Students, and Administrators.*

Dwayne Gardner is the executive director of the Council of Educational Facility Planners, International, and adjunct associate professor at Ohio State University. The Council of Educational Facility Planners, a non-profit organization, assists both public and private agencies with the planning, designing, creating, equipping, and maintaining of the physical environment of educational facilities. Dr. Gardner formerly served in several positions with the U. S. Office of Education and with the State Department of Education in North Carolina and Nebraska. In 1972 he received the Council of Educational Facility Planners "Planner of the Year" award. He is an honorary member of the American Institute of Architects. He is the author or co-author of many publications dealing with planning in the areas of education, school insurance, and facilities for early childhood programs, elementary schools, and secondary schools.

Samuel Halperin is a widely known and respected commentator on the politics of education in the United States. He earned his Ph.D. in political science and taught at several universities before going to Capitol Hill as a member of the professional staffs of congressional committees on education. He later was named Assistant U. S. Commissioner of Education for Legislation and Congressional Relations and served in the U. S. Department of Health, Education and Welfare as Deputy Assistant Secretary for Legislation. He won two Superior Service awards and the Distinguished Service Award for his work in government. Dr. Halperin has been with the Institute for Educational Leadership, Washington, D.C., since 1969. He served as the Institute's director from 1974 to 1981, and as its first president (1980-81). He has published and lectured widely on the professional development of educational policymakers. He currently serves on the U. S. Peace Corps Advisory Council and the Secretary of the Navy's Advisory Board on Education and Training.

Laurence Iannaccone is a professor in the confluent education program of the graduate school of education, University of California, Santa Barbara. He has served on the faculties of the University of Toronto, Harvard University, Claremont Graduate School, Washington University, and New York University. He is the former editor of the *Review of Educational Research* and was the 1980 recipient of the Cooperative Professor of the Year Award of the American Association of School Administrators. His many books include *Education Policy Systems: Guide for Educational Administrators, Politics in Education, The Politics of Education* (co-authored with Peter Cistone), and *Public Participation in Local School Districts: The Dissatisfaction Theory of Democracy* (co-authored with Frank Lutz). Dr. Iannaccone is former acting dean and chairperson of the Department of Education at the University of California, Santa Barbara. He has made many presentations to national groups on various political aspects of education and served as a consultant to state departments of education, national committees, universities, schools, and private industry.

Vasil M. Kerensky is a Mott Professor and director of the Center for Community Education Development at Florida Atlantic University, Boca Raton. He studied at Central Michigan University, the University of Michigan, and Wayne State University, where he received his doctorate as a Mott Fellow in 1964. He has been a teacher, high school principal, assistant school superintendent, and college professor. In 1979 he was appointed by Governor Bob Graham of Florida to chair the Governor's Task Force on Community Schools. Dr. Kerensky has published many articles on the relationship between schools and their communities and is the co-author, with Ernest O. Melby, of *Education II—The Social Imperative*.

Edith K. Mosher is a specialist in the politics of education. She received a Ph.D. in educational administration from the University of California, Berkeley, in 1967. She has had administrative experience in the federal government and was formerly on the staff of the Far West Laboratory for Educational Research and Development. Dr. Mosher is co-author, with Stephen K. Bailey, of *ESEA: The Office of Education Administers a Law* and recently contributed chapters on intergovernmental relations in education to two books: the 1977 Yearbook of the National Society for the Study of Education, *Politics of Education*; and *Understanding School Boards*, the report of a research symposium of the National School Boards Association. She is co-editor with Jennings Wagoner of *The Changing Politics of Education*. She contributed to the 1982 edition of the *Encyclopedia of Education Research*, sponsored by AERA "The Federal Influence on Education." She recently retired as professor of education, University of Virginia.

William L. Smith was a teacher, counselor, and principal in the Cleveland, Ohio, public schools for 12 years. He has served the U. S. Office and Department of Education for 11 years. He was Acting Deputy Undersecretary for Intergovernmental and Interagency Affairs, Associate Commissioner for Career Education, Director of Teacher Corps, and U. S. Commissioner of Education. Dr. Smith currently serves as Administrator of Special Management Projects, Administrator of Education for Overseas Dependents, and Acting Director of Administrative Resources Management Services. He has received the Phi Delta Kappa Educator of the Year Award, the Association of Teacher Educators Distinguished Leadership Award, and most recently the Presidential Rank Award for Distinguished Senior Executives. He has published extensively in the areas of teacher education and multicultural education. Dr. Smith's international experiences including serving as U. S. delegate to the Organization for Economic Cooperation and Development (OECD), on the working committee for the International Management Training on Educational Change Project, Paris, France; as chairman of the OECD International Conference on In-Service Training and Educational Change, Paris, France; and as official guest of the Polish Minister of Education.

Jule M. Sugarman has served in management positions in many federal and local government agencies over the last 30 years. He was Vice President for Programs and Planning at the U. S. Council for the International Year of Disabled Persons (1981), Deputy Director of the U. S. Office of Personnel Management, vice chairman of the U. S. Civil Service Commission, Director of Project Head Start of the Office of Economic Opportunity, Chief Administrative Officer for the city of Atlanta, Georgia, and Administrator of the Human Resources Administration in New York City. Since July, 1981 he has served as president and managing director of the Human Services Information Center, a private agency dedicated to informing public officials and private citizens of significant changes in human service programs. He also holds the post of executive director of the Day Care Council of America. His most recent publications are *A Citizen's Guide to Changes in Human Service Programs* and *President Reagan's 1982 Proposals: White Paper No. 4.*

Helen R. Wiprud is Special Assistant to William L. Smith in his capacity as Administrator of Education for Overseas Dependents in the U. S. Department of Education. She is also the designated federal official for the Advisory Council on Dependents' Education, established by the Defense Dependents' Education Act of 1978, as amended, to increase participation by the school community in the administration and operation of overseas schools for military dependents. Before joining Dr. Smith, she served the U. S. Office of Education for 12 years in the field of international and intercultural education, primarily undertaking writing and editing assignments and special projects. Among these was the compilation of an inventory of the international education programs of the U. S. Government, a 1980 publication sponsored by the Federal Interagency Committee on Education.

AUTHORS OF REACTION PAPERS

Susan J. Baillie has held several positions at Syracuse University, including, Associate Director of the New York Center for Community Education, Research Associate at the Educational Policy Research Center, and consultant. Dr. Baillie has published articles on schools and social service delivery, educational leave policies, alternatives in education, school use by older adults, and futures intervention.

Sam F. Drew, Jr. is the Deputy Director for Education, Governor's Office, Columbia, South Carolina. His prior experiences include: business, education, as a teacher and principal, and Special Assistant to the U.S. Department of Education, Community Education Program. He was also a Leadership Development Program Fellow (Ford Foundation). He received the National Community Education Association's Outstanding Principal Award.

Sandra T. Gray is the Executive Director of the National School Volunteer Program. She formerly held several high-ranking positions in the U.S. Department of Education, including Special Assistant to the Under Secretary, Assistant Commissioner, and Special Assistant to the Secretary. She received the Outstanding Community Service Award from National Association for the Advancement of Colored People (NAACP).

Larry L. Horyna is the assistant professor and Director of the Oregon Center for Community Education Development at the University of Oregon. He received the Outstanding Service Award of the National Community Education Association and has made national and international presentations on community education.

Sterling S. Keyes is the Coordinator of New York City office of Elementary, Secondary and Continuing Education Services, New York State Education Department. His past positions include Acting Superintendent of Public Instruction and Associate Superintendent of Administration, Finance and Planning for the Baltimore City Public Schools. Dr. Keyes is an active member of several professional organizations and committees including the National Advisory Planning Board for the Simu-School Project and formerly the Freeport, N.Y. Board of Education.

George C. Kliminski is the Director of the Center for Community Education at the University of Wisconsin-Madison. He formerly directed the Center for Community Education at the Kent State University in Ohio. Dr. Kliminski received his doctorate from Western Michigan University. He has published articles in the area of community use of surplus school space.

Floretta Dukes McKenzie is superintendent of the Washington, D. C., public schools. She has held administrative posts in the District of Columbia schools, in Montgomery County, Maryland, and in the Maryland State Department of Education. From 1979 to 1981, she was with the U.S. Department of Education, where she headed the 25-member task force that planned the organization of all federal elementary and secondary programs in the newly legislated Cabinet-level department. She also served as deputy assistant secretary of the Bureau of School Improvement in the Department. McKenzie was the U.S. delegate to the 1980 UNESCO Conference in Belgrade.

Jack D. Minzey is chairman of the Department of Educational Leadership at Eastern Michigan University. He received his doctorate from Michigan State University and has held a variety of teaching and administrative positions in public schools and universities. Dr. Minzey is a past president of the National Community Education Association and a recipient of its Distingushed Service Award. He is the co-author, with Clyde E. LeTarte, of *Community Education: From the Program to Process to Practice,* and many articles on community education.

Everette E. Nance is Director of the Midwest Community Education Development Center and associate professor of education at the University of Missouri-St. Louis. He holds an Ed.D. in education administration and community education from Western Michigan University. He has been a YMCA director, counselor, regional coordinator of community education at Ball State University, and medical technician. He is a past president of the Missouri Community Education Association and currently serves on the National Community Education Association Board of Directors.

Susan C. Paddock is the Director of the Management Development and Training Program at Arizona State University. She is a former Research Associate at the Southwest Center for Community Education Development at Arizona State. Dr. Paddock has extensive experience in grants management and has published several articles in the areas of evaluation, competency-based assessment and training, and cost effectiveness. She is research editor for the *Community Education Journal.*

Steve R. Parson was the first full-time Cooperative Extension specialist with a responsibility for community education development. He has served as a resource consultant in many regions of the country. He has been at Virginia Polytechnic Institute and State University since 1974; his work there has centered on developing effective linkages between Cooperative Extension and community education. Parson received his doctorate from Western Michigan University.

John E. Radig is the Community Education Consultant at the Educational Improvement Center, Sewell, New Jersey and adjunct professor at Glassboro State College. He was formerly the Associate Director of the Center for Community Education Development at Eastern Michigan University. Dr. Radig is the author (with Lippencott) of *Community Leadership/Resource/Problem Identification Process.* He received the first Outstanding Community Educator Award from the Association for Community Education-New Jersey.

David A. Santellanes was the recipient of the National Community Education Association's Distinguished Service Award in 1981. He is the Director of the Community Education Mobile Training Institute, Coordinator of the Northwest Coalition for Community Education Development, and associate professor at the University of Oregon. Dr. Santellanes' publications have addressed evaluation and include *Doing Your Community Education Evaluation.* He has been a consultant for Migrant Programs, Indian Cultural Programs, and Teacher Corps.

Barry F. Semple is the Director of the Bureau of Adult, Continuing, and Community Education for the New Jersey State Department of Education. He is past chairperson of the Community Education Advisory Council of the U.S. Department of Education, past president of the Shrewsburg, New Jersey Board of Education, and past president of the Association for Adult Education of New Jersey. He received his doctorate from Eastern Michigan University.

FOREWORD

FOREWORD

Introduction

Contemporary economic, social, and political pressures are forcing local decision-makers concerned with education and community human services to seek out new approaches that make maximum use of shrinking resources. Increasingly, these decision-makers are showing an interest in community education, a process for involving community residents in the identification of local needs and local resources to meet those needs. Advocates of community education claim that the process, with its emphasis on citizen involvement and the use of existing resources, has the potential to affect many of the issues related to education and human services needs at a time of sharp cutbacks in public fiscal support.

The National Community Education Impact Project, conducted by the University of Virginia, Mid-Atlantic Center for Community Education, and funded by the U.S. Department of Education, Community Education Office, used an interdisciplinary approach to examine community education's potential impact in six issue areas. The project's major activities were:

- Surveying community educators and professionals in related fields to get their perceptions of the potential influence of community education in selected areas of concern.
- Commissioning major papers by experts in each of the areas of concern and reaction papers by persons both in and outside the field of community education.
- Convening the writers and reactors to refine the papers and to serve as a forum for audio and video recording of material suitable for the training needs of educators and other professionals.
- Publishing the papers and commentaries for national distribution to educational, policy-making, and governmental audiences.

Issues Addressed in the Project

The staff drew on the results of relevant research to identify the issues to be addressed in the project. For example, a 1979 study by Richard Remy found that educators judged the following issues to be the major ones affecting schools and communities:

- Loss of public faith in schools.
- Demand for student competency.
- Increased citizen participation in policy-making.
- General economic conditions.
- Declining school enrollment.
- Changes in family structure.
- Decline of a sense of community.
- New demands on education facilities.[1]

In a parallel study, Marian Clasby found that citizens perceived four major issues to be of key importance:

- Declining school enrollment.
- Transitions in family life.
- Fiscal constraints.
- Taxpayer unrest.[2]

These studies and other analyses of current policy problems in education were used to select issues that appeared to be closely related to community education objectives or to have potential for influencing the advancement of those objectives. The issues selected were:

1. The education programs of students.
2. School closings and shifting population patterns.
3. Political processes and citizen participation.
4. Coordination of the delivery human services at the community level.
5. Social issues affecting schools and communities.
6. Efficiency and cost effectiveness in the administration of community education.

Survey Results

The Community Education Impact Survey was mailed in October 1981, to approximately 300 community educators and professionals in related fields. The respondents gave their perceptions of the extent to which community education **has impacted** the issue areas and its **potential** for impacting them. They also identified writers and reactors in each of the six areas. Consistently, the respondents indicated their belief that community education has the potential for a much greater impact than it has yet had. Community education programs were perceived to have been most successful in improving the use of leisure time, increasing facility use, and decreasing school vandalism. In the respondents' judgment, community education has had the least impact in the areas of citizen participation in the political process, especially decision-making, governance, and confidence in schools; service delivery; and multicultural problems.

Questions Posed to Writers

The following statements and questions formed the framework given to the writers of the main papers:

- Schools have gone through many changes and adaptations over the years, and a variety of proposals for their future are being debated. What influence could community education have on the most likely projections for the future?
- Educational authorities in the United States are currently confronting the results of the decline in the school-age population and the geographical redistribution of the population in general. How should these and other demographic trends and projections be considered in educational planning and addressed by community education?

● Citizen participation in public affairs is an increasing phenomenon in education with the advent of block grants, collective bargaining, and changing priorities.

What do educators need to know to act competently and effectively in the political arena?

How can community education benefit from an understanding of the political process?

● The potential for schools' functioning as linking agents through interagency relationships is a key component of community education.

Does community education have as-yet-unidentified roles to play in providing services to local clientele?

What can community education learn from the experiences of other human service agencies?

Is community education still in the neophyte stage or has it advanced significantly?

● A myriad of societal changes have been accompanied by social problems.

How will pressing social issues such as rapid technological change, desegregation, immigration, and changing family structures affect education in general and community education in particular?

How will the shortening of the work week and increased longevity affect schools and communities?

● Proof of cost effectiveness and documentation of the tangible and intangible results of educational and human service programs are becoming requirements for resource allocation.

Can cost-effectiveness approaches in which effectiveness is measured in non-monetary as well as monetary terms allow for comparisons and rankings among potential programs?

What problems can be anticipated in adopting a cost-effective approach in community education?

Recurring Themes

Although each· writer concentrated on a particular topic, certain recurring themes or issues surfaced, some of them not anticipated in the original conceptualization of the project. For example, most of the authors believe that education and social, political, and economic trends are moving in the direction of community education objectives and view community education as a unique process for citizen participation in meeting new societal challenges. Most of the writers view community education as a reform, or change, whose long-range acceptance will depend on coalition building among political entities and agencies.

The writers stress the need to look for leverage points and to be aware of crucial timing. Several papers give examples and strategies for building on community education tenets to become effective political and economic facilitators of educational change. Many papers carry the reminder that change is usually slow and conservative.

Changing family structures, demographic trends, and declining resources are identified as areas in need of attention by community education, particularly in planning and problem solving. Community education is seen as having the potential to offer alternatives in resource management, shared facility use patterns, interagency coordination, and social service delivery.

Advancing technology can potentially affect every facet of education and society. Some authors suggest that community education can help bridge the gap caused by unequal access to advanced information systems and also address the equity needs of culturally diverse immigrants.

The issue of "unequal access" was also raised in relation to a diminished federal role in education. States have various revenue-generating systems and different education priorities, per capita expenditure formulas, curricula, etc. Writers asked where continuity, common values, common learning objectives, comparable fiscal support, and concern for equity for women and minorities will come from and who will ensure their enforcement? Should community education be concerned with these questions? Some authors say "yes" and advocate a federal role for community education. Others suggest that federal legislation is self-limiting that community education must, like civil rights concerns, be all pervasive, infused into every aspect of education, and that community educators' efforts should be directed to "spreading the word," and recruiting new advocates. They caution, however, against presenting community education as a panacea for education problems and social ills, instead of convincing people that the process is a viable approach to problem solving.

The project staff believe the following papers accomplished the objective of presenting challenges and recommendations for the future development of community education. For the reader, the final challenge will be to examine the options with an open mind, and to take them beyond rhetoric to new programs, processes, and practices.

D. H. S.
L. E. D.

NOTES

[1]Richard C. Remy, **The Role of the School in the Community: The Educators Perspectives**, Contract #P00-78-0660, USOE, Washington, D.C., February, 1979.

[2]Miriam Clasby, **The Role of the School in the Community: Community Perspectives**, Contract #41-USC252 (C) (3), USOE, Washington, D.C., July, 1979.

PART I

Educational Programs of Students

PART I: EDUCATIONAL PROGRAMS OF STUDENTS

SUMMARY

Mario D. Fantini presents a series of models through which American public schools have evolved and speculates about the next stage in educational evolution. Education in America began as a community activity, with home, government, church, workplace, and school each performing separate functions in the socialization and education of youth. This "Division of Labor" model of community education is the first educational model discussed by Fantini. The second model, termed by Fantini the "Delegation of Labor" model, has its roots in the industrialization of the 19th and early 20th centuries, when schools assumed some of the roles previously played by other community institutions. The idea of the "comprehensive school" was developed during this time.

Our schools have now entered the third, or "Coordination of Labor," model. Economic pressures and parents' desire to regain some authority over their children's education have combined to bring about a reassessment of the role of the school. The realization that the school cannot "do it all" has led to reductions in curriculum and an attempt to concentrate effort on what the school can do most successfully. The "back to basics" movement is a facet of this third model. Delegation of some educational services back to other community agencies and institutions is another. Schools are beginning to incorporate the idea of individualized education programs for increasing numbers of more students through flexible organization, the matching of teaching and learning styles, and the attempt to provide options and choices for learners.

Fantini sees movement toward a fourth model of community education, in which all educators are "community educators," devising, facilitating, and coordinating an individual education plan for each learner. In this model, each child could be offered an education appropriate to his own special abilities and talents, often outside the school building. Other community agencies and individuals and advance video and computer technology would take over a portion of the school's service delivery function.

Floretta McKenzie cites an effort currently underway in the District of Columbia as an example of Fantini's fourth model. The D. C. schools have gone beyond the traditional sources of cultural enrichment and learning to develop public-private partnerships to co-develop five career high schools.

McKenzie warns that Fantini's fourth model, characterized by self-directed, technology-assisted learning, with educators as facilitators, will face several obstacles. There are several prerequisites to such a model, she writes:

- Applications of technology to education must be developed and improved.
- Teacher training must be revamped.

- The view that the community, rather than the classroom, is the primary learning environment must be accepted.
- Careful long-range planning and anticipation of future educational needs must be undertaken.
- There must be alternate measures of educational success.
- Children must be prepared from an early age for self-directed learning.

McKenzie underscores Fantini's warning about the possible development of dual systems of education, one for the affluent and one for the poor. She believes that tax incentives for private education will undermine our traditional commitment to quality education for all.

John E. Radig is concerned that Fantini may define "community education" too narrowly. He stresses that community education relates education to real life experiences in the home and community as well as the school. Thus, solving a neighborhood rat problem is as much a community education activity as is planning for a child's self-actualization.

Radig agrees that our education system should move toward fuller implementation of Fantini's third model, and eventually to the fourth model. He discusses some ways to hasten progress in this direction:

- Public awareness and involvement.
- Delegation of educational service delivery to other community agencies and institutions.
- Strong leadership by those who recognize that changes in the structure and role of public education are necessary.
- Development of a national concensus on the type of public education system our country wants now and in the future.
- Community discussions of school problems and financial constraints.
- Improvements in individual and group communications skills.

Changing Concepts of Education: From School System to Educational System

by
Mario D. Fantini

The school model in the United States has evolved from the 18th century's one-room schoolhouse into today's vast educational complex, staffed by scores of professionals and designed to serve thousands of students. One current thrust in education is an attempt to restore the close family-school-community ties of earlier times and to incorporate into the formal structure of American public education some of the small-scale intimacy, individualized attention, and opportunity for nonformal education of the one-room schoolhouse. This thrust seems to be part of an effort to reconceive the relationship between education and the community, and to reestablish family-school-community ties in ways that are appropriate to our contemporary society.

A current preoccupation of America's schools is the broader political and economic aspects of education and society. Fiscal cutbacks have become the major concern of the educators, and the consequence of lower school budgets has been the curtailment of educational services. In Massachusetts, for example, recent state legislation known as Proposition 2½ affects local property taxes, which historically have provided the major support for public education. As a result of Proposition 2½, the state teaching force has been reduced by about 10,000 teachers, which has affected virtually all levels of the school system and caused cutbacks in such area as the arts, athletics, and bus services. This is clearly a difficult period for educators, who must balance the need to reduce services with the mandated demands for special education, bilingual education, and the like. But, it is also a time of opportunity because it represents a chance for schools to adapt their roles to changing times.

Schools have historically been asked to do more and more as other community agencies have provided less direct education. While the school-age population was rising and the economy expanding, the "more with more" approach was seldom questioned. As we now experience the limits of economic growth, a process of public accountability has led to a reassessment of public institutions. A familiar political cry now is that the schools must be more productive, must do more with less.

Two major movements could assist the schools in redefining their role; ironically, neither movement is generally perceived in this positive way. The first is the move to place economic limitations on school resources, and the second is the emphasis on "back to the basics." These two trends could actually be an impetus to modernize and update the schools.

Education has always been a *community* activity in our country. It is a process far broader than the activity of schooling, nonformal learning experiences, as well as the formal learning experiences of the schoolhouse, are a crucial part of an individual's total education. The quality of life in the community depends directly on the quality of education, because education empowers individuals as workers and as citizens, enables them to develop their potential, and imbues them with a sense of responsibility for others. Minzey and LeTarte give this general definition of community education:

> Community Education is a philosophical concept which serves the entire community by providing for all of the educational needs of all of its community members. It uses the local school to serve as the catalyst for bringing community resources to bear on community problems in an effort to develop a positive sense of community, improve community living, and develop the community process toward the end of self-actualization. [1]

To John Dewey, and to many others historically involved in community education, the school represents society in miniature. The school neither stands apart from its immediate community nor develops in directions unconnected from the larger society. The schools, in fact, reflect, serve, and redirect the needs and values of the larger society. As society changes, the responsibilities of the schools change. In the agrarian economy of the 17th and 18th centuries, the schools assumed a role suited to the social, economic, and political needs of the communities they served. As the industrial revolution transformed American society in the 19th century, urgent new needs arose and heavy new demands were made upon the schools. Because of the central, strategic, and coordinating position of the school in each community, the school came to assume more and more responsibility for filling in the gaps as other community institutions weakened or shifted away from their previous roles. In the United States, the schools had the additional task of introducing successive waves of immigrants, each with a distinct culture and ethnic identity, into the mainstream American culture and civic orientation.

An Historical Overview: The School in the Community

Increasing Responsibilities of the School in Society

Now, as we move towards the beginning of the 21st century, we see that our society has undergone further transformation. Many functions that were formerly the responsibility of other agencies in the community have settled uneasily on the schools. The family is no longer the unified entity it was earlier; the current divorce rate indicates that almost half of all marriages end in some form of separation. Family patterns established over generations have been disrupted by rapid urbanization. The economic realities of the 1980s impel increasing numbers of women to work outside the home, away from the homemaking careers that characterized the lives of middle and upper class women in the early 20th century. The family unit is no longer the nuclear family of the turn of the 20th century, when the family structure of a male bread winner and a female homemaker with two children represented approximately 75 percent of the population. Single-parent families, families with two working parents, and other family patterns have emerged. The family in which the male works outside the home and the female is a full-time homemaker represents less than 20 percent of today's American families.

As family structures have changed, the families themselves have delegated supervisory powers and responsibilities to the schools, with the understanding that the schools would perform *in loco parentis*. Increasingly, a sense of neighborhood ties and of community life has collapsed under the disorienting forces of advanced industrialization, a highly specialized job market, and geographic mobility.

As the manpower needs of the society evolved—and especially as apprenticeships in the workplace were replaced by extended training in the schools—the schools were given increased responsibilities for vocational training and college preparatory courses. An increasingly automotive society necessitated driver education. The advent of the space age and the international competition sparked by Sputnik in the 1950s brought demands for improved and accelerated education in science and mathematics.

In the 1960s, with the society's heightened awareness of poverty in the midst of plenty, the schools assumed a central role in compensatory and remedial efforts aimed at "disadvantaged" populations. Efforts to achieve racial integration and to mainstream students with special needs were mandated by law and brought into the schools. Responsibility for multicultural and bilingual education was assumed by the schools. Issues raised by the Watergate crisis led to an interest in moral education in the schools. The alarming increase in pregnancy, venereal disease, and drug and alcohol use among teenagers suggested a need for comprehensive sex and health education programs in the schools.

As computers and other electronic media have become a part of everyday life, the schools are increasingly called upon to provide computer literacy. "The basics" as definded by the demands of our highly technological society have been expanded from the "3 R's" to encompass a host of new skills and competencies.

There are also new demands on teachers and administrators. Teachers are expected to provide specialized information in response to the new literacies, administrators to orchestrate and balance a number of different interests operating at different levels. The interests and perspectives of teachers, students, parents, school administrators, and elected officals no longer coincide and, in some cases, are clearly in conflict. Teachers are increasingly aware of their own professionalism, and increasingly active in organizing along professional lines. The development and growth of teachers' unions has brought teacher strikes and other political action. As teachers and administrators have gained recognition as highly trained professionals with special credentials, their power and responsibilities have increased, but with this increased authority has come heightened expectations and greater demands for public accountability.

The School Model Overburdened and Outmoded

Because of the school's central position in the community and the growing disconnection between the other institutions and agencies in the community, the school has accumulated a load of increased responsibilities and tasks. As new needs have arisen, the schools have tried to meet them with programs added on to their basic structure. As the needs proliferated, the add-ons sprouted in all directions, developing in a makeshift manner rather than as part of a comprehensive system. But in spite of the dramatic changes growing out of industrialization and urbanization, the basic school model remains rooted in an agrarian economy and a rural society. (The maintenance of summer vacation is historically linked to the need for school-age youth to assist during periods of planting and harvest.) Thus, there remains a substantial degree of satisfaction with the schools in rural areas in which the society resembles the original agrarian society. In urban areas, the same model is overburdened and outmoded; the school as a model no longer reflects the society it was designed to serve.

Symptoms of the inappropriateness of the schoolhouse model in urban areas have emerged inexorably in the past several decades. The high percentage of school dropouts (in spite of the increasing necessity of a high school diploma in today's job market) and increasing rates of absenteeism, truancy, vandalism, and violence in the schools are symptoms of severe obsolescence. Disciplinary problems in the classrooms and the public's overall loss of confidence in the schools are indications of the same phenomenon, which would have been unthinkable in the days of the one-room schoolhouse. There are also increasing divisions in the internal structure of the school, with instances of debilitating struggle between management (administrators) and labor (teachers), and a destructively rapid turnover of administrative leaders. The extreme politicalization of the schools can be seen in the school receiverships that have occurred in recent years in Boston, Cleveland, and Trenton.

Changing Concepts of the Comprehensive Community School

The 1950s concept of the comprehensive school meant that each school should contain within its own walls, or on its own grounds, all of the educational services and educative environments needed for all of the students in the community. This reliance on the schoolhouse produced a general orientation that the only valid learning takes place in the formal chambers of the school. It is now clear that this expectation greatly overburdened the schools, that schools cannot be all things to all people, nor are they the only place for learning. Social, political, and educational factors have all played a part in the process of clarification.

The concept of "comprehensive" in the 1980s is likely to be very different from the earlier model. Ideally, the "comprehensive school" can become "comprehensive education," entailing a coordinated system that ties all of the educative agents and environments in the larger community into a community-wide educational network. One goal of this community-wide education is a breaking down of the traditional barriers and boundaries between the schoolhouse and the community it serves. During the '70s and '80s, citizens and families began to recall lost authority and to redefine their roles and the roles of social institutions. A growing spirit of self-determination began to take hold. There was a movement to return authority to the citizen, so that the citizen could exercise increased control over his or her own life.

The force of democratization—growing out of a concern for the civil rights of racial and ethnic minorities and women, and out of a concerted effort to provide for the needs of handicapped citizens and the elderly—has rekindled recognition of the need to empower individuals to control their own lives. As society becomes more complex and as the trappings of modern technology appear to take away a sense of direct control, the sense of empowerment **through education** becomes even more crucial; there is a growing tendency to transfer authority from the institution to the individual, and from a centralized administrative source to the locus of local communities.

The Community Schools and Comprehensive Community Education Act of 1978 added several new titles to the Elementary and Secondary Schools Act of 1965, recognizing the potentially pivotal role of the public school system in the evolution of a community-wide network of educational facilities and resources. In an attempt to transform the concepts of community education into public policy, Section 802 of the Act declares in its Statement of Findings and Policy:

1. *the school is an integral part of the local human service delivery system;*
2. *the school is a primary institution for the delivery of services and may be the best instrument for the coordination of frequently fragmented services, including benefits obtained by energy savings and parental involvement in the delivery of such services;*
3. *community education promotes a more efficient use of public education facilities through an extension of the school building and equipment;*
4. *as the primary educational institution of the community, the school is most effective when it involves the people of that community in a program to fulfill the educational needs of individuals of the community; and*
5. *community schools provide a great potential for the use of needs assessment as a basis for human resources policies.*[2]

The purpose of the Act was to provide for collaborative school-community programs in order to coordinate social services; make efficient use of school facilities; and support research and development programs with an emphasis on community education, optimally to serve as the basis for federal, state, and local policy on education.

Schools can, of course, draw on the work experience and professional expertise of community residents through field trips and other excursions into the community, and through such programs as parent volunteers in the classroom and performing arts troupes in the schools. Such efforts are not new. Figure 1[3] graphically represents the school structure, in which the school is the central institution to which students look for specialized training and through which community professionals offer students the benefits of their expertise and experience.

THE SCHOOL STRUCTURE

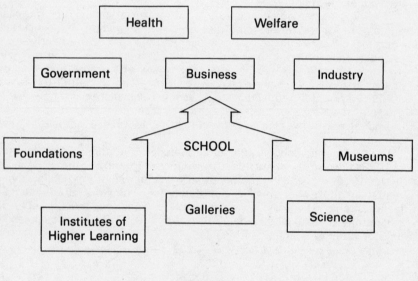

FIGURE 1.

This concept of the entire community as an educational resource can be extended much further, so the community is viewed as a series of learning environments (Figure 2).[4] The separate resources of the community could be viewed and, ideally, could be utilized as a community educational system open to learners of all ages whose individual needs impel them to look for expertise, experience, and environments outside the traditional school structure.

THE COMMUNITY

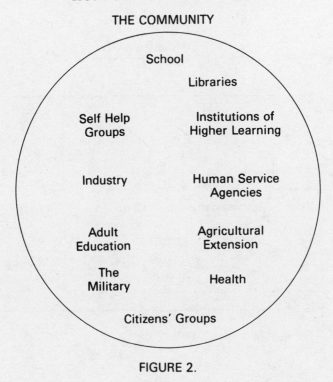

School

Libraries

Self Help
Groups

Institutions of
Higher Learning

Industry

Human Service
Agencies

Adult
Education

Agricultural
Extension

The
Military

Health

Citizens' Groups

FIGURE 2.

Four Overlapping Models of Community Education

One: A Division of Labor Model

Throughout the changing structures of education in the United States, there is a series of overlapping models of community education. While the society, the economy, and the schools have all changed dramatically, the community has always operated as the educational base.

In the agrarian economy of the 18th and early 19th century, homogeneous rural communities were united by common values under a dominant religious organization; the home, church, school, workplace, and local governing body all reflected similar values. Each separate agency within the community performed a separate function in socializing and educating youth (Figure 3). Primary control and accountability in this tight community network rested with the parents and the clergy. Children of all ages and abilities learned together in a one-room schoolhouse. The school curriculum emphasized the "3 R's," and religious values, if not religious teachings, were incorporated into the curriculum. Strict discipline, repetitive drills, and a didactic approach were accepted educational standards. Questions about who learns what and how, where, and when learning takes place were decided by the traditional values of the community as expressed by the family and the church.

DIVISION OF LABOR MODEL
FOR COMMUNITY EDUCATION

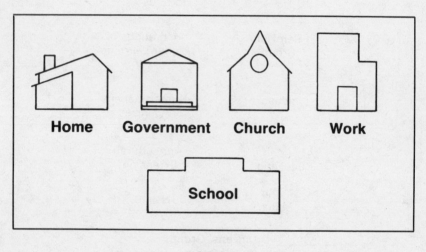

FIGURE 3.

Two: A Delegation of Labor Model

The second model for community education has roots in the industrialization and urbanization of society in the 19th and early 20th centuries. The rapid economic, political, and cultural changes occasioned by the industrial revolution affected the relationships of community institutions. Social and educational services that had been delivered by family, church, workplace, etc., were increasingly assigned to the school. In a series of add-ons to the school's structure, the curriculum was expanded, and power was transferred to professional educators. The school's role and responsibility in society were thus greatly enlarged as other community agencies that had previously functioned as educators delegated power and educative tasks to the school as shown in Figure 4.

COMPREHENSIVE SCHOOL MODEL

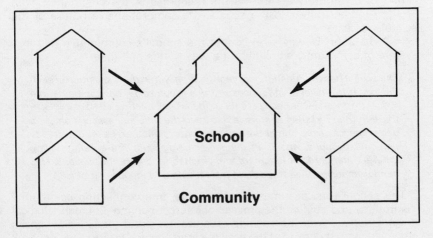

FIGURE 4

Increased Delegation of Responsibility from
Community to School

The idea of the comprehensive school developed at this time. As the content of the curriculum greatly expanded, standardization of curriculum and instructional methods emerged in an attempt to deal with the demands of mass schooling. From this standardization a system of human classification developed, with labels such as "winners" and "losers." Decisions about who learns, what should be learned, and when, where, and how learning takes place were controlled by the schools and school professionals. The educative power of other agencies continued to be recognized, but the school as an institution was viewed as the educative center of the community.

In the 1930s another dimension of the concept of comprehensiveness surfaced in the "community schools" pioneered by the Mott Foundation in the Flint, Michigan, public schools. Under the community school concept, the school opened its doors to the community for after-school, evening, weekend, and summer programming. Learners of all ages participated in recreational, vocational, and enrichment activities in the school as the center of community affairs. As the resources of the community were brought increasingly into the school, the comprehensive nature of the school was extended.

In 1916 John Dewey wrote about the school's coordinative role in a system of community education in a way that is still timely:

> The school has the function...of coordinating within the disposition of each individual the diverse influences of the various social environments into which he enters. One code prevails in the family; another on the streets; a third, in the workshop or store; a fourth, in the religious association. As a person passes from one of the environments to another, he is subjected to antagonistic pulls, and is in danger of being split into a being having different standards of judgment and emotion for different occasions. This danger imposes upon the school a steadying and integrating office.[5]

The school thus assumes a special role, interconnecting community institutions and guiding the process of interconnection. But technological developments, ever-increasing urbanization, and concurrent social changes have undermined the previously strong and interlocking network of human relations and civic units. A frequently conflicting diversity has replaced the homogeneity of earlier times. The role of the comprehensive community school is to coordinate diverse community institutions into a well-integrated and cohesive whole. As Dewey wrote:

> It remains but to organize all these factors, to appreciate them in their fullness of meaning, and to put the ideas and ideals involved into complete uncompromising possession of our school system. To do this means to make each one of our schools an embryonic community life, active with types of occupations that reflect the life of the larger society and permeated throughout with the spirit of art, history, and science. When the school introduces and trains each child of society into membership within such a little community, saturating him with the spirit of service, and providing him with the instruments of effective self-direction, we shall have the deepest and best guaranty of the larger society which is worthy, lovely, and harmonious.[6]

Unfortunately, we have not yet realized Dewey's goal of a larger society that is "worthy, lovely, and harmonious." As the school became overburdened with social and educational responsibilities, it developed a makeshift system of add-ons that were both ineffective and expensive. An inefficient system cannot be sustained in an era of public accountability and declining financial resources. We now appear to be in a transition period in which the development of diversity in public education, in both the schools and the community, is a major thrust. In the midst of a series of options and choices in education, the school serves a coordinative function.

Three: A Coordinative Model

A third model, with the school in a coordinative role, has its roots in the limitations imposed by our post-industrial economy and the demands of urbanization. New knowledge based on educational theory and practice have accompanied the political and economic changes to create a new concept of community education. The major change is the recognition that the school, as one institution among many in the community, cannot realistically attempt to "do it all." This has led to a reduction in the number of school-based programs and a concurrent attempt to concentrate the school's efforts and energy on what the school can do successfully. A number of recent school effectiveness studies have refocused efforts at school reform. A back-to-basics movement has ties to educational philosophy as well as to a tightened economy and political conservatism. But even as the role of the school in the direct delivery of social service has been reduced and emphasis on the "basics" increased, the complexities of modern life have made a host of new literacies—driver education, legal literacy, computer literacy, sex education, nutritional literacy, global literacy, and the like—as essential as the original "3R's." In an attempt to avoid duplication of effort and maximize efficiency, the schools are now beginning to delegate some educational services back to other agencies and institutions in the community. A more coordinated system of education, involving shared responsibilities and cooperative programs, is emerging as shown in Figure 5.

COORDINATIVE MODEL:
COMPREHENSIVE COMMUNITY EDUCATION

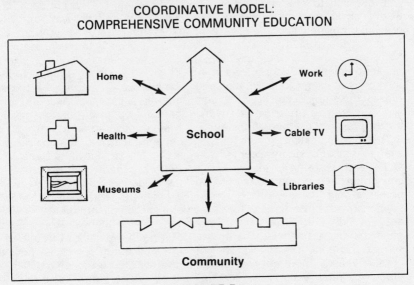

FIGURE 5

Linkage of School to Other Educative Agents
and Agencies in Community

Cooperative Programs

In this model, the curriculum in the school emphasizes the basics and learning how to learn so that students may then go outside the school and benefit from the other educative environments and opportunities. The schools coordinate the extended curricula with the help of other community agencies. Driver education, for instance, could be taught by insurance companies, drug education by health care professionals, and sex education by collaborative teams drawn from the health care professions, the social services, and the clergy. Moral education and ethics could be taught by an interdenominational group of clergy, and legal literacy by lawyers. Business and industry could supply the expertise needed for computer literacy, and, perhaps with tax incentives, could be encouraged to donate computers and ancillary equipment for student use. Most of these examples have been tentatively explored in practice; all of them emphasize the shared responsibility of community education.

Many agencies and institutions in the community have educative potential. And all community agencies have an educative responsibility. The school's central role is, first, to encourage and support the educative efforts of other community agencies and, second, to ensure that the students' experiences outside the school are indeed educative. The issues of who, what, where, when, and how then become the joint responsibility of parents, school professionals, and other agents in the community.

Flexible Structures and Programs

In addition to assuming a coordinative function, the school becomes flexible in its own organization. This flexibility is a shift away from the previous normative structure, with its standardized expectations of teachers and students and its non-variable approach to learning style. More and more, schools are incorporating the idea of individualized education plans. Pioneer efforts in individualized plans were made under the Education for All Handicapped Children Act (PL 94-142) and Massachusetts Chapter 766. Under these laws, parents, teachers, and specially trained professionals work together to plan a program that is custom-tailored to the abilities and interests of each student.

This kind of flexibility could be applied to benefit all learners and can be seen in the increasingly accepted practice of attempting to match teaching styles with learning styles, to provide, with sensitivity and expertise, a curriculum and an environment that fit a student's individual needs. A program might be devised, for example, for an exceptionally shy child, whose shyness interferes with his academic accomplishment and whose academic difficulties, in turn, diminish his self-confidence. Such a child might be given extensive one-on-one tutoring in the basics through the school and encouraged to participate in small group situations and to pursue outside interests that would enhance his self-esteem. Such a program would recognize education as a social, essentially community-based, process and would be well within the range of even a traditionally structured school.

Another flexible program might enable a child to develop a particular talent through the use of community resources and home education. A child exceptionally talented in music from an early age might join a musical group and be playing professionally while still in his teens. If this involved performing until 2:00 a.m., he would probably end up in conflict with the school, which might expect him to be in attendance by 7:30 a.m.. If he gave up his music, he would be frustrated and his potential thwarted; if he chose to develop his musical talent at the expense of basic high school studies, he would limit his future choices. But with a small degree of flexibility in school structure and recognition of the educative potential of the community, the child's professional work as a musician could be acknowledged as valid educative experience and the child's basic studies in the school supplemented by parental tutoring.

Expanded Parental Roles

In this coordinative model for community education, cooperative programs and flexibility in school structures are accompanied by a changing role for parents. Reclaiming many supervisory powers and educative tasks previously delegated to the school, parents are seeking more control over their children's education. Many parents want some choice in the kind of schooling their children experience. Once the choice has been made, some parents feel that the child's education is best left to trained professionals in the school and the community, while others take the more radical path of home education.

Exploring the growing phenomenon of home education in a recent book, John Holt begins by asking the basic question:

> Why do people take or keep their children out of school? Mostly for three reasons: they think that raising their children is their own business and not the government's; they enjoy being with their children and watching and helping them learn, and don't want to give that up to others; they want to keep them from being hurt, mentally, physically, and spiritually.[7]

Holt goes on to explore a number of the issues surrounding the controversial practice of home education—the politics and legality, strategies and philosophies, and reasons for and against choosing home education. Citing case histories from around the country, Holt demonstrates that while all sorts of people in all sorts of circumstances are educating their children at home, a consistent reason is the parents' insistence on their **right** to assume primary responsibility for their child and his education. Holt quotes parents as diverse as the wife of a U.S. Navy career officer, a foreign-born Muslim mother, and a retired physician. He sums up their desire to assume primary and direct responsibility for their children's education as simultaneously old-fashioned and contemporary. Their attitude harks back to the social structure that was in place before the development of our elaborate public school system, long before various social, civic, vocational, and psychological responsibilities were delegated to the schools and to school professionals. At the same time, their insistence on self-directed individualization within a system of community education is entirely modern.

Home education efforts **are** a part of community education. Many of the parents quoted by Holt reveal a stong antipathy towards official institutions including the school, along with a desire for a direct role in their children's education. In fact, community agencies are often involved in home education efforts. While we do not know how many children are simply "hidden away" illegally in home schooling, we do know that increasing numbers of parents are going through official channels, from local school boards to courts, to make arrangements for home education. Depending on the level of expertise of the parents, the attitude of the particular school authorities, and the laws of the individual state, arrangements between the home, the school, and the community vary greatly. More and more, however, the concept of joint responsibility for children's education is emerging, with the school, the community, and the parents all playing a substantial role.

Development of Alternatives
Whether the primary responsibility rests with the school or with the parents, it is imperative, given our current needs and interests, that the educational system provide a series of options and choices for learners. If there is no genuine variety in educational programs, the school fails to meet its responsibility. Schools cannot offer a quality education to all students with a single standardized program suited only to the needs of some. Realistically, the provision of alternative programs in public schools depends on the utilization of community resources through the coordinative efforts of the school.

Magnet schools are an interesting example of the shift toward defining and developing community resources as a legitimate part of the school setting. Magnet schools offer specialized programs intended to attract a diverse student body from throughout a school district. The specialized program may be talent-based with a curriculum emphasizing music, dance, or the visual arts, for example, or it may be based on career training, offering such courses as pre-law or preparation for medical or health care training. The magnet school may offer a specialized pedagogical approach such as mastery learning or independent study. Whatever form the specialized program takes, the educational emphasis is on individual interests and educational opportunities not available through the traditional school structure. Magnet schools also serve an important social function because their student populations are drawn from all over the school district. They attract a truly diverse student body, racially mixed with varied ethnic and socio-economic backgrounds. Furthermore, magnet schools are frequently located outside a specific neighborhood, at an appropriate site in the larger community. A school focusing on business career preparation, for instance, might be located in a city's business district, while a school offering courses in health care and medical technology might be located in or near a hospital or medical center. The community location of the magnet school serves as a "neutral" setting, emphasizing the fact that the quality of the program, not the socio-economic composition of the neighborhood, determines the quality of the school. The effort to provide quality education utilizing community resources thus promotes school desegregation.

Magnet schools have been developed in many cities across the country. One of the earliest programs, in Dallas, Texas, began with four diverse programs.[8] The Transportation Institute took over the facilities of a former automotive repair shop. The school's program includes a new car showroom, a fully operative repair center, and an automotive rebuilding center. The Business Management Center, located in the city's central business district, offers business and management training plus an extensive program of field employment. In the Creative Arts Academy, students explore the visual and performing arts, enjoying access to practicing professional artists in the course of their public school education. The magnet school devoted to the health professions gives students training in health-care skills that can be applied in jobs or serve as the basis for further training. In Denver, Colorado, a proposal currently under consideration incorporates an even more specialized series of programs and schools, including a Multicultural Heritage Center (for K-6), a Science/Math Academy (for grades 4-8), a Center for Computer Science (for grades 9-12), a Life and Health Sciences Center (for grades 9-12), an Institute for Aerospace Studies (for grades 9-12), and many other options.[9] The magnet school is only one of many forms education can take in attempting to draw on community resources, serve varied educational needs, and implement the ideal of choice in education.

Summing Up: Current Trends Under the Coordinative Model

Our expectations and emphasis in public education are shifting from the inherent limits of the schoolroom to effective use of the resources of the greater community. From the normative, standardized approach to mass schooling, there has been a shift to explore diversification and individualized education plans. From centrally administered and federally funded programs, there is a shift in the direction of decentralization in both administration and financing. The implicit emphasis on "learner fault" of the compensatory and remedial education programs of the 1960s has given way to the more enlightened concept of "program fault" or "institution fault." This shift incorporates three significant changes that have far-reaching implications for educational theory and practice. First, there is the idea that every child can learn and that, given the right educational program and the right educational environment, every child will learn. Second, there is the belief that access to quality education is a fundamental right for all learners, not a privilege for the few. And third, there is the idea that the school system is responsible for providing the "least restrictive environment" for the education of each learner. While these ideas have not yet received universal implementation in the schools, they posit serious structural changes in our system of public education.

Four: A Facilitative Model

We appear to be in a period of change, with an interest in increasing the number of educational options, offering individualized programs, and utilizing the human and material resources of the community to provide quality education equally to all learners. We also appear to be moving towards a fourth possible model of community education, one that makes use of all potential educators in the community and, in doing so, changes the role of the school and the responsibility of school professionals in the entire educational system. This fourth model for community education is based on our expectation of an automated global economy in the 21st century and projects a primarily facilitative role for educators in the overall division of labor in the community. In this model (Figure 6) the individual learner puts together his or her own program, working with advisors in the home and in the school. Thus the parents and professional educators, working cooperatively, help students assemble their own individualized learning environments in self-directed situations.

THE FACILITATIVE MODEL

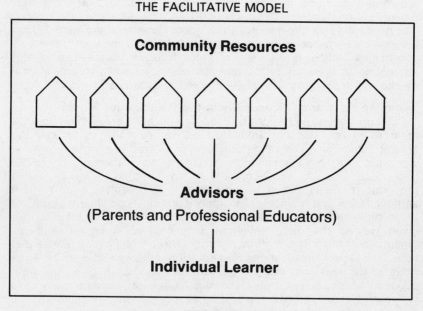

FIGURE 6

Educative Resources of Community Available to
Learner with Advisors (Parents and Professional
Educators) Assisting in Facilitation of Custom-Tailored Programs

Under a facilitative concept of community education, the individual who is cognizant of his fundamental rights to quality education is in ultimate control. Depending on his age and circumstances, the individual learner may seek the advice of parents and professional educators in planning an educational program. The learner may be shy or assertive, rich or poor, interested in the arts or in science, able to learn independently or in a group situation, oriented towards technology or the humanities. His closest advisors (parental and professional) will interact with him to plan a custom-tailored sequential educational program. He may need a tutor in some fields, a small group situation in others, a self-initiated experience in still others. He might work part-time, use home-based cable TV channels for specific subject matter, study in museums, or have a highly specialized tutor in ballet, music composition, or city planning. Another learner might take a "sabbatical," in which world travel is an essential learning experience. Others might rely heavily on home learning, perhaps with videotapes or videodiscs that represent a personalized library or the archives of the best thinkers of our time. Using the home as an "electronic cottage," the individual could learn foreign languages from a Berlitz-designed recording program and mathematics from a computer with interactive capabilities. Cable television could become the medium for specific programming in numerous fields. A learner might spend the morning at a computer terminal, the afternoon at a museum or library, and the evening at an art center.

Ongoing evaluation involving all partners in the educative process would lead to adaptation and self-correction in each individual program. The evaluation would probably be competency-based and related to the overarching goal of a quality education. Control would always rest with the learner, who would evaluate the efficiency of the program and the effectiveness of the advising. The role of the professional educator would be to facilitate the best possible educative experience for each learner. Converting work experiences into educationally relevant learning environments implies functional connection of the educator to the workplace in order to assure that the best interests of the learner are served. If the educator believes that the learning environment is inappropriate, he has both the right and the responsibility to so advise the individual learner. (What's best for General Motors in sponsoring on-the-job training programs, for instance, may not be what is best for the learner educationally.)

The whole range of human and material resources in the community—which now extends to the entire globe—becomes available to the individual learner, while professional educators facilitate programs that protect each learner's right to a quality education. The professional educator relinquishes direct delivery of most educational services to other educative agents in the community but is accountable for assuring the quality of the individual's learning environments and experiences. In this system of self-directed learning, the educational options are as extensive and diverse as the contemporary society. Quality education can be seen as a means of personal empowerment based on the individual's sense of control over his own life and the responsible caring for others, linked to a multitude of literacies and talent development. Learning can thus be seen as a lifelong experience. In the optimal learning society, members serve as educative resources for each other, and the society becomes an educative environment, promoting growth towards fulfillment of the positive potential of each individual. An educative community develops when various educative environments are linked together and consciously coordinated to deliver quality educational services to all learners.

Community Resource Management: Doing More With Less

Ironically, the forces that must be harnessed to bring about this contemporary concept of community education are economic and political. The current economic situation dictates that schools do more with less. "Doing more" means that the educator, while continuing to be responsible for delivering direct service in the school must also provide indirect service by linking with the other educative resources in the community. Pioneers in tapping the rich learning resources of the community are the Parkway Program (the School Without Walls in Philadelphia), and Metro High School in Chicago. These efforts recognized the city as educator and harnessed the various educative environments of the community into a comprehensive system of public education. They did more with less; without school plants of their own, they saved millions in construction costs. They established linkage with museums, libraries, communications centers, insurance companies, etc., offering more options to students, parents, and teachers.

In addition to the economic impetus of diminishing resources, another contemporary force shaping community education is political. While various groups in a pluralistic population agree on quality education as an end, they are divided on the best means to attain that end. Instead of imposing one model of education on the community, public schools now have the opportunity to offer **choice**. The right to choice has become a rallying cry for more educational options. This means that professional educators must become accustomed to offering alternatives within the public schools, ranging from the matching of teaching and learning styles to offering a whole series of optional classroom environments. It also means that they must accept educative environments outside the schools and learn to tap the economic and political currents for educational purposes.

If an environment fails to support positive human development or actively thwarts it, the environment is **miseducative;** this adds another dimension to the role of the professional educator. Inside the schoolhouse, a classroom dominated by competition rather than concern for learning is a miseducative environment for many learners. The inaccurate information about sex and drugs that many children and adolescents receive from their peers is miseducation. In the context of the larger community, ongoing miseducation tolerates and fosters prejudice and discrimination and allows illiteracy—academic, social, moral—to flourish. Television, which has such great potential as an educational tool in both the school and the community, more often than not serves miseducative commercial purposes.

To nullify the impact and ultimately transform the effects of miseducative environments, positive learning environments must be organized and coordinated. The goal of quality education is to allow the individual to achieve a level of potency that will permit him to eradicate miseducative environments and construct learning environments, experiences, and programs that support and encourage the full development of his human potential. Dewey noted this special goal of education as an ongoing, community-oriented process:

A society of free individuals in which all, through their own work, contribute to the liberation and enrichment of the lives of others, is the only environment in which any individual can really grow normally to his full stature. An environment in which some are practically enslaved, degraded, limited, will always react to create conditions that prevent the full development even of those who fancy they enjoy complete freedom for unhindered growth.[10]

The system of community-wide education suggested by a facilitative role for educators is not some visionary projection but, in fact, a reflection of the educational needs and potential of our society. The continual need for change in educational systems, concomitant with changes in the larger society, goes far back, as can be seen in Dewey's efforts to define the interconnection between educational reform and social conditions:

Can we connect this "New Education" with the general march of events? If we can, it will lose its isolated character; it will cease to be an affair which proceeds only from the over-ingenious minds of pedagogues dealing with particular pupils. It will appear as part and parcel of the whole social evolution, and, in its more general features, at least as inevitable.[11]

Financing a comprehensive system of public education will rely on a sharing of economic responsibility. Business and industry have been developing their own educational system; medical centers are increasingly emphasizing education; electronic technology is slowly turning from entertainment to education; museums, libraries, and other institutions are increasingly budgeting resources and personnel for education. The main thrust of these efforts will be toward the delivery of services. In public education, a major thrust has been to return fiscal and supervisory power to the local level through decentralization, deregulation, and federal block grants to the states. As the federal government returns increased control to the states, the states are giving greater authority and control to the individual family. In the early stages, decentralization appears to take the form of tuition tax credits and modified tuition vouchers. Thus the individual, perhaps with the advice of parents and others, will have the purchasing power to attain a customized education in keeping with his needs and aspirations. In this case, the public schools become major advisors and a major resource to the home and the individual as educational decision-maker. The school, instead of expecting all families to adjust to a standardized pattern, will function as counselor, looking at the resources available in the immediate and global community. In the future, then, an individual child may purchase day care or a parent, male or female, may elect to stay at home, perhaps alternating child care responsibilities. More leisure time and more education for adults could mean that all adults will be prepared to be teachers and resources to one another. Basic information could be computerized and instantly retrievable in the home. Great libraries may be accessible through home computers. Home computers, videotapes, and videodiscs will make learning available in the comfortable and intimate setting of the home. Where businesses and industries have set up day care with strong educative environments, children may accompany their parents to work. In a "do it yourself" home-based approach to education, financing methods give purchasing power to the individual, who can then decide when, how, and where education takes place.

Marvin Feldman, president of the Fashion Institute of Technology, makes the following observations on the trend toward increased self-direction in industry, which has parallels in the increased emphasis on the individual in education:

> At about the same time, another elemental social trend reversed itself. Self-employment, which has been declining for more than a century, began to increase faster than conventional employment. Before the Civil War, industrialization had barely begun. The overwhelming majority of Americans worked for themselves on farms or in small family enterprises. Then, with an almost frightening rapidity, the pattern shifted. People left their farms to work in factories, many of them driving Henry Ford's Model-T's (which he built in part because he hated farming so passionately).
>
> Soon, America became not the nation of independent yeoman farmers Jefferson believed might keep us free, but a nation of employees. We crowded into cities; we crowded into factories. We made miracles of productivity, but part of the price was a heartbreaking agenda of public problems. But now that pattern is changing. Self-employment is increasing faster than conventional employment. People are becoming more independent, self-supervising—entrepreneurial.[12]

Furthermore, Feldman sees promise in the trend toward utilization of educational technology that relates to developments in society:

> As the society becomes more information-intensive and as the electronic means for handling information becomes more and more cost-effective, people who work at great distances from each other can be linked electronically as easily as if they were in the same room. We no longer need to bring the people to work, in expensive, energy-consuming, atmosphere-polluting vehicles. We can bring the work to the people— electronically. It is cheaper, conserving of non-renewable resources, and ecologically benign. And, most important, it offers the hope that some of the intractable social problems associated with industrialization and urbanization may now become more manageable.[13]

This view of future possibilities rests firmly on needs and demands that are evolving today. The shift from schooling to a system of community education is made imperative by the diverse needs and complex interdependent realities of our post-industrial society. The "community" we must utilize in community education today is indeed a global community, embracing specialized environments and technology unheard of in previous eras and underutilized even today. Engineering a community education system that links together all of the educative environments of society through the facilitative agencies of the home and the school offers a genuine challenge. It is a challenge we must meet, because our failure to do so will threaten the essential fabric of our society. If we do not diversify our system of public education, develop options and choices, and encourage individualization, the public will turn increasingly to the private sector for educational services. The public's demand for choice in schooling is well documented by the rise of an entrepreneurial and consumer-oriented approach. Private sector education has expanded despite the increasingly hard financial times of the 1980s; a system of alternative schools and alternative programs has developed inside the public school system; revived interest in voucher plans and tuition tax credits is evident at the federal level. As the middle class leaves the public school system, a dual system of education will develop: an expanded private sector for the upper and middle classes, and public schools for the poor and the handicapped. This dual system would have dire consequences for both the individual learner, whose full potential would go unrealized, and the society, which would soon have to deal with an undereducated underclass. To avert this tragedy, we must diversify our educational system and develop a community-wide network of interlinking educative environments, coordinated by school professionals working in close collaboration with the home and the community to provide quality education programs for all learners.

The author wishes to acknowledge, with graditude, the editorial efforts and research assistance of Ms. Laura Holland.

NOTES

[1]Jack D. Minzey and Clyde E. LeTarte, **Community Education: From Program to Process to Practice** (Midland, Michigan: Pendell Publishing Company, 1979), pp. 26-27.

[2]Section 802 of Title VIII—**Community Schools** (PL 94-561), "Community Schools and Comprehensive Community Education Act of 1978."

[3]Mario D. Fantini, Elizabeth Loughran, and Horace Reed, "Community Education: Towards a Definition" (unpublished paper), p. 13.

[4]Ibid., p. 14.

[5]John Dewey, **Democracy and Education** (New York: The MacMillan Company, 1916), p. 26.

[6]John Dewey, "The School and Society," in **The Child and the Curriculum/The School and Society** (Chicago: University of Chicago Press, 1956), p. 29.

[7]John Holt, **Teach Your Own: A Hopeful Path for Education** (New York: Delacorte Press, 1981), p. 13.

[8]**Mario D. Fantini,** "History and Philosophy of Alternative Schools" **Magnet Schools: Legal and Practicadl Implications,** Nolan Estes and Donald R. Waldrip, eds., (Piscataway, New Jersey: New Century Education Corporation, 1978), pp. 18-20.

[9]Denver (Colorado) Public Schools, Board of Education, **Total Access Plan,** submitted to United States District Court, 1981.

[10]John Dewey, "Need for a Philosophy of Education," in Reginald Archambault, ed., **John Dewey on Education: Selected Writings** (New York: The Modern Library, Random House, Inc., 1964), p. 12.

[11]John Dewey, "The School and Society," p. 8.

[12]Marvin Feldman, "The Homecoming of America" (unpublished paper, undated), p. 2.

[13]Ibid., p. 3.

Reaction Paper to: Mario D. Fantini's

"Changing Concepts of Education"
by
Floretta Dukes McKenzie

Communities and schools have been inseparable throughout the history of public education, as Dr. Fantini has precisely documented. Given the record that education has directly reflected community needs and values, the term "community education" is redundant. While the role of the community in education has varied over time, the presence of the community in public education has been constant. Thus education in many ways has always been "community education."

"Community education" was coined as a distinct term on the basis of efforts in Flint, Michigan, to extend the use of school buildings beyond the regular classroom hours and to focus on the school as an agent for providing a range of community services. However, as Dr. Fantini notes, community education has evolved beyond expanded hours of operation and enlarged service populations.

A brief discussion of one new educational thrust in the Washington, D.C., public schools will illustrate the emergence of a further refined view of community education. This particular undertaking focuses on the need for private sector involvement in the educational process.

The District of Columbia public school system has recognized — through its private-public partnerships efforts — that the more traditional sources of cultural enrichment and learning (museums, galleries, universities, etc.) are not the only education agents available to the schools. As Dr. Fantini points out, industry, businesses, medical centers, libraries, and technological systems are all developing — or have developed — educational components.

American businesses spend an estimated $60 billion annually on training employees. A large part of that amount is spent to upgrade employees' basic skills:

- AT & T spends an estimated $6 million to teach 14,000 employees basic writing and arithmetic during office hours.
- Metropolitan Life devotes more than 40 percent of its training and development program to English usage and arithmetic.

Employee recruitment, hiring, and turnover costs are estimated at more than $100 billion:

- General Motors hired 9,000 employees to fill 1,500 jobs in one year.
- Most entry-level training programs are not cost effective because too few employees are retained past the break-even point for training costs.

Obviously, today's student is tomorrow's employee. Improperly prepared students become problems for employers. Business and education are interdependent. Previous efforts to benefit from this interdependence have led educators to seek gifts and grants from businesses and foundations.

Philanthropy, however, does not adequately serve business needs and does not necessarily improve education. Asking for grants is a win-lose situation. But education is not a zero sum game; it is possible to have a win-win business relationship through investment, not philanthropy.

Educational leadership and design support, rather than financial support, are the more valued and less expensive roles for major employers. This kind of support is not as quick or as tangible as a financial contribution, and it implies accountability for new products, but our national economy is at a crossroads in the world markets, and a corporate check is no longer proof of corporate responsibility, much less a guarantee that any substantial return will accrue to either the company or the students.

The D.C. public schools' early efforts to secure corporate partners have been directed toward identifying lead companies to join us in co-developing five career high schools which opened in September 1982. Negotiations are under way with lead employers representing major local employment sectors. Represented are national companies such as General Motors and Control Data Corporation, as well as large firms with a substantial local presence, such as IBM and Blue Cross/Blue Shield. Interest in this investment approach has been high and sustained and lends support to Dr. Fantini's view that "a comprehensive system of public education will rely on a sharing of economic responsibility." In line with Dr. Fantini's analysis, the D.C. public schools are carrying this charge a step further; all aspects of education, not just financial concerns, must be shared efforts. Thus, in Washington, D.C., the school system readily acknowledges: "*Schooling* is our business, *education* is everybody's business."

This example of expanded community involvement is consistent with Dr. Fantini's projection of community education as a precursor to the fourth model. The private sector involvement occurring in the D.C. public schools addresses the fourth model's requirement of tapping other potential educators in the community, yet does not adopt the "community educator as facilitator" aspect of the model.

Dr. Fantini describes this future model of education as one in which "the individual learner puts together his or her own program, working with advisors in the home and in the school. Thus the parents and professional educators, working cooperatively, help students assemble their own individualized learning environments in self-directed situations." This vision of education relies heavily on technological advances. The importance of technology in the future of education is undeniable. One small example is evident in the findings of a Montgomery County, Maryland, task force on educational technology. The task force recommended that by 1990 elementary students use a computer a minimum of 50 minutes a week, middle school/junior high students a minimum of 90 minutes, and high school students a minimum of 135 minutes.

Unfortunately education is lagging far behind other fields in the applications of high technology. Thus, realization of Dr. Fantini's vision of learning through electronic assistance will require acceptance of some dramatic changes in the traditional methods of educational delivery. The advent of self-directed, educator-facilitated education will demand even greater alteration of many fundamental assumptions about learning.

Thus, the evolution of the fourth model will face several obstacles. Enumeration of some of these obstacles, or prerequisites is essential to reliable projections about the course of public education and an understanding of why the fourth model may be forestalled, postponed, or never accomplished.

Prerequisites to self-directed, educator-facilitated education

1. *Applications of technology to education.* The field of education today still relies on "paper and pencil" learning. Despite the ever-increasing presence of computers in daily life, education has not yet widely accepted advanced technology as a learning tool.
2. *Revamping educators' training attitudes.* Longheld, entrenched views of the teacher as the imparter of knowledge will make acceptance of the educator-as-facilitator difficult. To many educators, the facilitator role will appear to mean relinquishing control. Educators will have to be trained differently, not only technically but attitudinally if they are to serve as facilitators and effectively tap the range of community resources.
3. *Acceptance by other institutions and community groups.* The view that classrooms are the primary environments of learning is shared by many outside the education field. If these institutions are to be a valuable part of the learning resource network, they must abandon the still-prevalent notion that schools are places to keep children between the hours of 9 a.m. and 3 p.m. for 10 months of each year.
4. *Adoption of anticipatory and participatory behaviors.* Education, like many institutions in society, is crisis-reactive. The demands on schools rarely allow or encourage educators to "take the long view." Successful adoption of the fourth model will require careful long-range planning and anticipation of future educational needs. Such planning is currently lacking in approaches to world problems, let alone educational ones. Furthermore, despite evidence that parents and communities want more personal control of education, such participation is not yet well developed. The fourth model will need a more active recognition by the public that "education is everybody's business."
5. *Alternate measures of educational success.* The contemporary reliance on standardized test scores to measure academic success or failure will be less appropriate under a self-directed model of education. Today, proof of learning resides in many measures other than test scores. Unfortunately, the current preoccupation with scores often obscures the other indices of true learning. In Dr. Fantini's fourth model of education, the test score "evidence" would have to be substantially supported by additional means of measuring learning.

6. *Preparing children for self-directed learning.* Describing the fourth model of education, Dr. Fantini states, "Control would always rest with the learner." In order for the learner to apply such control effectively, the principles of self-initiation and the tools of inquiry must be taught and encouraged early in life. The development of self-reliance, motivation, and information-seeking behavior will have to be elevated on the list of educational priorities.

These prerequisites do not foreclose the possibility that a self-directed model of education will emerge, but they do point to the serious, substantial groundwork that must occur before such an occurrence.

A more diversified approach to education is overdue. Furthermore, as Dr. Fantini notes, achievement of educational diversity is essential to the continued success of public education. Unquestionably, public education today faces many threats and challenges. Our communities, in their attempts to widen educational opportunities, must be wary of proposals such as education vouchers and tuition tax credits, which give the illusion of greater diversity but in practice will offer more options to a few at the expense of many.

Dr. Fantini's warning about the possible development of a dual system of education, one for the affluent and one for the poor, is not to be taken lightly. Tax credits for parents who send their children to private schools would undermine this country's traditional belief in providing quality education for all. The advantages of advanced technology are accompanied by a threat of unequal access to that technology. Although the once-prohibitive price of computer technology is declining, the "electronic cottage" remains the more likely province of the rich. Communities, therefore, must adopt an outlook that will recognize the importance of access for all people and ensure that education congruent with future societal needs is available to everyone, regardless of individual economic backgrounds.

As the role of education has changed over time and been reshaped by the prevailing political and societal realities, one constant may be identified and must be reiterated today: education — meaningful, enriching, and practical education — remains essential for *all* people and therefore is vital to the continued success of the society at large.

Reaction Paper to: Mario D. Fantini's
"Changing Concepts of Education"
by
John E. Radig

Complete Understanding

Fantini describes community education in somewhat narrow, educator-to-educator terms. Although the familiar Minzey and LeTarte definition is used early in the paper, the philosophy throughout is linked to John Dewey. It is important to note that community education emphasizes the practice of other disciplines that activate education in the home, the neighborhood, the community and, yes, the school.

Community education is both an educational philosophy and a system for community development. In the late 1960s and early 1970s, both theoreticians and practitioners realized that the "lighted schoolhouse" and the "community school" would realize their full potential for school and community improvement only when they were coupled with progressive education, community organization, interagency cooperation, and other strategies. This holistic approach to defining and then solving individual, group, and community problems integrates those disciplines and others. Saul Alinski's views are just as relevant to educational improvement as are John Dewey's. Involving citizens and community resources in a neighborhood rat problem is just as valid a community education activity as determining how and where a shy child should receive his education. Educators can learn much about quality instructional programs by being involved in community life.

Public Involvement Essential

Fantini states that economic and political forces can meld community education and quality education for children and youth. Who will really transform these forces into institutional change? The public, of course, because educators are unlikely to move public education into Fantini's "coordination of labor" or "facilitation of labor" models. The public has been increasingly involved in transforming the operations of public schools. National groups such as the Institute for Responsive Education and the National Committee for Citizens in Education are two of many national organizations causing change in public schools. Similarly, there is a national revitalization of neighborhood organizations and community development/anti-poverty groups fueled by the "new federalism" initiative. Their increasing numbers and strength are making a difference in community life. Many are finding that school and community problems are interrelated and are taking action on both the "rat" and the "instruction"aspects of their neighborhoods.

Now is the time for educators and community leaders, especially in those states that have experienced state funding cuts, to challenge established norms, to start the change process by making the public aware of how it is possible to have more for less. When the public understands that deteriorating economic conditions can be used to improve the quality of education, local policy makers will respond with program diversity and individual instruction ". . .that links together all the educative environments of society."

Community education philosophy states that people are willing to be organized around the problems that confront them. Certainly, the efficient expenditure of tax dollars is sufficient motivation. Community education offers the rationale and approach; its documented practice in school and community settings shows that it can have an impact on public policy at the state and local levels. If an idea has merit, the public will act, and only then will local policy makers be willing to try new approaches to meet society's changing needs.

A New England school district faced with rapidly rising fuel costs and public resistance to increased taxes recently took dramatic and illegal action to lengthen the school day and shorten the school week to four days. The state legislature decided not to interfere, hoping that the anticipated failure of the move would restrain other districts contemplating similar action.

Instead of failing, the four-day week was a success in almost every aspect. The school day starts earlier and ends later on Monday through Thursday. Friday is a day off. The community and its educators may soon realize the potential for independent learning in the community on Friday, with the schools coordinating the educational use of local resources. The salient question is whether local and state community education leaders will take the initiative to pose the questions and propose the solutions suggested by Fantini and others.

Fantini states that the schools are beginning to delegate some educational services to other agencies and institutions in the community. Does he mean that this delegation has already started? Or that the time is right for it to begin?

Federal dollars for public schools are drying up, and state legislatures and local governments have not yet geared up to provide a significant part of the shortfall. Indeed, local and state resources may never be able to fill the gap. Most school officials have pulled their wagons into a circle and are preparing for a long seige. I suggest that Fantini is talking about pulling the wagons aside so the kids can go into the community to learn how to live in the world.

The Leadership Imperative

Strong leadership is imperative if taxpayers are to be convinced that restructured schools will offer greater program diversity, increased individual attention, and greater efficiency. Leaders outside public education must recognize that changes in structure and role are necessary; leaders in public education must be willing and ready to give change a try.

The risks of such leadership are great. Local initiatives will be greatly aided if state and national leaders discuss ideas such as Fantini's in the light of new roles for those who seek improvement in education for the 21st century.

A number of national organizations are discussing ways to increase confidence in public education. The Education Leaders Consortium, a coalition of the nation's major education associations, and the new intergroup task force on Community Education for Building Public Confidence in America are two such groups. These groups should be asked to define the kind of system that will produce the best public education program now and in the future in the light of our economic, social, and political environments. I believe their conclusions would not differ greatly from Fantini's visions. Such a discussion would not only increase public confidence, but would give credibility to the leadership efforts in the New England community and 40+ school districts nationwide that have adopted a 4-day school week, with Friday viewed as a "non-learning" day.

Professional community education leaders must move from a state of opportunity to a state of action. (Note: I define a "professional community educator" as a person who applies the principles of community education to his/her professional role; i.e., superintendent, mayor, principal, social agency director, citizen, parent, etc.) Some of the school improvement and effectiveness studies now receiving great attention will be adapted and replicated at the local level. During this period of self-examination, community educators should involve the community in discussions of school problems and the need for accountability and restructuring to meet financial constraints, and in generating alternative ideas for using the community to provide learning experiences.

In school districts in which community education is well established, a core team, perhaps lead by a principal or a director/coordinator with facilitation skills, could lead a community and local school district towards full implementation of community education in a few years. Similarly, a mayor or another political leader could contribute to school improvement and change by leading discussions on the needs of children and youth; the need to maintain or reduce tax levels while improving the quality of education could provide the impetus. Further, a civic leader might be effective in dealing with the initial furor that can be expected from teachers' associations and other groups that will need time to examine and test the implications of a coordination and facilitation role. Resistance to change is normal. A supportive local political leader will give the change agents (the core team) the support and time necessary to change the structure of the school. Combined school-community leadership is likely to result in better decisions that more accurately reflect the whole society.

Interagency Relationships: The Importance of Communications Skills

Fantini describes four models of community education as they relate to changing social contexts. He suggests our current state is somewhere between Model 2 and Model 3.

In Model 2, at least within the community school movement, coordination between school officials and community agencies is implied and is, in fact, often successful, occurring more often in the realm of service delivery than in student learning. In Model 3, this coordination is explicit in every subject outside the "basics" and is implicit in the basics as well. Model 4 takes public educators beyond coordination to facilitation and culminates in "a community-wide network of interlinking educative environments, coordinated by school officials working in close collaboration with the home and the community." Improvement in communications skills will be required to increase the likelihood of success in Models 2, 3, and especially 4.

The development of productive, efficient interagency relationships is one of the fundamental goals of community education. Each interagency relationship is unique, developed according to indentified need; available resources; current practices, policies, and law; the complexity of the problem or event; the disposition of those in authority; and other variables. These relationships involve varying degrees of communication, from none at all to highly complex forms:

Stage 1 — No communication or dialogue.

Stage 2 — Communication: continuing communication or dialogue but no decisions for action.

Stage 3 — Cooperation: action undertaken to work on one-time or occasional events determined to be mutually beneficial. Complete agency autonomy; no formal structure or agreement.

Stage 4 — Coordination: continuous action follows established procedures, resulting in interdependence between agencies in affected areas. Specific informal or formal agreements.

Stage 5 — Collaboration: action towards common goal(s) resulting from intensive planning between agencies for the purpose of sharing personnel, financial, administrative, and program/service responsibility. Individual agency autonomy may or may not be limited. Interdependence between involved agencies within scope of defined program/service area(s). Formal agreements detailing responsibilities and procedures. A small, ongoing group representing the involved agencies directs the collaborative effort.

Full involvement of the community in the teaching-learning process is obviously complex, and many public educators lack the communications skills they need to make interagency relationships productive. How often do teachers, administrators, and policy makers actually communicate with the public? What conceptual, human, and technical training have they received from institutions of higher education? What communications skills do they need? Educators' communications skills may well have been dulled from lack of use and from a lack of reinforcement by both peers and the establishment itself.

Action Now

The rewards of relevant, exciting, and self-motivating learning experiences for students are not far away. It may be necessary to take action without waiting for change in the entire education system. Every educator can do something, however small, to involve the community. Success will spread.

Contributing enthusiasm and ideas to the school and to community improvement activities may be an effective way to begin.

National resolve is also needed to harness the potential of the community for educational improvement. National organizations must promote innovative practices and disseminate the results of the research conducted by such programs as Teacher Corps, Title I, and the Community Schools and Comprehensive Community Education Act. The National Committee for Citizens in Education, for example, recently compiled the findings of over thirty-five research studies on the impact of parent involvement on student achievement in **Parent Participation—Student Achievement: The Evidence Grows.** The experience of state-mandated citizen advisory councils in California, Florida, and South Carolina must be studied and communicated to local school and community leaders.

Fantini is rightly concerned about the possibility of a dual system of education. Leaders who inform and motivate educators, parents, and other community members regarding the potential of the community as an educational resource will help us through the critical period of redefining and testing new school-community relationships; their initiatives will open up new structures and options for learning for all. Finally, a heightened sensitivity to the complexities of interagency relationships will increase the probability of success.

PART II

School Closing and

Shifting Populations

PART II: SCHOOL CLOSINGS AND SHIFTING POPULATIONS

SUMMARY

William DeJong and Dwayne E. Gardner discuss recent demographic trends that have had an impact on the planning of education and other public facilities. Advances in medicine and nutrition have increased life expectancy and thus increased the proportion of the population in the older age ranges. The number of students enrolled in adult education in the U.S. doubled between 1970 and 1980; 21 million adults, or about 13 percent of the adult population, are taking classes.

The U.S. birth rate fell during the 1960s and '70s but is now rising. Some of the schools closed in the last decade will have to be reopened in the next. Changes in child care needs have accompanied the entrance of increased numbers of women into the workforce and the increased numbers of single parents. Central cities are regaining population previously lost to the suburbs, and the North has lost population to the South and the West. All of these demographic shifts have caused changes in facility needs.

Before 1970 interagency use of school facilities was rarely considered in facility planning. But continued experimentation in the last 10 years has demonstrated that housing diverse services under one roof leads to a greater probability of cooperation and the elimination of duplicate services.

The problem of declining school enrollment and concomitant surplus space have been dealt with most successfully by community involvement and interagency coordination. DeJong and Gardner believe that the school facilities of the future will reflect that influence of community education. They will be planned cooperatively by community residents, educators, and architects, and will provide opportunities for lifelong education and the delivery of human services.

George C. Kliminski writes that public education will not be responsive to community change unless there is in place an organizational structure accountable to the general community. Accepted principles of community education—citizen involvement in decision-making and two-way communication between citizens and institutions—provide such a structure. Kliminski says that communities need a community educator with a processing role to detemine community priorities and appropriate resources to deal with those priorities.

The population shifts cited by DeJong and Gardner have contributed to citizens' beliefs that schools should be open to the general public for a broad range of services. Kliminski cautions that as the school-age population increases in the years ahead, space allocated to community services in times of declining enrollment cannot suddenly be reclaimed for K-12 use.

Energy shortages mandate a community-wide view of energy use because decreased energy use in one institution may be offset by increases in other institutions or by individual consumers. Kliminski cites studies that have shown that locating a public service near where people live increases the percentage of people taking advantage of the service by about 25 percent.

Sterling Keyes notes that demographic trends are subject to change but agrees with DeJong and Gardner that energy-related problems will have to be dealt with for the foreseeable future. He says that research in New York state confirms their closing schools to save energy is likely to increase energy use in the community served by the school, and concurs with the community-wide approach to conservation described by DeJong and Gardner.

Keyes cautions that our nation's poor and less well-educated must be given opportunities to express their needs and desires and to participate in the identification of community needs and the best ways to respond to them. He also warns against a crisis approach to problems and calls for long-term planning. He points out the particular needs of poor families. Keyes believes that community education can have an important influence on future educational, social, and political policy.

DEMOGRAPHICS AND USE OF PUBLIC FACILITIES
by
William DeJong and Dwayne E. Gardner

Better use of public facilities, especially schools, has been a central theme of the community education movement for many years. The examination of demographic trends can provide a clearer understanding of where to apply our resources in the years ahead.

Demographic Trends and Use of Data

Planners and demographers have been rightfully accused of making poor decisions by ignoring "soft" data, the attitudes and perceptions of people. The failure of low-income housing projects in the late 1960s can be attributed to a failure to consider soft data and hard data (facts and figures) simultaneously. During the 1960s, planners and decision-makers determined statistically that people were poor and housing was dilapidated; they proceeded to raze vast urban areas and build low-income high-rise buildings. Ten years later many of these same planners looked at the statistics and again identified people as poor and the housing built 10 years earlier as dilapidated. The planners had neglected the soft data; if they had asked the people if they wanted to live in high-rise apartment complexes, the result might have been different.

Many people involved in community education can be characterized as "soft data planners," planners whose decisions are based on the attitudes and perceptions of community members. The Council of Educational Facility Planners was recently asked by a school district to assist in developing a new community school to be financed by a proposed bond issue. When asked why a new community school was needed, the planners responded that residential development was increasing, which implied that there would be more school-age youngsters. When hard data were collected, however, it was clear that there would be no increase in the student population; fertility rates had declined faster than housing had increased. The point is that both hard and soft data must be taken into account in planning.

Planners must also be aware that demographic trends are subject to change. The most significant factors affecting demographic trends are social, political, and economic. A classic example of a social factor that altered demographic patterns was the rapid acceptance of "the pill" and other new forms of birth control.

The cautious use of demography is critical. Without a clear understanding of the future in relation to the past, decisions made today could become albatrosses tomorrow.

More than at any time in our past, events are occurring at a rapid pace. We are dealing now with more information and with many more variables, especially relating to the construction of buildings. Nearly 80 percent of the buildings that will be in use in the year 2000 are already built, and almost every one of them is energy inefficient. But, through computer technology, we also have greater capabilities for analyzing data and better educated people to deal with the challenges of understanding the future.

Increasing Population

The population of the United States is increasing.

U.S. POPULATION

1950	150,697,361
1960	179,323,175
1970	203,235,298
1980	226,504,825

Life has been prolonged, immigration from Mexico, Asia, the Carribean, and other parts of the world is continuing, and babies are being born in increasing numbers.

The current world population is approximately 4.3 billion, up from 2.5 billion in 1960. It is projected to be 6.2 billion in the year 2000 and to double in less than 30 years after that.

More Older People

As our population has increased, the mix of people has changed. There are more elderly and fewer young people. During the baby boom of the '50s and '60s, about half of the people in the U.S. were under the age of 18. By 1990 it is estimated that four out of five Americans will be over 18.

One speaker recently summed up the situation this way:

> The youth culture is over. Go to any shopping mall or golf course on Monday and notice that patrons have crow's feet, liver spots, big bellies, bald heads and bifocals. While you are shopping, check out the decline of youth oriented products. Circus World has doubled its **adult** toy market. The acne creams, the baby foods and the diapers are being replaced by optometrists, wigs and toupee shops and health food stores.

> Airplane attendents have suddenly matured. A list of the ten most beautiful women in the world included no one under thirty. Jackie O. has turned fifty. Juvenile crime has decreased and Gerber Baby Food now sells life insurance. The Boy Scouts are down about 2 million members in the last six years. And the Grey Panthers are flexing their number power on behalf of the elderly.

> When it came time to vote for taxes for public education during the 1960s, over fifty percent of the households had children in schools. By the end of the '70s, it was less than thirty percent and in the state of Florida only about twenty percent.

FIGURE 1.

Percent Distribution of the Resident Population, by Age and Sex: April 1, 1980, and April 1, 1970.

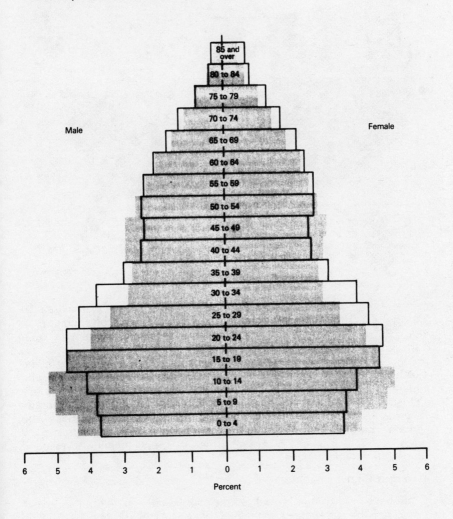

FIGURE 1.

Percent Distribution of the Resident Population, by Age and Sex: April 1, 1980, and April 1, 1970

1970
— 1980

Male

Female

85 and over

80 to 84

75 to 79

70 to 74

65 to 69

60 to 64

55 to 59

50 to 54

45 to 49

40 to 44

35 to 39

30 to 34

25 to 29

20 to 24

15 to 19

10 to 14

5 to 9

0 to 4

6   5   4   3   2   1   0   1   2   3   4   5   6

Percent

Source: 1980 and 1970 censuses.

Migration to the South

Within the United States, there has been a dramatic shift in population from the North to the South and West.

FIGURE 2.

Percent Change in Population by State: 1970 to 1980

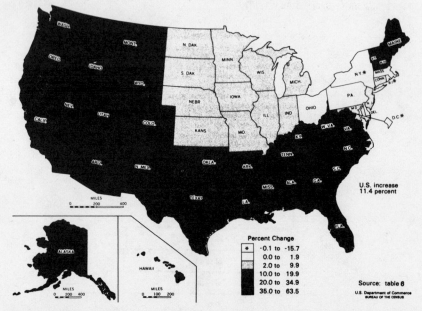

Percent Change

* -0.1 to -15.7
  0.0 to 1.9
  2.0 to 9.9
  10.0 to 19.9
  20.0 to 34.9
  35.0 to 63.5

U.S. increase
11.4 percent

Source: table 6

U.S. Department of Commerce
BUREAU OF THE CENSUS

Many of those who have moved are older people, but the young are also moving. This migration is far greater than that of the wagon train days of the 1800s. A number of variables—the economy, retirement, and especially mobility—are primary reasons.

Mobility has caused a series of problems for both North and South. The North has begun to lose one of its most valuable resources, its people, and thus the base of its economy. Even though there are fewer people and less industry, streets must still be planned, libraries run, and other essential services provided. These needs translate into higher taxes for those who remain. The South and West, on the other hand, have been confronted by water shortages, a lack of essential services, and inability to respond quickly to new demands.

Boom or Bust

We have lived through two dramatic population shifts within a 35-year time span: the baby boom and the baby bust. The U.S. fertility rate dropped from an average of 3.7 children per family in the late '50s to 1.78 in 1975, less than the minimum replacement rate.

FIGURE 3

Estimates and Projections of Annual Total Fertility Rate: 1960 to 2000

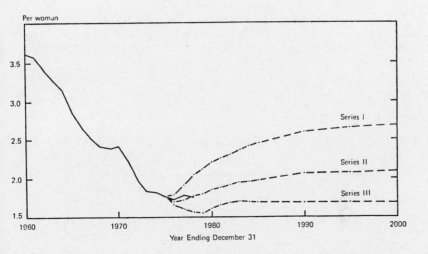

Source: 1960 to 1973 from: Robert L. Heuser. *Fertility Tables for Birth Cohorts by Color: United States, 1917-73.*
1974 to 1978 from: Unpublished tabulations of the National Center for Health Statistics.

The number of annual births began to decline, with only an occasional slight upswing, after an all-time high of 4.3 million in 1961. The number of annual births declined precipitously during the next decade and ranged between 3.1 and 3.2 million in 1973-76.

In calculating projected birth, both the fertility rate and the number of women classified as potential childbearers must be taken into consideration. The number of women of prime childbearing age (15-44) continues to increase:

Year	
1970	42,447,000
1975	47,403,000
1980	51,683,000
1985	54,775,000

Even if the fertility rate were to stabilize at the 1975 level, there is potential for a large percentage increase in births because of the increase in the number of potential childbearers. The number of births in 1980 (approximately 3.6 million) was nearly 4 percent higher than in 1979, and in the first six months of 1981 the birth rate was nearly 2 percent higher than it had been in the first six months of 1980.

Two social changes could dramatically affect future fertility rates. First, it might become more fashionable for middleaged women to have children. Second, abortions might become illegal, causing a dramatic increase in the number of live births.

FIGURE 4.

Estimates and Projections of Annual Number of Births: 1960 to 2000

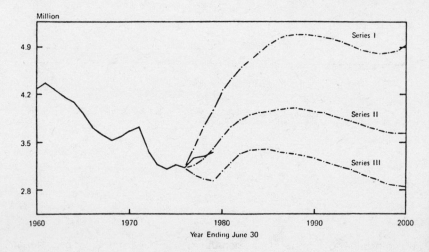

Source: Current Population Reports, Series P-25, No. 704; No. 870.

FIGURE 5.
Changes in the Components of Fertility:
1970-75 and 1975-80

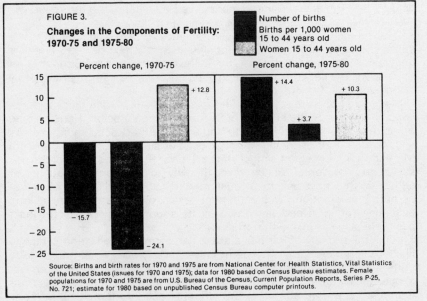

FIGURE 3.

**Changes in the Components of Fertility:
1970-75 and 1975-80**

Number of births
Births per 1,000 women
15 to 44 years old
Women 15 to 44 years old

Percent change, 1970-75 — Percent change, 1975-80

Source: Births and birth rates for 1970 and 1975 are from National Center for Health Statistics, Vital Statistics of the United States (issues for 1970 and 1975); data for 1980 based on Census Bureau estimates. Female populations for 1970 and 1975 are from U.S. Bureau of the Census, Current Population Reports, Series P-25, No. 721; estimate for 1980 based on unpublished Census Bureau computer printouts.

The Death of the Suburbs

Migration from city to suburbs has occurred on an even greater scale than the migration from North to South. The suburbs are primarily residential or "bedroom" communities; in fact, most suburban homes have three, four, or five bedrooms built in response to the baby boom of the '50s and '60s.

Table A.   Central-City and Suburban
Migration: 1970-75
and 1975-80

(Numbers in thousands)

	1970-75	1975-80
Central cities:		
Immigrants	5,987	6,891
Outmigrats	13,005	13,237
Net migration	-7,018	-6,346
Suburbs:		
Inmigrants...................	12,73	13,628
Outmigrants	7,309	8,627
Net migration	+5,423	+5,001

As the size of the average household shrinks, it is increasingly obvious that we have built too many large homes, many of them bought as an investment, a hedge against inflation. Adam Smith suggests in **Paper Money** that the age of "cheap money" is over, that in the future we will build homes as places to live, not as investments.

Over the last several decades, central cities have lost population to the suburbs, but suburbs may lose population in the next decade. Whether people will move back to the city, out to the country, or to the Sunbelt is yet to be seen. The decline in suburban population will be caused primarily by the movement of young people.

Many suburban areas were built rapidly, and one of their biggest needs was for schools. In the suburbs of Detroit, Chicago, Boston, Houston, and other cities it is not uncommon to find an elementary school within every square mile. Half of them are now closed or slated for closure by 1985. More than 80 percent of school staff will be at the highest level of the pay scale, and residents will be taxed heavily to maintain the quality of education they have become accustomed to. Lacking a distinctive cultural or ethnic orientation, and with high taxes, overly large homes, long distances from jobs, and high energy costs, suburbia may well be the least desirable place to live within the next 15 years.

In contrast, many of our cities are experiencing revitalization, which is likely to continue. Large homes in cities have been divided into smaller units suitable for smaller families. There are incentives to restore housing, shops, and factories. Condominiums, revitalized retail areas, and electronic industries are all attracting the affluent back into the cities. In many cases, revitalization has had the unfortunate effect of displacing the poor, who can not afford the housing and other necessities, and the blue collar worker, whose older manufacturing plant has given way to industries oriented to a computer age.

Uncertain Energy Supplies

There are three major threats to the future of our planet: the world population explosion, nuclear war, and reliance on petroleum as the major energy source. World oil consumption has increased from about 3.7 million barrels a day in 1950 to more than 35 million barrels today. Oil is a finite resource, and its availability is extremely susceptible to political and economic influences.

Continued oil price increases, the cutting off of imported oil, or continued consumption at current levels would substantially decrease the standard of living in this country and affect every city, every household, and every person in the United States.

Trends in Education

The effects on U.S. education of the change from a younger to an older population are immense. The number of students enrolled in adult education doubled from 1970 to 1980. More than 21 million adults, 13 percent of the adult population, are now enrolled in classes.

During this same period there was a comparable increase in the number of women in the labor market, creating new demands for preschool and after-school child care programs. There was a 70.5 percent increase in preschool enrollment between 1970 and 1980.

These two trends—to an older population and to greater numbers—have generated debates in nearly every local board of education. How is "public education" defined? Is it only for those between the ages of five and 18, for six hours a day, or is it for everyone, for lifelong learning? If the latter, who will pay for it, especially when money is tight? And if public education is not broadly defined, will taxpayers who do not have school-age children (now 72 percent of the voting public) be willing to support it? The debate goes on.

Techological changes are forcing a review and revision of curriculum and the way in which education services are delivered. Because rapid change has become characteristic of our society, the so-called "basics" may become secondary to listening and coping skills and the ability to deal with change. Mandatory attendance may become obsolete. There is speculation that by the end of the century 12th grade will no longer be part of the high school sequence, but will be absorbed by college or trade and vocational schools, or dropped entirely.

The composition of the family has undergone so many changes that it is hard to predict how "family" will be defined in the future. Fewer than 15 percent of Americans now live in a traditional nuclear family in which the father works, the mother is a housewife, and there are two or more siblings. Nearly half of our youngsters will live with a single parent sometime during their school years. Yet most of our educational system is still based on the premise of the traditional family. Today's youth will live through more change in their lifetime than they would have experienced had they been born at the time of Christ and died after man landed on the moon.

The "Unknown Trend"

The trend likely to shape our lives more than any other is the one we are still unaware of. No one projected the baby bust or the acceptance of the pill or, for that matter, OPEC—induced oil gluts and shortages. These trends appeared suddenly in the last 25 or 30 years. New discoveries, such as food from the oceans to solve world hunger problems, medicines to prolong life, or advances in genetics, could drastically alter our future. What we don't know suggests that we must be receptive to new ideas, information, and change.

FIGURE 6.

Labor Force Participation Rates for Married Women
16 to 44 Years Old With Husband Present, by
Presence and Age of Children: 1960, 1970, and 1980

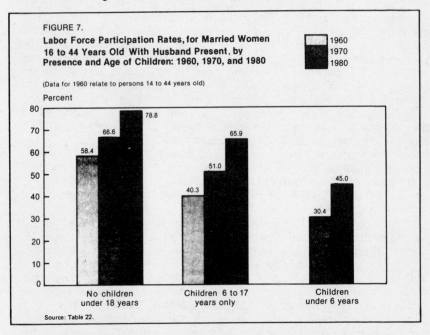

FIGURE 7.

**Labor Force Participation Rates, for Married Women
16 to 44 Years Old With Husband Present, by
Presence and Age of Children: 1960, 1970, and 1980**

1960
1970
1980

(Data for 1960 relate to persons 14 to 44 years old)

Percent

No children under 18 years: 58.4, 66.6, 78.8
Children 6 to 17 years only: 40.3, 51.0, 65.9
Children under 6 years: 30.4, 45.0

Source: Table 22.

Community Education and Use of Public Facilities

Much has been written on declining school enrollment, school closings, the conversion of surplus school facilities to community centers, and interagency occupancy of surplus schools. What follows will be a scenario of what community education has and has not accomplished regarding the use of facilities and what might be accomplished during a time of changing demographics.

Community education has the flexibility to respond to both growth and decline. From a facility planner's perspective, community education is not a separate program, such as special education or adult education, but a concept that applies to the delivery of education and other human services in the most effective, efficient, and humane manner. During a time of declining enrollment and school closings, this concept may be directed to converting school buildings into community centers to respond more adequately to broader education and human services needs. During a period of growth, the same concept may be applied to planning and building facilities, with agencies working together to respond appropriately to community needs.

The Past, the Present, and the Future — Community Education and the Use of Public Facilities

From 1935 to 1970 broadened use of public facilities was usually applied only to public schools. This period can be described as the "extended use" or "lighted schoolhouse" era, when school buildings were used after regular school hours for a variety of community-oriented education, enrichment, and recreation programs.

The arguments of those involved in community education at the time could not be dismissed: public schools were being used only 30 percent of the time during the school year and not at all during vacations. This was an obvious waste of the taxpayers' investment, especially when other community needs were not being met. Community education became an appendage, its programs added on to the regular school day. Within the professional education community, the community education concept was not fully recognized. When new school buildings were planned, planners, with few exceptions, did not consult with community educators, nor did they include the needs of other community programs in their specifications. Little or no thought was given to non-school programming until after the facility was built, and function followed form.

In the late '60s and early '70s a new concept began to emerge in educational facility planning—the human service center. About a dozen very large complexes housing a variety of education and human services were built in urban areas. In most instances these facilities included education, recreation, municipal, employment, and welfare services. The Pontiac, Michigan, Human Resources Center, the John F. Kennedy Community School, Atlanta, and the Thomas Jefferson Community School in Arlington, Virginia, are examples. The connection of this new facility concept with the community education concept was obvious, underscoring as it did the need for both comprehensiveness and flexibility in response to changing community needs.

The concept of human service centers or interagency facilities made sense for a number of reasons. First, housing agencies under one roof increased the probability that they would work more closely together and eliminate duplication. Second, clients had one location to go to for assistance with their educational and social needs. Third, housing agencies under one room was cost effective in terms of capital investment and operating expenses when compared with developing and maintaining separate facilities. Fourth, space utilization increased when agencies shared common areas, such as offices, conference rooms, and classrooms, and when space was used for an increased number of hours.

Thus, the period from 1935-70 provided two phenomenal contributions to public facility planning: (1) the extended day and evening use of school facilities for a variety of community needs; and (2) introduction of the concept of interagency use of facilities.

1970—Present

The period from 1970 to the present has been a time of continued experimentation with the interagency use of new facilities, continued development of the lighted schoolhouse concept, and tremendous opportunities opened up by declining school enrollment. The community education concept gained much greater sophistication, especially in its influence on the way facilities are planned.

The community education movement has missed many opportunities it could have capitalized on, however, most notably in the public works and community development block grant programs and in opportunities for use of surplus schools. Even today, as legislation is being drafted for "enterprise zones," community education is passing up yet another opportunity.

Community education has gained recognition in the area of school closings, a highly emotional and difficult topic for the traditional administrator to address. The most successful method for dealing with this issue has been to apply the community education principles of community involvement and interagency cooperation. In this era of declining enrollment, community education has taught us that decline need not be viewed as a negative condition but may be seen as an opportunity to redefine the quality of life in our communities so that changing neighborhood needs may be met.

Community education has proved valuable for other reasons. The population in our communities has not necessarily decreased, although the population mix has changed, and community education is capable of meeting the changed educational needs of community residents. And as a school-based movement, community education is less threatening to school administrators than a community-based movement.

The influence of community education has been felt in the years since 1970 as more than 7,000 school buildings with a real estate value of approximately $6 billion and a replacement of value of $20 billion have been closed. Not all of the 7,000 buildings have become community centers or interagency facilities, of course; in some cases, the community worked with agencies and found that such a facility was not needed. The important contribution of community education was that agencies and communities began to work cooperatively and, where needed, to share facilities to provide community services.

Community education has made significant contributions to the development, use, and reuse of public facilities. One of the most notable contributions has been a change in our planning methods. Traditionally, administrators and consultants have provided input to the architect, working in isolation from the community. The notion of "cooperative planning," in which community members, professionals, and decision-makers work together to determine community needs and how they can best be met, has provided a rebirth of public participation in many communities.

Another contribution of community education, with its emphasis on shared space, is the phase in/phase out concept, which is just beginning to gain momentum. As traditional education programs are phased out because of enrollment decline, other compatible programs, such as adult education, preschool, and recreation, are phased in. Declining enrollment doesn't have to mean an abrupt discontinuation of education services. Through community education, an education program can be delivered effectively and efficiently in concert with other community programs.

Community education also provides an opportunity to adapt unneeded school facilities to non-public uses, such as private housing or commercial development. Application of the principles of community involvement and interagency cooperation does not mean that every facility must be interagency community center, but rather that every facility will be used in a way that best responds to community needs, whether public or private.

Community education may also offer an answer to declining financial resources. As money for social programs continues to dwindle, agency "turfdoms" will eventually crumble, and new forms of cooperation must evolve if basic social needs are to be met.

Community education has made contributions to energy conservation. Less total energy is consumed if services are based within neighborhoods, if agencies are housed collectively, and if facilities are more efficiently used. The extended use of public facilities may seem to be in conflict with energy efficiency, but recent energy studies show that extended use is highly cost effective, especially in the snowbelt.

As a result of community education, new facility legislation is being written daily. New Jersey is currently considering legislation that would prohibit any public agency from building a new facility without considering the availability of existing public space. The legislation includes financial incentives for interagency projects. Florida already gives preferential treatment to multiagency projects. In New York, South Carolina, California, and other states, community involvement is required in planning and decision-making related to public facilities. Other states are moving to eliminate codes, regulations, and financing methods that inhibit the development of multiagency projects and community centers.

Beyond 1985

During the past five years, maintenance, new construction, capital improvements, and renovations have been deferred, chiefly because of shrinking school enrollments and a depressed economy. The backlog of new construction and renovation projects is so large, there could be a tremendous construction boom if the economy of the nation improves. For the first time in our history, we would see large-scale new construction, renovation, and school closings occurring simultaneously in different parts of the country. Regional and local differences, differences between North and South, and differences based on growth and decline patterns within standard metropolitan areas will determine what happens where.

The impact that community education may have on public facilities beyond 1985 has been determined in part by its past contributions. The lighted schoolhouse will be with us for some time to come, as will the interagency facility, the community center, and the recycled school.

Community education is unlikely to influence future demographic trends or, for that matter, social, economic, and political trends. But its principles can help meet the challenges of tomorrow. How well it does that will depend on how well community educators comprehend the future and how well they communicate to others the application of its principles.

A year ago the Committee on Architecture for Education, a joint committee of the American Institute of Architects and the Council of Educational Facility Planners, International, met in Cincinnati for two days to discuss the school building of tomorrow. After spending a half day discussing demographic, technological, social, and economic trends (with a little infusion of some community education concepts), the group broke into design teams to conceptualize and draft tomorrow's schools. The terms used to describe the design concepts were "one-stop shopping centers for human services," "expressways" with multiple entries and exits based on the number of times an individual would be involved in education for training and retraining, "learning/resource centers," "lifelong learning centers," and others. Every team concluded that traditionally defined schools would no longer exist.

The times are ready for community education. The question is, are those who embrace the community education concept ready for the times?

REFERENCES

American Education, vol. 15, no. 1 (January/February 1979).

CEFP Journal, vol. 17, no. 3 (May/June 1979).

CEFP Journal, vol. 19, no. 3 (May/June 1981).

Council of Educational Facility Planners, International, Energy Use in Community Schools, (Columbus, Ohio, 1980).

Nancy Cook, Facility Use Patterns. (Mid-Atlantic Center for Community Education, School of Education, University of Virginia, 1979).

Council of Educational Facility Planners, International, Surplus School Space—The Problem and the Possibilities (Columbus, Ohio, 1978).

National Center for Education, Digest of Educational Statistics (Washington, D.C. February 1981).

Smith, Adam, Paper Money (Dell Publishing Company, Inc., NY, 1980).

Steele, Marilyn, "Cooperative Community Planning To Respond to Use of Surplus Schools" (speech, San Diego, California, February 1980).

The Structure of the U.S. Economy in 1980 and 1985, no. 1831 (U.S. Governing Printing Office, 1975).

U.S. Bureau of the Census, Current Population Reports, p. 20, no. 359-368, (January 1981-January 1982).

Reaction Paper to: William DeJong and Dwayne E. Gardner's
"Demographics and Use of Public Facilities"

by
George Kliminski

DeJong and Gardner show how demographic trends and the use of public facilities, particularly public schools, have changed over time, generally in response to changing community values and needs. Rapid social change must be reflected in the institutions responsible for meeting the needs of a changing society. The question is not whether institutions should change, but how they can change efficiently and effectively. This paper will focus primarily on the role of the public school in a time of change.

The Role of Public Schools

A community cannot respond to change unless it has in place an organizational structure that is accountable to the general community for responding to change. An accepted principle of community education is that community residents should be involved in decisions that will affect them. The concept of a well developed two-way communication structure between community residents and community agencies and institutions is inherent in the involvement principle. If the community lacks a working accountability model that can assure two-way communication, change will be seen from different perspectives by community residents and agency personnel. Experience has shown that the public school is potentially suited to be an accountable organization that could take on the communication role. Unless both the public school and the community agree upon this new role for the public school, or for some other community agency, there will be no effective and continuing two-way communication.

Some public schools have adopted a community education-based policy in which they define a new role and relationship with their communities. The new role usually includes the following major components:

1. *Extended use of public school facilities: board of education support for and involvement in development of the local community education plan, including extended use of public school facilities for community residents.*
2. *Citizens involvement: mechanisms that provide for continued, cross-aged citizen input into program planning and development. This includes, but is not exclusive to, the use of a representative community advisory council.*
3. *Leadership: a qualified person(s) with training in community education having a work role based on a community education job description.*

4. *Interagency cooperation: a regular contact with community agencies and organizations for the purposes of (a) joint planning, (b) avoiding duplication of efforts, and (c) insuring expanded community services through existing service systems.*

5. *Needs assessment and planning: a documented community planning effort involving a cross section of community residents and including a sequence of needs and resource assessment, goal prioritizing, and evaluation.*[1]

Demographic Trends

DeJong and Gardner point out that "soft" data reflecting attitudes and perceptions may be as important as hard data about populations in determining how public schools and other public facilities are designed, remodeled, and used. Major changes have occurred in people's beliefs about the purposes of school buildings; it is now abundantly clear that community residents believe that school facilities should be available to anyone in the community on an organized basis. A 1979 study in Wisconsin[2] found that 90 percent of Wisconsin residents believe that schools should be open to the general public for a broad range of services. The question that should be paramount to all public administrators is how we can change traditional schools into public facilities open to all community residents, offering programs designed to meet the needs of the local population. Further, how will agencies within the community share responsibility for the general financing and upkeep of the facility? How will the costs of community services be met, and what mechanism will be adopted to ensure that the services are meeting identified needs?

Population Changes

In addition to dramatic changes in both the numbers and ages of people in the U.S. and the world, other important population changes are occurring. More people are immigrating into the U.S. than immigrated during the second decade of this century. Ten percent of the school population in Ramsey County, Minnesota, is of Asian descent. St. Louis Park, Minnesota, has more residents 65 years old or older than it has school-age children (5-18 years). Recent statistics indicate that the number of live births in the U.S. is increasing at a higher rate than previously expected, and that school enrollments will begin to increase by 1987.

Long-Term Commitment and Planning

Schools must change to reflect population changes in their communities. But changes made to accommodate schools during declines in enrollment should be accompanied by implicit commitments to maintain the added services even if K-12 enrollments began to grow again. The schools cannot suddenly decide that all available space must be used for the K-12 population and that services housed in previously underused space must find new facilities. There must be agreements between agencies involved in multipurpose community facilities. The following procedures developed by the National Recreation and Park Association are essential for continued interagency cooperation:

- *top-level commitment from the citizen boards and the administrative boards of service agencies;*

- *a written cooperative agreement that includes goals and objectives, provisions for joint planning committees and procedures, joint policies, guidelines, and requirements;*

- *continuous communication between the two or more agencies at all staff and board levels;*

- *mutual understanding and respect for each other's roles, responsibilities, and resources, including a positive attitude toward all aspects of the cooperative program; and*

- *regular evaluation and reassessment of the joint or multiple program.*[3]

The continuing commitment of schools and other community agencies to be responsive to changing community populations is not new, but it is more complex than it was when society was simpler and more stable. Administrators and leaders can no longer afford to create empires in isolation from each other; economic realities have forced them to work together to serve their constituents in the most efficient and effective manner.

Energy

The consumption of diminishing energy resources should be viewed from a community-wide perspective rather than from the perspective of individual persons or agencies. It has already been documented that when a community as a whole concentrates on decreasing energy consumption, a single agency's consumption may increase. For example, if a college class is offered in a local community building instead of in a centralized institution, the instructor may have to drive some distance to the students, rather than have the students drive to the central institution. The college will use and pay for more energy than if the class were held on its own campus, but the net amount of energy consumed by those involved in the class will decrease.

Adult Education

The trend towards offering services in decentralized locations is related to growth in the number of programs for adults. As larger numbers of adults (52 percent of students in college credit courses in 1980 were over 25) attempt to enroll in classes of all kinds, it becomes more important to offer decentralized services. Studies have shown that bringing a service to people rather than forcing them to go to the service will increase use of the service by about 25 percent. This would indicate that locating a service in a public school, library, church, city hall, private business place, or any other facility within walking distance of a large number of people would greatly increase the number of people using it.

Other Programs

Many community services—educational, cultural, social, and recreational—could be delivered in decentralized locations. Decisions about which services, and which agencies should deliver them, require the prioritizing of community needs and wants and the identification of potential resources.

New Personnel — The Community Educator

Communities that decide they want to develop a systematic approach to the problem of changing demographics (hard data) and changing values and attitudes (soft data) usually find that no person currently employed has either the time or the professional commitment to develop the two-way communication necessary to determine community priorities and the appropriate resources to address them. A solution has been to create the position of Community Education Director (the title may vary). This person has primary responsibility for matching community needs and resources. This role should not be confused with a **programming** role in a specific program area such as adult education, recreation, social services, day care for the young and elderly, etc., but must be seen as a **processing** role. The two roles are distinct and usually cannot be combined.

A community agency other than the public school could be responsible for hiring the community educator, but experience has shown that the public school is eminently capable of assuming the community education process as part of its community responsibilities. A major reason for the success of the public school in community education is the fact that schools are the public facilities most likely to be located close to the greatest number of community residents.

Problems and Opportunities

The major obstacle to community education in carrying out new functions and roles in communities is a lack of recognition by public administrators and community leaders in the need for these new functions and roles. A question in the minds of many is whether schools are capable of accepting the challenges mandated by change. Although the change process is slow, many communities have begun to accept a redefinition of the role of the public school and other community agencies. The potential for creating a better service delivery system through the concept of community education is tremendous. Public schools have the opportunity to relate to the total community and, using existing resources, to deliver programs in a more efficient and effective manner. The challenge is to provide services to people of all ages and to improve the quality of community living.

The Future

DeJong and Gardner indicate clearly that the demographic picture in the U.S. is continuing to change rapidly, and that schools and other public facilities are changing in the types of services offered and the kinds of people served. A larger question remains. How can public facilities adapt to rapidly changing community needs and remain efficient? A major need is for institutional leadership that is responsible for communication with community residents and agency personnel and accountable to the public. In many communities, the need is not for a new service provider but for a facilitator responsible for building a bridge between community needs and community resources.

The public schools appear to have the potential for taking on this facilitating role, but they will face many challenges as they redefine their role to encompass all of the people in a given geographic area. Someone has said that what we now think of as public schools can become community facilities that are sometimes used for the education of children. What an interesting and practical thought.

NOTES

[1]**From Community Education Models in Wisconsin** by Kliminski, Smith, and Gierach (Wisconsin Department of Public Instruction, 1981).

[2]Francis B. Evans, **Public Opinions About Education: A Statewide Poll of Wisconsin Residents** (Wisconsin Department of Public Instruction, 1979).

[3]From **A New Foundation — Perspectives on Community Education** by V. M. Kerensky and J. D. Logsdon (U.S. Department of Education, 1979).

Reaction Paper to: William DeJong and Dwayne E. Gardner's

"Demographics and Use of Public Facilities"

by
Sterling S. Keyes

As we examine demographic trends and the influence they have on planning for facility use, we must be cognizant of how our perceptions affect the interpretation of these trends. The interpretaton of demographic trends is subject to the same admonition Edward Hallett Carr advanced about the interpretation of facts.

Carr writes:

> History consists of a corpus of ascertained facts. The facts are available to the historian in documents, inscriptions, and so on, like fish on the fishmonger's slab. The historian collects them, takes them home, and cooks and serves them in whatever style appeals to him. . . .(But) facts are really not at all like fish on the fishmonger's slab. They are like fish swimming about in a vast and sometimes inaccessible ocean; and what the historian catches will depend partly on chance, but mainly on what part of the ocean he chooses to fish in and what tackle he chooses to use—these two factors being, of course, determined by the kind of facts he wants to catch.[1]

Demographic trends are, as DeJong and Gardner warn, "subject to change." One thing is clear: we are dominated by energy issues and the economic, social, and political ramifications of those issues. It is obvious that we must combine and conserve. We must seek ways to convert buildings to more efficient uses. A report issued by the New York State Education Department in 1978 recommended flexibility in school calendars:

> Since none of the alternative school calendars under study appears to be superior in all aspects—energy conservation, fostering learning, social acceptance, and maximization of use of facilities—it would seem unnecessary for the [New York] Board of Regents to change the method by which individual school calendars are presently selected. Instead, the Board of Regents should seek enabling legislation which would allow school districts to operate experimentally, at the discretion of and with the approval of the Commissioner of Education under a calendar not presently deemed permissible.[2]

It is easy to say that we must combine and conserve; accomplishing it may be more difficult.

DeJong and Gardner trace the past, present, and future of community education in relation to the use of public facilities, and suggest that community education "has provided a rebirth of public participation in many communities." I concur with this idea, but a word of caution is in order. Too few of our poor and less well-educated are considered able to contribute to the determination of their own needs. Poor decisions are later identified as decisions of the poor. The authors provide an excellent example in "the failure of low income housing projects in the late 1960s." Our attitudes must be changed to the extent that we believe that all people are capable of expressions of aspirations, that all people are capable of expressing what they believe to be their needs. Perhaps more importantly, we must believe that all people have a right to the opportunity to help plan for their future. DeJong and Gardner might have stated the "community planning" imperative more strongly. In the case of energy conservation, the nature of the savings, the manner in which energy uses are combined to reduce costs, and the consideration of such factors as the fostering of learning, meeting community needs, and sharing facilities must be studied thoroughly by all of the parties affected by the decisions.

DeJong and Gardner's contentions that the extended school day may actually conserve energy is supported by the New York State Department of Education:

> . . .Closing of school buildings during cold winter months may be counterproductive to total saving of energy. . . .Energy consumption, as measured in the homes of children, was somewhat more when schools were closed.[3]

Although the evidence "cannot be considered conclusive"[4] because of the small sample of school buildings, doubt is cast on the wisdom of closing schools in the winter as a way to save energy. Perhaps schools should be kept in operation for longer periods of time, especially during winter, to reduce the amount of energy consumed in the homes of the pupils. Other experts write:

> The community school idea is an important one. It's an idea that schools and other agencies and organizations and groups can serve neighborhoods and communities better if they cooperate in planning and delivering their services. It's. . .founded in the belief that not only is this a better way to serve people, but also a more efficient way to use resources—people, buildings, energy, and money.[5]

In discussing urban revitalization, DeJong and Gardner express some concern about the displacement of the poor. I share their concern. An example is contained in the presentation of demographic data in a proposal for multiservice health facility for a section of Brooklyn.[6] In 1970 the population of the area, 111,071 persons, represented 4 percent of the population of the Borough of Brooklyn. The median age was 28.43. There were 41,833 households: 24,671 families of two or more persons, and 15,224 one-person households. Recent data show a 4.6 percent drop in total population to a current total of 106,000.[7]

The multiservice health center proposal states:

> . . .These statistics show that there is a high increase of fetal death, early infant disease and deaths under one year of age. Statistics further reveal high occurrence of sickness and disease, pneumonia and influenza together with accidents which are most prominent.

Another dimension of the urban problem is stated in a publication of the National Urban league:

> . . .Finally, the dreadful condition of families headed by black women should be a matter of serious public concern. Part of the problem is due to marital disruption: proportionately more than twice as any black as white women were separated or divorced (19.0 percent compared with 7.4 percent). When a marriage is broken, nearly half of black families are thrust into poverty. In March, 1977, one of every three black families was headed by a woman. About three out of five of the black families with children were living in poverty.[8]

What does this mean for our future? It means a radical change in our thinking and in our way of responding to crisis. And we must be careful, as we attempt to solve one problem that we do not create another. Mario Fantini, writing on "our crisis approach to urban education" made a statement that has, I think, broader application:

> . . .If we do not act to establish an integrated public policy for urban education, we shall continue to lurch from one crisis to another—spending money too inefficiently to make any lasting difference and allowing the gaps separating classes and races to widen. By default, a dual system of education may devlop, with one set of schools for the poor and the handicapped and another for the wealthy and the middle class. . . .Our crisis-oriented approach to fuel conservation is an appropriate analogy. In our efforts to save gas, we build smaller, more fuel-efficient cars. . . .Since their introduction, automobile fatalities have doubled. Our response to one crisis led to another.[9]

DeJong and Gardner raise intriguing questions about future populations, not only in the United States, but in the world. What will be the needs of an American population when "four out of five Americans will be over 18"? The population issues raised by fertility and abortion trends are startling in their implications. All of these population considerations have their greatest impact when considered against the backdrop of uncertain energy supplies.

Education, like energy, affects every man, woman, and child in the world. The New York State Board of Regents is currently studying a draft proposal for **Education for a Global Perspective, A Plan for New York State**. Lifelong learning, what to teach and what to learn, and who does each, are included in discussions of enrollment, budget, and psychological and sociological issues. The rapid changes in our society outlined by DeJong and Gardner are clearly relevant to this kind of planning.

I differ with the authors' assessment that "community education is unlikely to influence future demographic trends or, for that matter, social economic and political trends." The real question, as the authors suggest, is whether enough of us who believe in community education can convince others that community education is ready for the difficult times to come.

NOTES

[1] Edward Hallett Carr, **What is History?** (New York, Vintage Books, 1967), pp. 6, 26.

[2] The University of the State of New York, the State Education Department, **A Study of School Calendars,** (Albany, New York, December, 1978), p. 2.

[3] The University of the State of New York, **A Study of Calendars** (State Education Department, Albany, December 1978), p. 9.

[4] Ibid, p. 9.

[5] Ellen Bussard, Alan Green, and Graham Parker, "The Influence of Community Use of Schools: Some Clues", **CEFP Journal,** vol. 20, no. 2 (March/April 1982), p. 12.

[6] Sylvia Rivers, Waldaba Stewart, and Carol Keyes, **The Development of a Multiservice Health Facility for 205 Ashland Place,** Research, Development and Technical Assistance Department of the Mid-Brooklyn Health Association (Brooklyn, New York, 1982).

[7] Ibid, p. 11.

[8] Bernard E. Anderson, "Economic Progress," **The State of Black America 1980,** (Washington, D.C.: National Urban League, Inc., January 1980), p. 1.

[9] Mario D. Fantini, "Toward a National Public Policy for Urban Education," **Phi Delta Kappan,** vol. 63, no. 8 (April 1982), p. 546.

PART III

Political Process and Citizen Participation

PART III: POLITICAL PROCESS AND CITIZEN PARTICIPATION

SUMMARY

Edith K. Mosher says that community educators must understand the key concepts of power, politics, and policy if they are to "come to grips with the realities of the political arena." Mosher describes relevant theories of policy-making, including Dye's "models of politics" (i.e., institutionalism, interest theory, elite theory, rationalism, incrementalism, game theory, and systems theory). She posits that understanding and influencing policy-making may be more of an art form than a science.

Lindblom's "Play of Power" theory is presented and discussed. Topics covered include: the distinction between policy-makers and citizens; the dependence on rules; persuasion, exchange, and authority; and mutual control and adjustment.

The final section of the paper addresses "the community education connection." Mosher sees process as power; she recommends developing an extensive information base and a "sense of timing," learning how to deal with conflict, and promoting coalitions. She concludes that community education's capacity for future impact will depend on its "finding its way" in new paradigms.

Samuel Halperin discusses the following agenda for community educators in the next two decades:

1. Reassertion and redefinition of a federal role in education. Describing the federal role at the end of the Carter administration as a "highly fragmented, crazy quilt of federal aid programs," Halperin asserts that our first task is to reconceptualize appropriate federal involvement in education. He believes that an overriding federal objective is essential to achieving "our professional equity goals in this country." He notes that the unequal resources and capabilities of the various states demand leadership and an equalizing role for the federal government.
2. Restoration of public confidence in education.
3. Proselytizing within the educational family breaking down the parochial walls between various specializations in education. This will require getting rid of some of the "intellectual splay" evident in community education literature.
4. Achieving greater internal consensus on the nature and limits of community education.
5. Adoption of "a strategy of treating community education as a process rather than a program"—a process that would seek to influence all of education and schooling.

Laurence Iannaccone postulates that American polities, including school districts, have cyclical sequences of quiescence and discontent; periods of discontent provide favorable conditions for policy changes. The stages of the cyclical sequence in school districts are:

- Quiescence.
- Rising voter discontent, often foreshadowed by change in socioeconomic and demographic composition of the district.
- A triggering election—the first election in which one or more school board members are defeated.
- Involuntary turnover of the superintendent following policy conflict between the superintendent and the new board.
- The articulation of a new policy mandate by the new board and new superintendent.
- An election in which the new mandate is tested.

It is important to recognize "turning point election periods" (TPEPs), as different strategies are appropriate and effective at different stages of the cycle. During a TPEP, there is increased public awareness of educational issues and heightened concern about citizen access to policy-makers and school system responsiveness. According to Iannacone, these factors create a favorable climate for advancing community education principles.

Steve R. Parson speculates that successful community education intervention to resolve conflict and provide direction for desired change could, in fact, alter the TPEP stages, or eliminate TPEPs altogether. He observes that the community education movement does not require either a liberal or conservative posture in order to carry out its goals. Community councils, in fact, should endeavor to remain politically neutral, in order to be able to work effectively with all political factions. Periods of policy realignment, superintendent turnover, and articulation of new policies offer opportunities for an expanded role for citizen involvement because special interest groups will be mobilizing to promote particular interests.

Community educators should work initially on problems identified by school district personnel, thus demonstrating the effectiveness of community education in expanding citizen participation to achieve school goals. Parson warns that there are hazards in following an Iannacone suggestion to work outside the system to promote or defeat certain issues. He recommends developing a base of support for community education in the community and letting that support base deal with the political system.

Samuel Halperin disputes Iannacone's turning point election period theory on the grounds that it lacks utility to community educators in search of national, not local, impact, and that it is, in itself, invalid as an explanation of American political behavior. Halperin believes that election results more often reflect candidates' personalities than they do voters' assessments of crucial issues. He characterizes American politics as "notoriously personalistic," and refutes a "mechanistic" explanation of political change.

POWERS, POLITICS, POLICY:
PERSPECTIVES FOR COMMUNITY EDUCATION

by
Edith K. Mosher

... The attempt to separate the two categories of 'process as problem-solving' versus 'process as power' is to fail to recognize that one of the key techniques in the development of problem solving is the use of power. ... We need to recognize that the employment of legitimate power in problem solving is an acceptable and appropriate way to bring about change.
Jack D. Minzey in John W. Warden **Process Perspectives, Community Education as Process.** *(Charlottesville, VA.: Mid-Atlantic Community Education Consortium, 1979), p. 64.*

The ideology and the practices of the community education movement have the contemporary cast of the 1980s, but their roots actually lie in the municipal government reforms of the late 1800s and early 1900s. Educational historians have amply documented the effects on the schools of the widespread effort to replace management by rascally politicians with management by trained administrators whose watchwords would be honesty, efficiency, and non-partisanship.

The public generally endorsed the view that the schools, as "sacred" institutions responsible for the well-being of children, should be divorced as much as possible from the "profane" rough-and-tumble of local and state politics, which determined the fate of other public enterprises. In this climate of opinion, thousands of school districts acquired powers of management and taxation that were largely independent of general government, and political scientists called them "the fourth branch of government." Concurrently, the school systems, though highly diverse in size and resources, greatly expanded both their tasks and their resources, and took on the familiar characteristics of bureaucracies. Other governmental agencies followed a similar trend away from grassroots management by local citizens. What changed least in the last six or seven decades was the conviction, embraced by ever-increasing cadres of professional educators, that policy making for the schools should be non-political, however the term might be defined; that is, it should be fully rational, idealistic, respectful of expertise, and free of partisan conflicts.

Community education advocates today are critical of the adverse effect of official bureaucratic practices on community well-being and deplore the isolation of schools from other community-based agencies. But, like most educators, they are still reluctant to confront the implications of their own use of political power or to come to grips with the realities of the political arena. They have yet to accept the view, now widely shared by other social activist groups, that attention to the nature of power and its exercise in a democracy is central both to understanding and influencing public policy. As Minzey points out, the aloofness of community educators from this trend could be a serious deterrent to achieving their change-oriented goals. To employ "legitimate power in problem solving," as he recommends, requires not merely a shift in attitudes but a better understanding of "power as process" Achieving that understanding is neither a casual nor an easy task.

Power and Policy: The Research Focus

The terms "politics" and "power" have almost as many applications and meanings as users. Political scientists have come to regard them as "slippery concepts," difficult to objectify and unwieldy as bases for generalizing about political life. Many employ instead the concept of "policy" and undertake to study the range of actual circumstances in which people interact to exercise control or influence over each other in the formulation of issues and in making and implementing public policy. According to Thomas R. Dye, their intent is "the **description** and **explanation** of the causes and consequences of governmental action."[1] This analytical task contrasts with many other currently popular approaches to policy questions, such as rhetoric, dialogue, confrontation, and direct action.[2]

My reading of the writings about community education suggests that people in the field are already cognizant of the latter approaches; thus I will attempt in this paper to describe some relevant aspects of the research focus on policy making, indirectly, on the exercise of power, and to relate these concepts to the concerns of community educators. It will be read as a very modest effort to map a highly complex area of study.

Empirical investigations of public policy questions, even when narrowly defined, necessitate collecting and ordering a great volume of data. To accomplish these troublesome tasks, researchers have necessarily made use of various conceptual frameworks, some originating in traditional forms of political research, others traceable to more recent behavioral science orientations. Their eclectic choices do not add up to theoretical coherence, and they cause considerable confusion among both the producers and consumers of policy studies. Dye has undertaken to provide "some help in thinking about public policy" by offering an inventory of seven "models of politics"[3] cautioning that they are not to be considered competitive in the sense that any one is "best." In fact, an adequate explanation of any specific policy issue or event generally requires an artful combination of at least two or more of the models.

Dye's models of politics are as follows:

Institutionalism. Traditional political science concentrated on the study of governmental institutions—Congress, the Presidency, courts, states, cities, political parties, etc.—their structure, organization, duties, and functions. This approach involves detailed attention to constitutional and legal arrangements at all levels of government, but also extends to studies of the linkage between governmental institutions and public policy. This linkage is typically close because the institutions confer legitimacy on policy decisions and use force if necessary to ensure citizen compliance. The institutions embody stable patterns of behavior for groups and individuals, and may be structured to facilitate certain policy outcomes and inhibit others.

Interest Theory. When individuals with common interests band together to press their demands on government, they become "political" in the theoretical sense and are considered in this model to be the basis for all significant political activity. That is, the task of the governmental system is the management of conflict among groups, and public policy at any one time is an equilibrium reached in the struggle among group interests. Changes in the equilibrium will move in the direction desired by those groups that are gaining in influence and away from the direction desired by those losing influence. According to Dye, the influence of groups on public policy is determined by their numbers, wealth, organizational strength, leadership, access to decision-makers, and internal cohesion.

Elite Theory. Some theorists regard public policy as a reflection of the values and preferences of a governing elite, usually a small group of privileged citizens who may or may not be officeholders but who shape mass opinion and acceptance of their policy decisions. Responsibility for mass welfare rests on their shoulders, and the citizenry at large has only a very indirect influence on policy. Competition among elites may exist; however, it tends to be within a narrow range of issues because all elites share a strong interest in preserving the existing system and in preventing rapid or major changes.

Rationalism. Policy is considered "rational" when it results in a higher positive ratio between values achieved and values sacrificed than any other policy alternative. This view of rationality is synonomous with efficiency, but it does not refer merely to a dollars-and-cents frame of reference. Rather it extends to all social, political, and economic values, and is illustrated in this volume by the papers dealing with cost-benefit analysis.

To arrive at a truly rational policy, policy makers would have to: (1) know all the value preferences of society and their relative priorities; (2) know all the policy alternatives and the consequences of each; (3) calculate the ratio of achieved and sacrificed values for each policy alternative; and (4) select the most efficient alternative. Since it is assumed that the value preferences of the entire society—not just those of some interest groups or elites—are relevant, this model is sometimes referred to as "rational-comprehensive" or as embodying "the scientific vision" of policy making.[4]

Incrementalism. The model of incrementalism, views public policy as the continuation of past practices, with relatively minor modifications over time. In this model, constraints of time, intelligence, and cost make the requirements of the rational-comprehensive model impractical; instead, policy-makers use limited forms of policy analysis, support familiar policies, and are satisfied with accomplishments that are below optimal levels.

Such governmental action characterizes extended periods of stability and is not conducive to coping with social change. Thus it is not uncommon to find in some polities periods of incremental policy making interspersed with episodes of explosive political activity, as Iannaccone illustrates in his paper on the politics of local school districts.

Game Theory. Game theory is an abstract and deductive model of decisions making that describes how policy makers would make decisions in competitive situations if they were completely rational. It is thus a variant of rationalism applied to situations in which there is no objectively best choice that one can make. Instead, the "best" outcomes depend upon what others do, based on the values each player seeks to achieve. Game theory's narrow assumptions and conditions for analysis of conflict are seldom found in real life; its principal utility for policy analysts has been to suggest interesting question and to provide a vocabulary to describe and explain policy making in conflict situations.[5]

Systems Theory. The most comprehensive model of policy-making is systems theory which also incorporates aspects of the other models. Systems theory is based on a broad conception of public policy as the response of any political system, however defined or delimited, to forces brought to bear on it from the environment.[6] The political system and environment are interrelated; that is, the system can respond to its environment and must do so to survive. The environment may be modified by the policy outputs of the political system, which also, in time, have the potential of modifying the nature of the political system.

This dynamic view of the sources and impact of the policy-making process implies that an identifiable set of institutions in society, official and unofficial, functions to transform environmental pressures, or demands, into authoritative governmental decisions, or outputs, which the citizenry will support by, for example, accepting election results, obeying the laws, and paying taxes. It recognizes that various sectors of society hold values that are more or less in conflict and that they will press, through organized interest groups, their conflicting demands for governmental action. An on-going political system must be able to arrange and enforce settlements among these contending groups; and, as the incrementalists point out, the process of negotiation usually produces a series of marginal policy compromises, not policy revolutions. As suggested by Kerensky and Fantini in the papers in this volume, growing pressures from a changing social environment constitute major "paradigm shifts." When these lead to a restructuring of demands on the political system, the customary incremental strategies are inadequate to resolve them and more radical policy modifications are likely to occur.

Dye's seven models provide clues to the tasks needed to produce meaningful research about political processes and influence. For particular situtations, such inquiries must identify the relevant institutions and individuals responsible for making and implementing public policy and the ideas and activities of the interest groups that have a stake in the policy outcomes. Analysts must give attention both to previous initiatives and settlements that shaped present public policy and to the potential for changes that are emerging from the environment. Policy makers may lean heavily on past experience in making policy choices. In today's technological society, policy analysts are expected to produce information about more rational, research-based alternatives. Perhaps their most difficult challenge is to grasp the way a political system functions as a whole—i.e., its interactions and modes of conflict resolution—at the same time as they seek out and describe its constituent parts. Discovering the political dynamics of even a small locality is a severe test of analytical skill. More demanding still is the task of the activist who wishes not only to understand the policy making system but also to influence the policy choices. For such a person, policy making becomes less of a science and more of an art form.

The Play of Power

Charles E. Lindblom, the political scientist who formulated the model of incrementalism in the 1960s, has with David Cohen, written more recently about the relationship between policy analysis and social problem solving.[7] His seminal, The **Policy-Making Process,** published first in 1968 and revised in 1980 provides a useful analysis of what he calls, in metaphorical rather than theoretical language, "The Play of Power".[8] This expression stresses both the "game-like" nature of the policy making process and suggests closer and more complex interconnections between people who seek to influence and control each other than does the neutral term "interaction" or the generic term "politics."

Lindblom identifies these fundamental features of all political systems:

1. The distinction between policy makers and citizens.
2. The dependence of the play on rules.
3. The methods by which people control each other, especially persuasion, exchange, and authority.
4. Mutual control and adjustment among participants.

What follows is a very condensed discussion of each of these features.

1. **The distinction between policy makers and citizens.** In almost all political systems, participants in the policy making process fall into two distinct categories. The active, immediate, or proximate policy-makers, most of whom have some form of legal authority to carry out their responsibilities, make up an elite that is only a small proportion of the adult population. In modern industrial states, their participation at various levels of government is highly specialized; they serve, for example, as members of legislatures, elected or appointed officials in the executive branch, judges, or leaders of political parties. The governmental tasks they perform are also specialized, such as: initiating, approving, or implementing policy; planning and coordinating program operations; establishing or constraining policy agendas; adjudicating conflicting interests; and setting budget priorities and limits. Other participants—leaders of interest groups, journalists, party workers, foreign officials, etc.—occasionally exert direct forms of influence on the policy process.

With numerous participants performing specialized roles and tasks, policy can be made only by complex feats of cooperation. And, in a democratic government of divided powers, replete with checks and balances among the protagonists, such cooperation is attained only with great difficulty. Any one of the proximate policy-makers can easily impede the process merely by withholding the requisite collaboration at any stage of negotiations

The largest group of participants in the policy process are ordinary citizens, whose influence as individuals may be insignificant but whose combined influence on the policy process is highly important. In democratic political systems, they delegate the tasks of government to the proximate policy makers, who typically expend much effort to determine and respond to citizen preferences. Voters retain the option to organize and change the proximate policy-makers through elections. Under extreme provocation, they may launch campaigns of civil disobedience. In fact, citizens often need neither to speak nor to act in opposition if their representatives fear that they may be aroused to do so.

Lindblom points out that, while some sectors of the population have greater access to the policy-making process than others, no straightforward relation exists between what citizens want and the policies they get. The conversion of citizen demands or preferences into governmental decisions and activities is mediated by aspects of the play of power **within** the policy making system. Lindblom states: "The rules of democracy throw important powers and liberties into the citizen's hands, but confer only a loose control of policy."[9]

The Dependence on Rules. The play of power in political systems specifies the roles and powers of the players—i.e., the proximate policymakers at all levels and ordinary citizens—and what each role player is allowed to do or prevented from doing in that role. The rules that control the play may have constitutional or legal status, or maybe moral imperatives or matters of custom and expediency. People obey them for various reasons: they see them as necessary to carry on legitimate forms of cooperative action; they are afraid of the consequences of violating them; or they wish to gain practical advantages through reciprocal agreements. A political system in which citizens ignore the rules or violate them with impunity becomes increasingly fragile and unlikely to survive. If a weakened political regime and its rules are over thrown, the revolutionaires must inaugurate a new set of rules to govern the new play of power.

Persuasion, Exchange, and Authority. Lindblom treats these three methods by which people control each other as relatively equal in importance in political life. He recognizes that persuasion may take the form of threats or deceit or may be based on an honest analysis of possible gains and losses. The efficiency of threats and deceit is subject to legal and other constraints, but the honest analysis of possible gains and losses—called "partisan analysis" by Lindblom—is a principal means by which people successfully influence each other.

Two aspects of "partisan analysis" differentiate this concept from Dye's model of rationalism. First, all participants in political interaction, including individual citizens, are considered to have "partisan" points of view and a set of interests that derive from their values and other life experiences. "Partisan" in this sense indicates policy preferences, not political party affiliation. Second, the purpose of the partisan analysis is to collect and organize information about issues and problems that will clarify a partisan's own preferred courses of action, and also help to persuade other participants to support them. The analysis extends to determining the interests and preferences of the other participants in the policy game, and the best ways to win their approval. It has much in common with the sales pitch of advertisers whose mission is to persuade people to buy things they weren't even aware of previously.

While partisans use analytical resources to further their own interests, they are also interacting with other partisans who are doing the same things in behalf of their preferences and priorities. The need of proximate policy-makers for valid information is so critical that they will be attentive to evidence coming from rival interest groups, especially those with a record of research probity. Some of the information generated in this competition of ideas tends to become the common property of all participants; the range of admissible alternative courses of action is widened; and partisan positions may be modified by persuasive evidence previously unheeded. Major groups of partisans, once working at cross purposes, may be persuaded to form coalitions and press for concerted action, if it appears that they may thereby be able to attain some, if not all, of their desired policy results.

Partisan analysis is a pragmatic strategy for influencing policy making. It need not go to exhaustive lengths to demonstrate that the policy in question is the correct or best policy; it need only go as far as necessary to persuade a policy maker with respect to what should be done about a pending decision task. Moreover, the partisans need not agree on broad policy goals, nor argue ideological differences. Rather, the analysis is a search for a connection between a limited set of shared objectives and a policy to serve them. It is not a viable strategy for finding accommodation on policy matters with protagonists commited to non-negotiable ideological positions.

By "exchange" as a method of control or influence, Lindblom means the exchange of benefits between participants in the play of power. Exchanges may take the form of favors or reciprocal obligations that constitute future claims on those involved. Even the ordinary citizen can expect more ready access to an official whom he helps to elect than to one which he does not support.

Money is an important and universally appealing medium for exchanging benefits and can be legitimately used to provide elected officials and interest groups with services that enhance their political influence. But the use of money is fraught with danger because those participants in the play of power who spend heavily may be able to overwhelm all the others. Recognizing that possibility, most governments restrict the exchange of money for such political benefits, as votes or favorable decisions from judges, juries, legislators, and administrators. However, these restrictions have the effect of driving the buying of political favors underground, so that the actual influence of money on policy making is very hard to determine.

Governments are basically authority systems. In the play of power, Lindblom relates the concept of authority to another feature of political systems, namely, their dependence on rules. This means that a person carries out, by the rule of authority, what another requires him to do, and it is not necessary for the latter to invoke his powers of control on each specific occasion when compliance is sought. Authority is defined as follows: individual X has authority over Y if Y accepts the rule of obedience to X. Standing rules of obedience are exemplified in every sphere of governmental activity, from the acceptance by Congress of Presidential vetoes to the appearance of arrested motorists in traffic court.

Authority, so defined, is a highly efficient method of social control and, according to Lindblom, any lasting, highly-powered government depends on many wide-ranging rules of obedience and on the response of subordinate to superior officials. Persons in positions of authority are also generally in a stronger position than others to use persuasion or exchange of benefits as means of influence. Grants of authority to them are not unlimited, however, these are specific to the role and tasks of the various participants in the play of power. Those who overstep their limits may expect to encounter disobedience and even punishment for their infractions. Since exercise of authority is, by definition, considered to be a concession from those who agree to obey, political systems are considered to be highly vulnerable if proximate policy makers are lax in carrying out their responsibilities or if sufficient numbers of activitists in the political system withdraw their grants of authority.

Mutual Control and Adjustment. The foregoing discussion suggests that it would be highly simplistic to view power as running exclusively from the top of a political hierarachy to its lower levels. Policy making, in fact, involves processes of mutual adjustment among participants in the play of power at all levels, and all participants use various avenues and means of influencing each other. Proximate policy-makers are especially likely to become aware of their interdependence and the need for collaboration, so that, according to Lindblom:

> . . .all tread warily, all try to avoid policies certain to stir the strong objection of the others, all look for interests that all can share so that each can pursue his desired policies without resistance from the others, and all store money in the bank by doing favors for others when possible. All this mutual adjustment can occur without a word between them. . . .[10]

Process as Power: The Community Education Connection

It should now be apparent that theorizing about power ranges from very comprehensive systems thinking to a narrow emphasis on the role of elites in political life; from abstract models like game theory to the empirically-derived tenets of incrementalism; from exclusive reliance on scientific tools of analysis to the employment of limited (and some would say opportunitistic) forms of partisan analysis. It is well to recall Dye's caution that no one conceptual model is best and that the study of political events and activities typically involves guidance from two or more of them.

What help is all this to the political activist, specifically to the community educator seeking to relate his own theoretical views about "process as problem solving" to "process as power?" A research focus on the use of control and influence in the policy making process is not of course, intended to produce a set of "how-to's" for a practitioner. In fact, it creates skepticism about treatises that give simplistic advice to non-researchers.

Certain theoretical concerns and concepts recur, however, in research-based writings about politics, power, and policy making; and it is possible for the informed and thoughtful activist to see their relevance to his own particular problems and surroundings. Moreover, through awareness of them he may more readily accept the legitimacy of political activity, a state of "self-affirmation" that Halperin considers essential to effective use of power.[11] What follows are a few examples of the ideas that profitably command his attention.

An Almost Limitless Information Base. A partisan (using Lindblom's definition) who ventures into the play of power without doing his homework is never really in the game at all. The necessary groundwork requires, at a minimum, familiarity with the workings of relevant public agencies, their formal powers and actual operations, with electoral histories, environmental characteristics, the identity and peculiarities of relevant proximate policy makers and interest groups, the traditions and policy preferences of the citizenry, and so on. There is virtually no limits to the potentially usable knowledge about a policy problem and its context. As partisans, community educators have an especially difficult "boundary role"; that is, they are seeking to span boundaries between the world of the government official and the world of the citizen. To do this, they need command both of the organizational expertise of the proximate policy makers and the knowledge and skills of facilitators of community involvement in problem solving. The acquiring of such competence is not an end in itself. Rather, it is a way for the activist to discover leverage points for dealing with proximate policy-makers: gaining their attention and access to their important deliberations; providing opportunities for persuading them to support partisan concerns, and furthering collaboration with others in solving significant, rather than trivial or marginal problems.

Timing. Related to the need for relevant types and sources of information, the activist needs a sense of timing, a sense of when it is feasible and appropriate to delay initiatives, to remain on the sidelines in the play of power, or to take actions of various kinds. This is an especially important concern for the community educators whose policy agendas have both short-range and long-range objectives for community change. Decisions about timing involve speculation about the motives and actions of others, and finesse in methods of influence and risk of failure. The stronger the activist's grasp of political realities and of changing environmental circumstances, the stronger his prospects for bringing influence to bear at a propitious time. Good timing is in some circumstances a function of patience and settling for small gains over a period of time, because the building of solid support for long-range reform efforts like community education tends to require painstaking nurture. Decisions may be poorly timed if they win support for short-range advantages but render longer-range goals more difficult to attain.

The Ubiquity of Conflict. If politics at its core is nothing more nor less than the process of distributing society's scarce resources, then conflict, however manifested, is inevitable among the claimants. Many political theorists make a strong case that conflict, diversity among contenders, openness of public discussion and debate, and employment of improvisational strategies are society's main assets in social problem solving. Community education has experience in encouraging openness and diversity of contributions to problem solving efforts. What may be needed is a clearer recognition that consensus is normally temporary, given the ever-present prospect of renewed conflicts. It may be hard to regard dissension among community groups as "healthy" when it disrupts policies and activities which were long and difficult in the making. Coping with such insecurity is an inescapable hazard for all partisans or interest groups whose efforts are directed not just to the easy goal of winning some concrete advantage, but rather the far more demanding task of marshalling citizen energies to attain more broadly-conceived process objectives.

Coalition Building. Community educators are well positioned to join and even promote coalitions among individuals, interest groups, and public agencies that share common goals for constructive citizen involvement in public affairs, particularly education. The concept of mutual adjustment suggests that the ideological fervor some partisans may bring to the coalition have to be modified in the search for ways to work with those who are defensive about or resistant to reformist zeal. Relationships with school officials are apparently prone to tension and difficulty on that score. The concept of mutual adjustment may also suggest that instead of seeking to influence issues defined by community education criteria, its partisans should look first for ways that community resources can enhance specific instructional objectives of the schools. This would provide a basis for seeking reciprocal support from school officials. The same non-ideological, flexible approach to other community agencies would facilitate alliances and concerted forms of action with them.

The Prospects for Change. The elitist, incremental, and systems theories of politics all project conservative conceptions of political life, implying that public policy changes gradually. In other words, the cards are stacked against reform efforts that seek to bring about major changes in a short time. Obviously, this view is not congenial for community educators, especially when they maintain their confidence that the resources of community remain untapped. Fortunately for the morale of social reformers for a faster pace of change in political systems is expected by some theorists, who believe that it can be accelerated by new demands from the environment or by alterations in some of the basic structures or interrelationships within the political system. As Halperin points out in his paper in this volume, rapid policy changes occurred after the passage of the Civil Rights Act in the 1960s. Some of the "new federalism" proposals of the Reagan administration for greater decentralization of responsibility for policy making to the states and localities envision similar possibilities. Such occurrences offer partisan groups opportunities for new leverage on the system, if they are well prepared to provide timely and reliable information about problems that need attention, contribute to the revision of the rules of the game, build new alliances, and, in effect, exert influence through and understanding of the play of power. Several of the writers in this collection link the future impact of community education to its capacity to find its way with regard to new paradigms now emerging in the social and political arenas. Some of the shifts in public attitudes discerned by these writers are congruent with ideas that community educators have advocated for two decades. Thus, mastering the use of "process as power" is the next logical move toward achieving reform.

NOTES

1. Thomas R. Dye, **Understanding Public Policy** (Englewood Cliffs, New Jersey: Prentice Hall, Inc., 1978), p. 5.

2. Ibid., p. 8.

3. Ibid., Chapter 2.

4. Charles E. Lindblom, **The Policy Making Process** (Englewood Cliffs, New Jersey: Prentice Hall, Inc., 1980), pp. 34-37.

5. Dye, **Understanding Public Policy**, pp. 34-36.

6. Ibid., pp. 36-37.

7. Lindblom, **Usable Knowledge** (New Haven, Connecticut: Yale University Press, 1979).

8. Lindblom, **Policy Making**, Chapter 6, 2nd edition; and Chapter 5, 1st edition (1968).

9. Ibid., (2nd edition) p. 63.

10. Ibid., p. 55.

11. Samuel Halperin, **A Guide for the Powerless and Those Who Don't Know Their Own Power** (Washington, D.C.: Institute for Educational Leadership, 1981), pp. 1-13.

A National Agenda for Community Education

by
Samuel Halperin

There are several benchmarks that should be included on a national agenda for community education in the next two decades. The following five considerations are what I'd like to see on the agendas of every community educator.

1. **We must reassert and redefine some kind of federal role in education.** We have never really had agreement in this country on the nature and priority of federal responsibility in education. As recently as 1961, the entire budget of the U.S. Office of Education was only $360 million. Then came an explosion of education programs, reaching a level of $15 billion in the Department of Education and a total federal expenditure for education of more than $25 billion under President Carter. On the other hand, no one I know predicted the speed and extent of the far more rapid dismantling under Mr. Reagan of 20 years of explosive growth. And no one I know believes that after Reagan everything will return to **status quo ante**. While there is support for once again tapping the U.S. Treasury for billions of dollars, there is hardly any for restoring the highly fragmented crazy quilt of federal aid programs.

Therefore, the first task of all concerned with the provision of education and other human service programs is to reconceptualize and reassert the nature and extent of future federal involvement. I would posit the desirability of far fewer programs than we had in 1980. Future federal programs should be far less prescriptive than most of those designed in the previous two decades. (Apparently, the relative flexibility and intelligent administration of the Community Schools and Comprehensive Community Education Act were not widely shared.)

But regardless of the number and breadth of future programs, the first task is to reassert the legitimacy and necessity of a vigorous federal role in education. We simply will not reach our professional goal of educational equity without an overriding federal objective. Nor shall we accomplish any of the things President Reagan urges upon us—strengthened national defense, modernization of our economic plant and equipment or reindustrialization, improved productivity and exportability—without strengthening the one government all Americans share. Educators of all types must rethink the questions of which educational functions should be financed at the state and local levels and which can only or best be financed nationally. Having dealt in different ways with the Soviets, the Japanese, the Germans, and others, I simply cannot accept the current Administration's notion that education is almost **solely** a state and local responsibility.

In community education, as in almost every other area of educational endeavor, there must be—at a minimum—a strong federal responsibility for leadership activities: research and development, dissemination, technical assistance, information collection and sharing, model building, and leadership training. Educators must reassert the essentiality of a federal leadership role that does not dictate one "right" way, yet capitalizes on the learning, the successes and failures, of our 50 diverse laboratories of educational service delivery.

Educators must also reassert the legitimacy of a strong equalizing role for the federal government. It is unacceptable as we approach the 21st century that citizens of Connecticut and California benefit from an educational investment that is twice that of their fellow Americans in Alabama and Mississippi. Money does buy opportunity and privilege and, therefore, if we mean to be one people we must resist with all our might the Reagan notion that it is an illegitimate function of Washington to equalize and compensate for state and regional imbalances of resources. Unless some larger measure of equity can be restored—and progress was being made in this direction in the '60s and '70s—all education, community education and human services included, will increasingly become the unequal birthright of some at the expense of others of our people.

2. **Educators of all types must pitch in to repair the damage caused in past years to public confidence in educational investment.** The vicious canards of academicians and politicians alike to the effect that all or most social programs are failures have become deeply entrenched. In fact, the evaluation data increasingly show that most federal education programs have produced positive results as educators have learned how to operate them. Head Start, less than a generation old, is not alone in its long-term successes. The annual evaluation reports of the Department of Education have, literally for years, carried good news of program success after success. Yet all of us are guilty of a massive loss of self-confidence in the power of education. All of us are guilty of letting the politicians and media hypes spread cynicism and rejection because it was not **our** program that was being held up to ridicule on **Sixty Minutes** or in the pages of **Human Events**.

3. **Community educators must do a better job of telling their story to other educators in order to break down the parochial walls that have until now kept educators divided and far less effective than they could be.** According to Thomas James, President of the Spencer Foundation, there is currently underway "one of the most remarkable surges of interest in the study of schooling in our entire history." James lists 14 current national efforts to reassess and rethink the purposes, content, and operations of American schooling.[1] What is being done by the community education profession to shape the thinking and the outcomes of these studies? If community education is even a fraction as good a notion as its true believers say, then it is a sacred professional obligation to proselytize within the education family. For, make no mistake, at least some of these studies are going to help shape the nature of policy discourse and public policy for years to come.

As a non-community educator, I read the community education literature to see what community educators were saying about themselves. I found a great deal of self-awareness, a fairly widespread recognition of what ails community education today. For my money, Robert Shoop summed it up best in an incisive one-page article two years ago in the **Community Education Journal:**

> Community education faces three serious dangers: the danger of being defined so broadly that it loses clarity and effectiveness; the danger of being defined so narrowly that it becomes just another program; and the danger of becoming centralized, with the decision making power resting in the hands of the professionals.[2]

The literature of the community educator contains abundant examples of the first danger. In **Community Education: The Federal Role**, the National Community Education Advisory Council grandiosely proclaims that the "sleeping giant" of community education "is just beginning to awaken" with the capacity to help solve the central problems of the nation: "...neglected senior citizens and juvenile delinquency...polluted waterways, shrinking energy sources, values clarification in a rapidly changing society, understanding the rest of the world."[3]

Then-President of the National Community Education Association (NCEA), Sidney Miller, also urged community educators to go beyond "fine and noble beliefs," "majestically nebulous terms and nonthreatening ideas" to take clear and specific stands on such controversial issues as funding for the disadvantaged; educational programs for women, minorities, and older Americans; legislation affecting housing, health programs, etc. Should NCEA go so far, she asked rhetorically, as to enter the political process and use its leverage in the form of "money, votes, endorsements, or some other form of influence? Isn't it time that we made some concrete statements on the pragmatic issues that relate to our beliefs?"[4]

What a far cry from the views of C.S. Harding Mott before the U.S. House of Representatives' Committee on Education and Labor only half a dozen years earlier, when he spoke approvingly of an Arizona community education program that offered Mexican aliens a class in knitting followed up by a class in U.S. citizenship. For Mr. Mott, and perhaps many other advocates, community education lodged in the schools was inherently "nonpolitical." Indeed, he assured the Congress, "working through schools and under their public aegis we think we avoid political, religious, racial, and similar hang-ups. In urban areas particularly we are convinced that by working through the established school system there is created a much-needed sense of 'community,' of identity, of 'belongingness.' "[5]

What a giant leap from Charles Stewart Mott's 1936 grant to keep five Flint schools and their playgrounds open "after hours" to the community education scene depicted by Shoop two years ago:

> In the rush to enlist support for community education, the professionals in the field are running the risk of being charged with quackery. Too often community education is sold in the same manner that snake oil was once sold from the back of a medicine wagon. We pull our wagon into town, gather a crowd of people, and start our spiel.

"Do you suffer from juvenile delinquency, vandalism, defeated bond issues? Are you regretful of the past, alienated from the present, afraid of the future? Is your divorce rate up and community support rate down? Are your high school graduates illiterate, your senior citizens forgotten, and your marriage boring? Then step right up and receive the elixir of life, the panacea for all of your problems—community education."[6]

Again, for my money, insufficient good can come from any movement that has as much intellectual splay in its literature as I think I have detected.

4. **The leaders of community education must seek greater internal consensus on the nature and limits of their approach to education.** Key concepts are used interchangeably and without sufficient definition to assure effective communication. Take the notion of parental involvement or participation. What does it mean to community educators? Is it involvement with the education of one's own child? Volunteerism in the regular educational program of the schools? Participation in the array of school-community-human service interfaces? Participation in educational decision-making? Or is it limited to "advise and consent?"

5. **Community educators should adopt a strategy of treating community education as a process, rather than a program.** Shoop warned of "the danger of being defined so narrowly that community education becomes just another program," and by benefit of hindsight, I think it may have been a most serious mistake for community educators to sell some of their intellectual and political heritage in the annual struggle to get a mere $3 million of federal pottage. In the process, community education may well have ceased to be a dynamic, cross-cutting movement and become just one more program claimant—and a small one at that—at the federal financial trough. Community educators should resent enormously, being lumped in the public's and policymakers' mind with environmental education, driver education, consumer education, career education, et al.

Therefore, for the future, I would counsel a strategy of seeing community education as a set of pervasive and powerful principles about the educational process that would infuse **all** of education in much the same way that the Civil Rights Act of 1964 and Section 504 of the Vocational Rehabilitation Act Amendments of 1972 seek to leverage **all** educational delivery programs. Regardless of the amount of money available for programs specifically labeled "community education," this approach would seek to influence **all** of education and schooling. As a program, community education will always be restricted to a small box on an organizational chart at the federal, state, or local level, each box buried under layers of bureaucratic trivia, each box competing for resources unlikely ever to be adequate to the tasks at hand. I would prefer to see community educators as a small, crack cadre of educational missionaries, ombudsmen, expediters, disturbers of the comfortable, comforters of the disturbed, who see their mission as the slow but sure conversion of the mindsets of educators and policymakers.

Again, I see a parallel to the civil rights efforts of the '60s and '70s. After the passage of the Civil Rights Act of 1974, then-U.S. Commissioner of Education, Francis Keppel convened his senior staff to debate how the provisions of the Act ought to be reflected in the organizational chart of the U.S. Office of Education. One school of thought advocated a strong centralized enforcement office. An opposing view maintained that a central office would soon become just another program office, competing for limited resources and attention. Moreover, under a centralized enforcement plan, civil rights would become the responsibility of the "other guys," relieving the bulk of federal personnel of the task of modifying their pre-Civil Rights Act behavior. Again in hindsight, I believe the correct side lost the organizational argument. Civil rights, instead of becoming a process of attitudinal and behavioral adjustment affecting the entire federal bureaucracy and the recipients of all grant funds, became too often just another hurdle to be surmounted, another competing program area to be manipulated.

From my reading of the excellent community education materials sent to me by the project staff, I conclude that community education has far more to offer to the American people than the narrow, self-imposed limitations of another program. Community education deserves to soar, suffuse, and scintillate rather than merely survive in the bureaucratic maze.

NOTES

[1]Thomas James, **Highlights of the 1981 Cleveland Conference** (mimeo, March 29, 1982). The 14 studies are:
1. **A Study of High Schools**, directed by Theodore Sizer.
2. **A Study of Schooling in the United States**, directed by John I. Goodlad.
3. **An Education of Value**, directed by Stephen K. Bailey (now deceased).
4. **The National Commission on Excellence in Education**, directed by Milton Goldberg.
5. **Exellence in Education: A Study of the American High School**, directed by Ernest Boyer.
6. **Minority Students in Catholic Secondary Schools**, directed by Andrew Greeley.
7. **Project Equality**, directed by Adrienne Bailey.
8. **Project on Alternatives in Education**, directed by Mary Anne Raywid.
9. **Project Paideia**, directed by Mortimer Adler.
10. **Redefining General Education in the American High School**, directed by Gordon Cawelti.
11. **Secondary School Improvement Project**, directed by Gilbert Johnson and Gary Phillips.
12. **The High School and Beyond**, directed by James S. Coleman.
13. **The Urban Education Studies**, directed by Francis S. Chase.
14. **The Stanford Study of the Schools**, directed by J. Myron Atkin and Donald Kennedy.

[2]Robert J. Shoop, "Remember, We're Not Selling Snake Oil...", **Community Education Journal**, vol. VII, no. 3 (April 1980), p.15.

[3]National Community Education Advisory Council, **Community Education: The Federal Role** (HEW, 1979), p. 1.

[4]Sidney Miller, "NCEA Report," **Community Education Journal**, vol. VII, no. 3 (April 1980), p. 29.

[5]C.S. Harding Mott, "Testimony on the Community School Center Development Act" in Hearings before the Subcommittee on Education of the Committee on Labor, House of Representatives 93 Cong. I sess. (Sept. 6, 1973) pp. 33-38.

[6]Robert J. Shoop, "Remember, We're Not Selling Snake Oil ...".

Community Education and Turning Point Election Periods (TPEPs)

by
Laurence Iannaccone

One of community education's fundamental goals or assumptions is that schools should be viewed as more than instruments of schooling; schools should be viewed as an expression of the community, and educational government should play an important part in the development of communities, in the sense of community, and in the awareness of communities in America. There are three core strands of ideology in community education literature:

(1) an interest in the optimum responsiveness of the school to the felt needs of citizens;
(2) concern for citizen engagement; and
(3) commitment to increased social and civic solidarity in communities through citizen participation, especially around the schools.

These three ideological strands are interdependent. Stated simply, the community education movement is interested in the social reconstruction of knowledge, especially the interdependence between the school, its government, and the community.

When I took on the assignment of examining the potential impact of community education, I asked myself what I know about the social reconstruction of knowledge from a research base in political science and the politics of education that would be useful to community education advocates. Clearly, community educators need an expanded conceptual awareness of the dynamics of policy premises, particularly the changing of those premises during periods of political paradigm shifts—changes in the fit, the configuration, the Gestalt of relationships among socio-economic and political assumptions.

The first part of this paper is a general statement of theory-related policy paradigm shifts characteristic of American polities. The second part takes a more detailed view derived from studies of local school districts. Finally, the paper examines the significance of turning point election periods and the paradigm shifts that occur during them. Awareness of transitions already underway is important information for those who would develop effective strategies and tactics.

The current national concern for turning from the public to the private sector offers opportunities to community educators who want to maximize grassroots involvement. The paradigm shifts now underway open opportunities for new input and, ultimately, for influencing the social reconstruction of knowledge.

An educational polity's turning point election period (TPEP) provides unusually favorable opportunities for community education. This assertion rests on four premises. First, American polities experience cyclical sequences of political quiescence and discontent. Second, significant changes in their politics, readjustment in policy-making processes and structures, and redirection of policies take place during eras of discontent. Third, these changes are lawful (in the scientific sense) and cyclic adaptations of the polity's policies and service delivery that more accurately reflect changed social conditions. Finally, the predominant political characteristics of such eras are turning point elections that express the discontent of enough of the polity's citizens to open the door to future redirection and establish the feasible parameters of that redirection.

Turning point election periods (TPEPs) produce unusually favorable conditions for the articulation of new mandates. They unleash driving forces for citizen involvement in political processes and are characterized by increased voter turnout and heightened public awareness of policy options.

TPEPs in the Politics of Education

The chief mechanism for managing tension in the American political system is a turning point election period. Turning point election periods are preceded by a growing imbalance between political and socio-economic systems; balance is restored through realignment elections that result in turnover of the chief executive office.

TPEPs are characterized by increased political conflict over competing philosophies of government. The prize at stake is the power to define the issues for the public. The significance of a TPEP for educational policy-making is that its politico-economic assumptions and ideological premises may guide educational policy long after the TPEP has ended.

Research on local school district politics during TPEPs is based on a large number of TPEPs because of the large number of American school districts. In all American polities, TPEPs are cyclic, patterned over time—not random.[1] In a typical school district, short TPEPs of expanded political conflict alternate with longer periods of low political conflict. Critical realignment elections are intense disruptions of traditional voting patterns. In the local school district, the shift in voting behavior is seldom concurrent with the replacement of a superintendent. Given the appointive nature of that office and the cost of terminating a superintendent's contract, some time usually passes between the board election and the replacement of the superintendent. It is only when the new superintendent is in place that the local district's policy-making system becomes a functional equivalent of the national policy-making system produced by a realignment election.

Policy-Making in TPEPs and Quiescent Periods

The policy-making process during long periods of political quiescence is aptly called incrementalism by Lindblom. Ideological premises are widely shared by the citizens of a polity during such periods. As Lindblom points out: `

> Any even loosely organized set of interlocking generalizations of principles...politico-economic organization—is of enormous help to policy analysis. . . .In effect an ideology takes certain beliefs out of the gunfire of criticism. . . .These. . .can thereafter be introduced into policy analysis as though they were settled fact.[2]

Although dependent on shared premises, incremental policy-making is, over time, increasingly influenced by precedents that reinforce the ideology. The precedents, rather than the ideological premises, become the focus of political conflicts.

In contrast to periods of political quiescence, turning point election periods are characterized by challenges first to recent aspects of policy and, later to earlier policies and their premises. As the politicization of TPEPs continues, political conflicts expand in scope and intensity.[3] The customary incrementalism is replaced by more abrupt, less consistent policy-making, reflecting polarized ideological positions, disrupted coalitions, and newly organized interests. Ideological premises are reintroduced into the gunfire of criticism as salient political issues. The incrementalism of quiescence does not cease, nor are its policy premises erased. The premises must, however, compete with other assumptions for a place in the next political paradigm of interlocking assumptions. The likelihood is that they will be subsumed in other elements involved in the ideological conflict. Incremental policy-making will be resumed only after the TPEP has produced another, different amalgam of interlocking principles supported by the voters. For years thereafter, policy will reflect the new premises.

Lessons from TPEPs in a Typical Local School District

Cumulative studies over 20 years illustrate the process by which the local educational mission is from time to time redefined by the local citizenry. Also, how the tendency of educational policy-making to be closed, is recurringly checked by voters.

A turning point election period in a local school district typically goes through five stages: (1) rising voter discontent; (2) a triggering election; (3) a realignment of the district's policy-making subsystem; (4) the articulation of a new policy mandate; and (5) a final test election of the new mandate.[4] The duration of each stage varies from school district to school district and from era to era. The occurrence of the first stage does not necessarily mean that there will be progression to the other stages. Politicization may diminish without completion of the five stages. However, the more common case is the sequence noted above. The final test election is followed by the end of the TPEP and a gradual return to political quiescence.

Rising discontent is usually foreshadowed by changes in the socio-economic and demographic composition of the school district some years before the discontent is manifested in voting behavior. A specific indicator is a significant change in the ratio of assessed valuation to average daily attendance, which may occur over a six- to ten-year period before significant evidence of voter discontent is seen. The school district may ignore or greatly underestimate the socio-economic and demographic changes and make none of the program adjustments required by the changing social composition of its citizens and their children. The gap between community demands and the actions of the board and superintendent may widen, and the school system may be seen as closed to change. Voter discontent may be measured in changes in the ratio of votes cast for and against incumbent board members, and in increases in the number of challengers running against incumbents. In some cases, the total number of votes cast for challengers may exceed those for incumbents, although the incumbents may be reelected because of splintered opposition.

The first election in which one or more incumbent board members are defeated may be thought of as triggering the defeat of additional incumbents in the next election and the one after that. A decision by two incumbent board members not to seek reelection has the same effect as an initial incumbent defeat after a period of political quiescence. Either event sets in motion the beginning of significant conflict within the school district's policy-making subsystem, the meetings between the board and the superintendent. Conflicts between the new member or members and the incumbents tend to expand rapidly into polarization. The superintendent often leads the older board faction in these conflicts, but incumbent members may swing over to join the new board members. Conflict within the board-superintendent subsystem brings to the surface other divisions within the districts and sharpens ideological differences related to the governance of the schools. Old ideas are challenged as inappropriate to changed conditions. Old board members and the superintendent tend to defend the programs they initiated or supported earlier. In the rhetoric of political conflict, defenders of existing programs are easily attacked as rigid and unresponsive. Often enough, however, the old board majority, led by the superintendent, has enough votes to maintain the direction of the past, even in the fact of bitter intra-board conflict. If the newer board members more accurately represent the district's developing educational ideology, the decisions of the majority go beyond the limits of tolerance citizens normally accord their governments. The conflicts continue and intensify until the legitimacy of the board and the superintendent are questioned. Incumbents are usually defeated in one or more subsequent elections, and a realignment of the school's policy system follows.

There is some empirical evidence that an election in which incumbents are defeated can be followed by a return to political quiescence. In these exceptions to the usual pattern, the following conditions seem to be present: (1) the socio-economic and political changes characteristic of voter discontent do not appear to precede the incumbent defeat; (2) the election campaign rhetoric highlights the personal characteristics of the candidates rather than educational policy issues; and, (3) incumbent board members are reelected and challengers defeated in the next election. If the school board and the superintendent understand the importance of an incumbent defeat and work quickly to change policies, the policy-making process, and school programs, the period of political conflict will be shortened, and the necessary balance between the schools and their publics will be restored.

The third stage in the TPEP is realignment of policy by removal of the superintendent. The incidence of involuntary superintendent turnover increases significantly in districts in which incumbents have been defeated in one or two successive elections. If this third stage is reached, the new superintendent will be chosen from outside the district. Research confirms that succession to the superintendency is much more likely to be from within the system in the absence of the first two TPEP stages. Carlson contrasts the conditions and board expectations of inside and outside executive succession:

> School boards elect insiders to the superintendency only when the judgment has been made that the schools are being properly administered. . .school boards will be satisfied if the insider keeps things as they are, but they expect and are satisfied with an outsider only when some changes are made.[5]

He also points out that boards give outsiders guidance in the general direction of the policy changes they expect.

The fourth stage in the progression of a TPEP is the articulation of a new policy mandate by the changed board and the new superintendent. Repeated turnover in the superintendency is possible if the district is experiencing rapid socio-economic and demographic change because the cross currents of clashing interests and ideologies may make the articulation of a new policy mandate virtually impossible for a time. The changed board may fail to provide the new superintendent with appropriate guidance, or the new superintendent may fail to articulate a new mandate, or delay its implementation. Sooner or later, a new mandate is articulated.

The articulation of policy requires a combination of a philosophy of governance, technical understanding appropriate to the enterprise, and the choice of pragmatic alternatives for implementation. Public discontent, which lead to the selection of an outsider, and the board's changed orientation, shared with the new superintendent, supply the basis for the needed philosophy of governance. The superintendent's professional training and experience supply the technical expertise and leadership for the pragmatic and programmatic definition of policy choices. Communication about the new policy is accomplished by the new chief executive in many ways: policy statements, personnel selection, revision of regulations, and school program changes. A clarification of values and a definition of the policy issues in effect places a new mandate before the voters.

The fifth stage of the TPEP emerges from the articulation of a new policy mandate and involves the aggregation of interests in a final test election in which voters choose between well-defined alternatives. They may support the board and, by inference, the superintendent, reject both, or stay home. From limited research, there appears to be a larger than usual turnout of voters in final test elections of a new mandate in local school districts. The victory of a new mandate in heavy voting appears to have the effect of suppressing opposition voting, and therefore incumbent defeat, in later elections. After a final test election, the new policies, policy-makers, and programs become increasingly more secure in their political support; political quiescence and policy incrementalism return until new voter discontent ushers in the next TPEP.

Some Strategic Considerations for Community Education

Several basic beliefs are pervasive in community education literature. These may be seen in statements about structural issues such as decentralization, public access to decision-making, citizen councils, and distinctions between roles and activities at the district and site levels; and in process issues such as citizen participation and involvement, and problem-solving collaboration between school professionals and community members. These structural and process concerns are related to program goals and desired educational outcomes.

The social and civic solidarity of any polity is likely to be at its lowest ebb when its citizens feel alienated from its decisions and their outcomes. The feeling of powerlessness and frustration in confronting autocratic power or a faceless bureaucracy inevitably increases the sense of being alone, and hence reduces awareness of community. A citizen thus alienated from civic life may have his sense of engagement restored by the inclusion in an election campaign of issues salient to him and candidates with whom he can identify. The responsiveness of a polity, the real engagement of its citizens, and the resulting social solidarity are functions of broadening rather than narrowing policy agendas and programs. That broadening requires greater appreciation of differences among citizens. There are strategic eras in the political life of any school district that are more amenable than others to this basic community education tenet.

The core features of community education's ideology—responsiveness, citizen engagement, and social solidarity—are shared by both liberal and conservative political traditions in America. An important strategic implication of that fact is that the community education movement does not require either a liberal or a conservative community in order to carry out its goals. A second implication is that community educators do not have to play a win-lose political game to champion their proposals. Differences between liberals and conservatives can be accommodated by the application of knowledge, intelligence, expanded awareness, broadened definitions of available resources, genuine appreciation of differences, concern for the rights of others, and flexibility in programs. Short-term conflicts can be survived without devastating political wars because of unifying basic values. Shared values do not assure reconciliation of differences, of course; this desirable outcome requires deliberate effort in addition to shared values. Mutually prized values can provide a basis for achieving reconciliation, while truly conflicting values demand a win-lose outcome.

The first triggering election of a TPEP in a school district may replace conservatives with liberals or liberals with conservatives. In either case, demands for increased responsiveness and expanded citizen participation and charges of citizen alienation are characteristic of the campaign rhetoric of the challengers. Consequently, general strategy to achieve community education goals can be discussed apart from the traditional political divisions.

The research suggests two broad strategic considerations for the community education movement in most school districts other than the largest urban districts with appointed boards. the first is deciding where the district is in its political life cycle. The second is judging the openness of the system's board members, administrators, and teachers to communications from citizens.

In periods of quiescence, specific program proposals whose goals and values are convergent with established policy premises obviously have a much better chance of adoption and implementation than do those with divergent goals and values. In such periods, the slow and steady nurturance of credibility with key policy and administrative actors in both the community and the school system is the best tactic. Implicit here is a plan of gradualism through educating people, and incremental modification of policies and processes. A specific tactic is for community educators to accept initially, the school system's identification of problems to be worked on jointly and the terms of the collaboration. This does not mean that community problems ignored by the school must be avoided. On the contrary, the immediate goal of this tactic is to demonstrate both to the community and the school system the value of expanded participation in problem solving. Rhetorical challenges, confrontation, and insistence on working on problems not identified by the school system are unwise tactics at this stage. The initial tactical goal is to legitimize expanded citizen participation through collaborative accomplishment. The risk of maintaining collaboration at this initial level can be reduced by keeping in mind the longer-term goal of incrementally broadening the range of problems and issues as well as the numbers and kinds of participants. This goal can usually be openly shared with others even in the initial collaboration as long as faith in it is not required of everyone. What is needed is willingness to make a start and then let the evidence speak. Except in the late years of quiescence, the cautious tactics of gradualism are likely to produce the desired long-term changes in participation. During the late stage of quiescence, most school systems display increased defensiveness, bureaucratic rigidity, and resistance to citizen demands; some systems may lack the political energy necessary to adjust to an altered social environment.

In a TPEP, change occurs rapidly as the school district goes through the five distinct TPEP stages. An effective strategy for facilitating the school system's adjustment to the community, to opening up its policy and administrative decision-making processes for long-term citizen participation, must take account of these changes, which will alter the district's policy-making system either quickly at relatively lower costs to the human beings involved, or more slowly, with greater political conflict, at greater cost to all concerned.

Policy conflicts in TPEPs usually begin as a reflection of the public value contradictions already present in the school's policies and programs during the late quiescent period. During the first phase of the TPEP—rising public discontent—citizens are clearer on what it is they dislike in established policies than they are about alternatives. As the TPEP progresses, new values and future policy premises become clearer, providing community educators with opportunities to influence the process of value clarification and to propose alternative new policies as different stages of the TPEP emerge.

The second major strategic consideration is whether and to what extent the community educator should work to increase the school system's awareness and understanding of what is going on. Given the basic community education tenet of working cooperatively with school boards and officials, this decision would appear at first glance to be simple. In practice, however, cooperation requires that at least two parties agree to work together.

The commitment of time, money, energy, and groups is fundamentally an economic decision about the best way to invest resources to achieve specific objectives. The community educator's choice is whether to use available resources to seek improvement in the school's responsiveness by increasing the awareness of the district's established policy-makers, or to allocate resources to the building of solid bases of support outside the system in order to change it through elections and referenda. There is some evidence that dividing one's resources equally between the two strategies at the same time may be the wisest course. In practice, however, the particular situation will have to be considered carefully. What are the probabilities that the awareness and understanding of the current policy-makers will improve? Will their enhanced understanding produce a new perspective? And will the new perspective be translated into changes in policies and programs or be applied to renewed defensiveness?

Each situation is unique. A wise strategy is to allocate some resources for initial testing before making the major choice between working primarily through the present key actors or outside the establishd policy and administrative system to change it. At some point during the early phases of a TPEP, it may be both inefficient and damaging to one's credibility to become closely associated with an establishment that is experiencing rejection by the citizens.

The following model summarizes the strategy choices described above:

Relationship of Two Strategies

Major resources allocations	Quiescence (1)	TPEPs (2)
Inside the policy system: collaborative influencing of key actors directly and and citizens indirectly	Convergence Incrementalism Basic consensus Begin with the system's defini- tions of tasks and collabora- tion	Contradictory policies Closed system with high degree of defensiveness fol- lowed by rapid and abrupt changes
	(3)	(4)
Outside the policy system: influencing voters directly and policy system indirectly	Probable failure	Divergence Abrupt change Clear discontent Lack of con- sensus on values; no crystalization of new mandate

This simplified model ignores the variations over time within the five stages of a TPEP, but it serves to suggest that working within the system to directly influence key actors and, through their actions, to enhance citizen participation and the system's responsiveness is the best-chance scenario in cell (1). Conversely, cell (4) suggests that the best-chance scenario is the allocation of resources to influence the citizenry directly and, through their voting behavior, the policy-making system. Thus, locating the district's politics accurately on the continuum from quiescent to final-stage TPEP, will guide the choice of best-chance scenario for long-term policy adjustment. Cell (2) of the model suggests that strategic resources allocated to collaboration may well increase the contradtions in the district's policies and hasten change by exacerbating and expanding growing political conflict. This may be a desirable short-term tactic for hastening the normal change process and reducing the cost of extended conflict, but it carries two risks, especially to longer-term considerations and goals. One risk is the loss of credibility with voters if the established leadership fails to adjust to the new challenges. A second risk, related to the first, is that collaboration will expand the contradtions in policy instead of yielding truly different policies in harmony with the felt needs of the citizens. Finally, cell (3) suggests that working primarily outside the system to influence it through voters during periods of quiescence is likely to be an unwise allocation of resources; expanding citizen participation and collaboration within the system is much more practical during such periods.

A detailed discussion of strategic considerations at each emerging stage of the TPEP is beyond the scope of this paper. A few examples of how awareness of these phases can help in making strategic decisions may be enough to convince community educators that TPEPs offer unusual opportunities. Take, for example, the rhetoric common to challengers on the eve of incumbent defeats. Challengers focus on educational goals and charge the system with being unresponsive to changing community needs and closed to citizen participaion in policy-making. Incumbents emphasize educational means, especially existing programs. Increased public attention to the goals of education and concern for citizen access to the system offer a favorable climate for community education goals.

A second example of the strategic importance of understanding TPEP stages relates to the weeks immediately following a triggering election. Research suggests that superintendents who survive the defeat of incumbent board members are likely to recognize the election as a mandate to adjust the school system and make program changes, while superintendents who are subsequently dismissed are likely to lead the old board members in fights against the newcomers. A strategy of expanding the awareness of incumbent board members and the superintendent may offer an opportunity for adopting community education goals and saving the superintendent and board at the same time.

A final example is the opportunity offered in the fourth stage of a TPEP, when a new policy mandate must be articulated. Typically, a new superintendent from outside the system must combine his expertise with the views and experience of the board; the new policy is often clearer in its rejection of the past than it is in its direction for the future. The guidance given the new superintendent by the board may be ambiguous and incomplete. Community education groups who are aware of this normal process and have knowledge of both the community and the educational programs can help reduce the ambiguity and expand the new superintendent's awareness of the community and even of program options. They can also begin to develop the broader citizen support systems necessary for the final test election ahead.

In sum, research in the politics of local school districts indicates that there are significantly different cyclical stages of policy-making and change in the life history of district politics. Awareness of these natural stages and processes can lead to the enhanced power that knowledge makes available if the knowledge is used appropriately. Evidence about TPEPs suggests that these eras are particularly propitious times for community education ideology and goals.

¹Larry W. Criswell, and Douglas E. Mitchell, "Episodic instability in school district elections," **Urban Education**, vol. 15, no. 2 (July 1980), pp. 189-213.

²Charles E. Lindblom, **The Policy-Making Process** (Englewood Cliffs, N.J.: Prentice-Hall, 1968), p. 23.

³E. E. Schattschneider, **The Semisovereign People** (New York: Holt, Rinehart and Winston, 1960).

⁴Ruth Danis, **Policy Changes in Local Governance: The Dissatisfaction Theory of Democracy** (unpublished Ph.D. dissertation, University of California, Santa Barbara, 1981). I am particularly indebted to Dr. Danis for her data on internal phases of TPEPs.

⁵Richard O. Carlson, **Executive Succession and Organizational Change** (Chicago: Midwest Administration Center, University of Chicago, 1962), pp. 69-70.

SELECTED REFERENCES

Gabriel A. Almond, and G. Bingham Powell, Jr. **Comparative Politics: A Developmental Approach** (Boston: Little, Brown, 1966).

William L. Boyd, "Community Status and Suburban School Conflict." in **The Polity of the School,**ed. by Frederick M. Wirt (Lexington, Mass.: D. C. Heath and Co., 1975).

D. R. Eblen, **School District Conflict and Superintendent Turnover in Transitional Suburban Communities** (Unpublished Ph.D. dissertation, University of Chicago, 1975).

Laurence Iannaccone, "The Future of State Politics of Education." in **Struggle for Power in Education**, ed. by Frank W. Lutz and Joseph J. Azzarelli (New York: Center for Applied Research in Education, 1966).

Laurence Iannaccone, "Three Views of Change in Educational Politics," in **The Politics of Education**, The Seventy-sixth Yearbook of the National Society for the Study of Education, Part II, ed. by Jay D. Scribner (Chicago: University of Chicago Press, 1977).

Laurence Iannaccone, and Peter J. Cistone, **The Politics of Education** (Eugene Oregon: University of Oregon Press, 1974).

Laurence Iannaccone, and Frank W. Lutz, **Politics, Power and Policy** (Columbus, Ohio: Charles E. Merrill Books, 1970).

David W. Minar, "Community Characteristics, Conflict, and Power Structures," in **The Politics of Education in the Local Community**, ed. by Robert S. Cahill and Stephen P. Hencley (Danville, IL: Interstate Printers and Publishers 1964).

Douglas E. Mitchell, and Laurence Iannaccone. **The Impact of California's Legislative Policy on Public School Performance**, California Policy Seminar, Monograph No. 5 (University of California, Berkeley, 1980).

Reaction Paper To: Laurence Iannaccone's

"Community Education and Turning Point Election Periods (TPEPs)"

by
Steve R. Parson

There are only two kinds of politics . . . the politics of fear and the politics of trust. One says: you are encircled by monstrous dangers . . . .The other says: the world is a baffling and hazardous place, but it can be shaped to the will of men.

Edmund Muskie

The basic premise of turning point election periods (TPEPs) theory is that public schools are political systems, subject to the cyclic process of periodic power realignment. The author identifies various stages that school districts go through in this cyclic process: (1) political quiescence, characterized by incremental policy-making and little political conflict; (2) rising voter discontent; (3) a realignment election in which incumbent school board members are defeated; (4) involuntary superintendent turnover, in which newly-elected board members oust the incumbent superintendent; (5) outside succession, the hiring of a new superintendent from outside the district; and (6) a final test election, in which voters confirm or reject the changes. According to the theory, after a school district has gone through the last phase, it begins the cycle all over again.

Iannaccone asserts that TPEP "provides unusually favorable opportunities for community education." It is obvious that his purpose is not to tell community educators how to take advantage of those opportunities but rather to help them understand the workings of the political system in which many of them labor.

I would like to isolate several points made by Iannaconne and suggest some possible implications for action by community educators.

● *Elections are the mechanism that restores the balance between political and socioeconomic systems.*

The author explains that turning point elections occur when enough of the citizens are disatisfied with established policies and services. This turning point opens the door for future redirection, and could be a point at which community education strengthens its role by providing vehicles for citizens involvement in the formulation of future directions for the schools.

It should be noted that this strengthened role is not without risk. Identification with one segment of the political community might leave community education open to retribution if political power is realigned at the next turning point election.

The renowned Neighborhood Councils of Independence, Missouri, believe that part of their success is attributable to the fact that they have not become a political organization. One of their recent publications states:

Since their beginning, the Neighborhood Councils have scrupulously avoided any kind of political activity, refraining from endorsing candidates for public office, taking stands on political issues, even refusing to sponsor candidates meetings. Encouraging folks to make up their own minds on such matters, the Councils have carefully followed a path of political neutrality, working with every political persuasion but endorsing none of them. [1]

The structures of community education (i.e., community councils) should perhaps strive for political neutrality in order to be able to work effectively with groups of all political persuasions.

● *Policy-making during periods of little political conflict is characterized by incrementalism.*

During periods of quiescence, to use Iannaccone's term, school systems often become more closed to outsiders and incremental in their decision-making processes. The implication appears to be that this is not the best time to promote community education as a vehicle for citizen involvement in decision-making.

On the other hand, an inventive community educator might choose to help school board members and superintendents understand the cyclic nature of the political system and anticipate the citizen discontent that tends to follow periods of quiescence. Community education could then be promoted as a means of involving community members in resolving conflict and providing direction for desired change. This might lengthen the period of quiescence and perhaps head off the abrupt change that follows turning point elections.

In a recent study, a colleague and I found that community educators may have a difficult time fostering a true democratic process if they are sponsored by a "closed" bureaucratic institution.[2] We also found evidence, however, that community education can have the effect of opening up the bureaucracy.

● *Superintendents can avoid "involuntary turnover" by adjusting policies, policy-making processes, and school programs immediately after the defeat of incumbent board members.*

A current school of thought holds that school administrators must abandon a technocratic model, in which their chief asset is technical expertise, and adopt a political model of administration. Don Davies of the Institute for Responsive Education identified these elements of the political model: reconciling a diversity of goals and values; dealing with conflict; mediating among conflicting interests of a diverse constituency; building consensus; bargaining and compromising; sharing power; providing services wanted by constituents; and recognizing that on many issues there is no one right answer morally or technically.[3]

Davies points out that the political administrator needs extensive parent and community involvement and a structure for providing it. Community education can offer that structure through its community councils. Therefore, after an election in which there is significant incumbent defeat, the community educator may be able to approach the superintendent with the idea of strengthening the role of the community councils.

● *The core features of community education's political ideology— responsiveness, citizen engagement, and social solidarity—are not the sole property of either American political conservatism or of American political liberalism.*

Iannaccone's point is an important one for community educators to ponder. It is my impression that community educators until recently tended to view their movement as appealing to the liberal side of the political spectrum. It is only recently, in the prevailing political conservatism, that they have become aware that the concept appeals to both camps. This reassessment may well have arisen out of a need to determine how to best survive during a period of political change.

Community educators need to examine what it is about the community education concept that appeals to each group, conservative and liberal. Then they must develop strategies based on the political leaning of the audience being addressed. This is not a call to dishonesty or a recommendation to become all things to all people, but a way of pointing out that community education is apolitical, facilitating as it does the involvement of people regardless of their political orientation.

● *After a turning point election, school system policy is realigned through the school superintendent.*

Iannaccone points out that incumbent defeats usually bring about a change in superintendents (a point that may be corroborated by noting that the national range of tenure for superintendents is less than 3-5 years). He says further that after significant political conflict and incumbent defeat, the new superintendent is usually hired from outside the system and given careful directions by the new board.

The period of formulating new directions offers the community educator an opportunity to propose an expanded role for the community education concept. This could be done through the community councils, whose members could approach new board members and the new superintendent. It should be noted, however, that others in the school political system are unlikely to miss this opportunity to promote their own special interests. The vocational educators, special educators, the advocates of programs for the gifted and talented, etc., will all be mobilizing. The difference could be that most community educators have in the past failed to recognize and take advantage of this opportunity.

● *The longer-term tactical goal for community educators is to build on early successes, incrementally broadening the range of problems and issues, and the numbers and kinds of participants.*

This advice is directed to the early part of a period of quiescence. Iannaccone states that "specific program proposals whose goals and values are convergent with the established policy premises of the school district obviously have a much better chance of adoption and implementation than do those with divergent goals and values." This should give some guidance to community educators as they work with community members in setting goals and objectives for the community education program. In fact, community education can benefit best, says Iannaccone, when community educators accept initially the problems the school district's personnel want to work on collaboratively. This may mean deferring work on problems in the community in order to demonstrate to school people the effectiveness of community education in expanding citizen participation in collaborative problem solving. This process will help legitimize the concept in the eyes of the school.

In practical terms this may mean devoting time and resources to organizing a school volunteer program before taking on a community crime prevention project. This policy of giving priority to school-identified problems will change as the school district moves through the turning point election period, and, as new values and policies are formulated after a turning point election, the community educator will have an opportunity to influence that process.

● *Two apparently conflicting strategies are identified for community educators during periods of growing citizen discontent with school policies. One is to try to improve the school's responsiveness to community needs by making school officials aware of what is going on. The second is to build support outside the system in order to change it through elections.*

Iannaccone tells us that there is some research evidence to support dividing one's resources equally between the two strategies. This suggestion causes me to shudder with visions of community educators getting caught playing both ends against the middle. It seems to me there is a danger in actively working outside the system to defeat certain board members or promote particular issues. I recommend developing a base of support for community education in the community, and then letting the support base deal with the political system. On the other hand, the strategy of seeking to increase the awareness of school officials, while likely to be frustrating at times, is both important and appropriate.

● *As incumbent defeats begin to occur during a TPEP, it may be both inefficient and damaging to one's credibility to become closely associated with an establishment that is experiencing rejection by the citizens.*

This is akin to saying don't stand too close to the target when the firing squad appears. It makes good sense but it may not be all that easy.

In many school districts community educators have become closely associated with superintendents, often because the superintendent is aware of the community educator's link with the community. The community educator must be careful not to be used as a "lightning rod," placed in the community to attract the fire and heat. A better role for the community educator is to help facilitate communication between the school system and the community, rather than to act as spokesman for either camp.

Iannaccone concludes that knowledge of the processes of policymaking and change in a school district can enhance the power of the community educator "if the knowledge is used appropriately." This knowledge will not give the community educator a how-to plan for success. It will, however, provide some valuable guidance in choosing a reasonable plan of action.

Idealistic as it may seem, community education might have as its long-range goal the elimination of turning point election periods (TPEPs). If the community education concept is securely in place, a school district has built-in mechanisms for helping citizens resolve conflicts of values and ideas without firing superintendents on a regular basis, or electing new school board members every time something needs to be changed. The only time a superintendent or board member would have to be replaced is when he or she was unwilling to support the community education concept of allowing citizens a share in the decision-making process.

Perhaps we all ought to take a lesson in political astuteness from that eminent political observer, George Burns, who said: "Too bad all the people who know how to run the country are busy driving taxicabs and cutting hair."

NOTES

[1] **Neighborhood Councils Service Center, Neighbors**, December 1981 (Independence, Missouri) p. 18.

[2] C. J. Dudley and S. R. Parson, **Open Bureaucracy or Process? An Empirical Investigation of Three Community Education Projects** (Research Report, Virginia Polytechnic Institute and State University, Blacksburg, Virginia, 1981).

[3] Don Davies, "Politics, the Public, and the Public Schools," **Principal**, vol. 61, no. 1 (September 1981), pp. 6-7.

Commentary on: Laurence Iannaccone's

"Community Education and Turning Point Election Periods (TPEPs)"

by
Samuel Halperin

I have two basic problems with Larry Innaccone's paper. First, in spite of my respect for his research methodology and his skills, I do not understand how his analysis of turning point election periods (TPEPs) can measurably aid policy makers, community educators, or the lay public, nor how it can further the objective of getting a national agenda for community education. Second, I am skeptical of the predictive power of cyclical explanations of human behavior. I believe that life is a great deal more chaotic, idiosyncratic, unpredictable, and unrepetitious than TPEP research implies.

Individuals with their unique abilities and their peculiar dreams, desires, and ideals, seem to me to be at least as decisive in determining outcomes as the mechanistic workings of a society allegedly governed by the characteristics of candidates rather than educational policy issues), seem to me more nearly the norm than the exception. American politics, after all, is notoriously personalistic. Far more often than not, the candidate *is* the issue. When policy planks and proposals are injected into a campaign, it is more often to see how the candidates' personalities are reflected and revealed by the issues, rather than to assess and plumb the merits of the proposals themselves. At the national level, who remembers that the major policies separating Herbert Hoover from Franklin Roosevelt in 1932 were the gold standard and prohibition? Was it the alleged missile gap or Jack Kennedy's style and "class" that beat Richard Nixon in the 1960 television debates? And was it Jimmy Carter's personality and perceived malperformance as President or Ronald Reagan's issues that carried the day in 1980?

Similarly, having watched almost a dozen D.C. school superintendents come and go in the past 21 years, I remain profoundly skeptical that issues and philosophies accounted for more than a token measure of the turnover in that disastrously unstable period. Rather, the struggle for political survival and dominance, and the interpersonal skills, or lack of them, of the major actors help explain what happened in the District of Columbia. Does the high standing of the current D.C. superintendent in the Washington political and educational community derive from a cyclical stage of the District's educational milieu, or is it, as I believe, a tribute to Floretta McKenzie's very substantial mastery of the political and social skills delineated by Don Davies (and cited approvingly by Steve Parson in his excellent paper)?

Was the vertiable explosion of federal social programs in the '60s and the '70s part of the "normal cycle" of social change or was it "aberrational," produced by a unique combination of social forces and dominant individuals unlikely to be duplicated again? Are Ronald Reagan and Reaganomics just a blip on the radar screen of upward social progress, or was the unprecedented growth of federal (and state) social programs really a long-term trend, interrupted briefly by a "turning point election?"

Whatever we may think of TPEP theory, the election of 1980 *was* a turning point of enormous significance for American society generally. Education, including community education, will never be the same. Deep in our hearts all of us know that our economic, social, and political problems are more deep-seated and intransigent than a simple replacement of Ronald Reagan will cure.

PART IV

Coordination of Human Services

PART IV: COORDINATION OF HUMAN SERVICES

SUMMARY

Jule M. Sugarman says that the current national debate over proper federal, state, and local roles will shape the human services delivery systems of the future. Demographic changes and advancing technology will also play a role in shaping the delivery systems. Changes in the age mix of the population, geographic mobility, the increased number of women in the workforce, and changes in the makeup of the family are causing increased demand for child-care programs and for the training of child-care providers. High rates of unemployment and underemployment may cause demands on government to create employment and necessitate adjustments in economic expectations and standards of living.

Community educators are particularly suited to fill the role that the economics, philosophy, and politics of the times are creating: that of community responsibility for the delivery of human services. Sugarman suggests a model for providing human services for which public funding is insufficient: a "Community Educator Corps" that would serve as an auxiliary to the local school system, and be available for assignment to public or private organizations involved in the provision of human services. Some functions of the Corps would be to educate, organize, motivate, resolve conflict, act as a catalyst to analyze problems, develop policy, and implement programs. Expenses for Corps services would be shared by the local and state education agencies and receiving organizations.

Jack D. Minzey notes that the federal role in public education has been a rather recent phenomenon, beginning in the 1950s. Community education, in particular, has had minimal federal recognition and only token federal support, and is more appropriately supported by the community.

Minzey says that the movement in the past two decades from a representative to a participatory democracy may be the most important change of the 1980s in its impact on our society; our political system is growing more responsive and more accountable. Changes in the age distribution of our population will mandate re-consideration of how public education uses its resources to address such issues as lifetime education.

Minzey defines community education as a set of beliefs and points out that the community school is simply one institution's attempt to respond to these beliefs. He cautions community educators to avoid trying to do things outside the realm of their training. He supports Sugarman's model for a Community Educator Corps but would modify it to emphasize a facilitating role for the community school director, who would ascertain that a needed service was not available before initiating community action to address the problem.

Susan J. Baillie agrees with many of Sugarman's speculations on the future but she does not believe that the Reagan Administration's proposals to phase out federal efforts in the delivery of human services are the wave of the future. She points out that public opinion polls consistently show support for federal social services (unless the word "welfare" is used). Baille points out that the current level of service is already inadequate and that the need is for expanded, not reduced, programs. She points out that successful models of community education include some that are independent of school systems. Baille believes that community education can have considerable national impact in the human services area if it develops its citizen participation component.

She lists six potential impediments to Sugarman's proposal for the expansion of community education: (1) general lack of knowledge about community education; (2) agency turfism; (3) service boundary disputes; (4) bureaucratic immobility; (5) the inefficiency of community participation; and (6) legal and financial problems.

ACHIEVING CRITICAL MASS IN COMMUNITY EDUCATION
by
Jule M. Sugarman

The question in my mind is whether the child has outgrown the parent. Community education, spawned and nurtured from its infancy by the public schools of America, is now mature and very robust. In fact, sister agencies such as recreation and community action have paid community education the supreme compliment of imitation. Yet community education's ties to its education parents may now be unnecessarily constraining its potential to achieve a critical mass of services in the future. Let me be very clear—I in no way recommend dissolution of the family ties. Rather, I want to consider whether some greater degree of independence of action and adjustment in institutional framework would not strengthen both child and parent. The breadth and depth of what community education is achieving throughout the nation demonstrates characteristics of flexibility and innovation that are critical to the expanded role I will suggest.

Speculations on the Future

We cannot plan for the future without speculating on what the nature of our society, our values, and our governments are likely to be. Our post-World War II experiences in predicting the future ought to be a cause for humility. Few can claim to have had any long-term success in anticipating the changes in technologies, the internationalization of society, the economic changes, and the turmoil in attitudes and values we are living through.

But with all humility I cannot resist the opportunity to think about the future, to consider those developments that are almost certain along with those that are highly speculative. My predictions are based on two assumptions: first, that the world will somehow find a way to remain at peace, and second, that the current recession will not become depression, that we will somehow restore the viability of our economy.

Government

There is currently no area more difficult to plumb than the future of our government(s). We are in the midst of a great national debate as to the future of government. There are two central issues:
- What are the proper responsibilities of American governments?
- How should those responsibilities be distributed among federal, state, and local governments?

Underlying both issues is the often unasked question of what is essential to the good of society. Similarly permeating the issues are questions of viable alternatives to government action.

During the middle of this century Americans put enormous faith and substantial investment into the premise that government, especially at the federal level, could solve any problem. With a fervor remarkably similar to the fervor American business brought to building America's industrial might at an earlier time, we applied enormous energy to using government to overcome all the defects we believed to exist in our society. Whether it was in education, health, social services, equal opportunity, economic security, life as a senior citizen, culture, recreation, or housing, we wanted the best for all—and we wanted it fast.

Now large numbers of people have developed grave reservations about what government, particularly the federal government, has been trying to do. For the first time in its history there is the possibility that the powers and activities of the federal government will be substantially reduced. Let me be very clear that this is not a certainty, for there are many other people who believe that the federal efforts have had highly positive results. They argue that, while refinements may be required, a vast amount has been left undone that only the federal government has the capacity to do (although it might use state and local governments and the private sector as allies and instruments to achieve its objectives).

President Reagan is the nation's leading spokesman for the view that government, particularly the federal government, should do less in human services. Although the precise limits as to what the federal government, in his view, ought to do are not explicit, the residual responsibilities seem to be:

1. maintaining the social security and unemployment insurance programs;
2. maintaining some degree of support for services to the aged, handicapped, and educationally disadvantaged, but at a considerably lower dollar level than in the past;
3. maintaining, for a time, the Medicaid and Medicare programs;
4. providing some support for medical, but not social, research; and
5. preventing intentional and substantial discrimination.

To the extent that other human services are essential, the President would assign both management and financial responsibilities to state and local governments. But his real preference seems to be that the private sector (i.e., business, philanthropy, and the churches) assume responsibility.*

To accomplish his objectives, the President has proposed a 10-year strategy. His proposal for fiscal year 1982 was to consolidate approximately 90 categorical programs into five block grants with an across-the-board reduction of 25 percent in funding. Congress substantially modified these proposals but accepted many of the principles behind them. (See Appendix B for a list of programs included in block grants.) In particular, Congress greatly reduced the authority of federal officials and granted state officials much greater authority over the use of federal money.

---

*Appendix A, which is drawn from the author's **Human Services in the 1980's (White Paper IV)**, provides more detail on those human service programs from which the President would have the federal government withdraw.

In his fiscal year 1983 budget the President proposes additional block grants and further reductions in funding. He also proposes, beginning in fiscal year 1984, creation of a trust fund to supplant 43 existing programs, 31 of which are human service programs. The programs range from general revenue sharing, mass transit subsidies, and sewer and water construction to education, health, social, community, and legal services. Their costs are estimated by the Administration at $28 billion. If approved by Congress (and this is far from certain), states would, beginning October 1, 1983, have three options on using their share of the trust fund. They could:

- *ask federal agencies to continue the program under federal rules until 1986 with reimbursement by the states (an option unlikely to be used by any state);*
- *use the money to carry on similar programs but under state policies as to eligibility, priorities, standards, and methods of service delivery; or*
- *use the money for any purpose the state wished (e.g., raising salaries, reducing taxes, constructing highways) without any requirement that the money be spent on human services.*

In 1987 the trust fund would be reduced by 25 percent, and by 1991 there would be no federal money. The President would have accomplished his objective of eliminating the federal role in managing **and** financing human services.

The trust fund is a popular idea with governors and legislators because it gives them virtually total control over how the money is used as well as over decisions on targeting, eligibility, fee scales, quality standards, and accountability. Their enthusiasm is constrained, however, by the disappearance of federal funding in later years. The White House and the governors are now negotiating possible modifications in the trust fund concept.

Many members of Congress are actively opposing the trust fund for other reasons. First, they do not want to appropriate large sums of money without knowing the specific purposes for which the money will be used. Many members have, over the years, helped create or support programs that enjoy strong constituent support. Some members are concerned that states will not give these programs the same priority the members would. Some feel that states will not perform well without close federal supervision.

Experience with the existing general revenue program has convinced some members that money not specifically targeted to particular programs is much more difficult to appropriate. This explains Congress' failure to appropriate the state portion of general revenue sharing in 1980. Congress felt that the states, at that time, were in good financial condition, and no compelling case had been made that specific damage would occur if the funds were lost. States should keep that example in mind as they evaluate the trust fund concept.

Whether or not a trust fund is approved, there is now a clear movement in the direction of giving states greater authority. The block grants enacted in 1981 were generally less restrictive on the use of funds than the categorical programs had been. Furthermore, the federal departments were told not to enlarge upon the legislative language through regulations. Congress believed that it had spoken clearly, but if there were any doubts, interpretation of the law was to be left to each state. This approach obviously creates a possibility that different meanings will be given to a law by different states and may set the stage for litigation testing whether Congress has provided "equal treatment under the law."

Congress also clearly signaled its intention to rely on the states for accountability. The states are required to make an annual report on their use of funds, but the content of the report is left entirely up to the states. As a consequence, our ability to make comparisons among the states is likely to be seriously diminished. Congress placed basic responsibility for auditing programs and fund expenditures on the states but did provide a complementary authority to the General Accounting Office and the Inspectors General.

It should be noted that Congress can undo what it has done. The original Community Development Block Grant contained few restrictions on grantees, but after a brief experience Congress became dissatisfied with the decisions and actions of state and local governments and added more federal requirements each year. In 1981 Congress again reversed itself and went back to a much less restrictive form of grant.

Demographic Changes

We know with a high level of certainty that a minimum of 29 percent of the people now 45-55 years old will live to age 85. If the gerontologists are right, most of these people will be physically and mentally healthy. They will both want and need to be an active part of society, although perhaps under different ground rules. Many of them will want or need to remain employed but may want a major shift in the type or conditions of employment.

At the other end of the age spectrum, the declining birth rate of the 1960s and '70s seems to be in the process of being reversed. The statistical evidence is not yet firm, but I suspect that shifting family values will soon raise the birth rate above the replacement level. We are not too far from the time when some schools will have to be reopened and some teaching staffs expanded. A higher birth rate accompanied by continuing growth in the proportion of women working would cause a sharp jump in the demand for preschool and after-school child care programs of many types. Our current difficulty in financing such programs is likely to be exacerbated by coming revenue shortfalls. Many more people who lack formal training may become care providers and require considerable training.

In the mid-years of life we will have, well beyond the year 2000, the largest number of individuals in the labor force that America has ever known. The implications of that fact are discussed under Employment, below.

Health

The 1970s appear to have marked the beginning of a new phase in health care, with a new emphasis on preventive care. Surgeon General Julius Richmond's landmark 1979 report on the state of America's health makes clear that the major causes of death and chronic illness can be greatly reduced by personal discipline and environmental control. Deaths due to heart disease, stroke, cirrhosis, cancer, and accidents are all directly tied to things we can do something about. Spending on preventive health care has clear promise of substantially reducing overall health care costs. But much of the payoff is long-term, and in the meantime our national medical costs may drive out spending for preventive programs. Clearly, an effective and continuing health education and advocacy program reaching into all age groups should be a part of our future. Private employers and private organizations may hold the key to mounting such a program because of their growing concern about the rising costs of health-care fringe benefits and the production losses attributed to drug use and alcoholism.

Employment

During the last decade, the American labor force passed the 100 million mark. Unfortunately, it left behind many people who would like to be a part of that labor force. Persistent unemployment in the under-25 age group and among minorities (particularly black and Hispanic males) was coupled with persistent underutilization of women's talents. At the beginning of the 1970s we talked hopefully of full employment with an unemployment rate of 3 to 4 percent. Before the current recession, the unemployment rate was about 7 percent; if discouraged workers (the unemployed who are no longer actively seeking employment) are included, the total number of unemployed would have been 8 percent. The discouraged were being sustained by an underground economy, or were living off savings of families and friends or through government financial assistance. No one knows their precise numbers, but they are a significant part of the population. Clearly, many of them are, however unwillingly, a drain on the public economy. It should be noted that a large part of this population does move in and out of employment, so the number of persons permanently unemployed is much smaller than the percentage indicates.

The labor market changed qualitatively as well as quantitatively between 1970 and 1980. Manufacturing activities and agriculture declined to 22.3 percent and 4 percent of the labor market, respectively. Public employment rose during the decade to a peak of 17.1 percent and then began to decline in the early '80s. Only the service industries showed sustained growth in employment. Although the current Administration speaks of the reindustrialization of America, the signs both here and throughout the world seem to indicate a continuing decline in manufacturing employment.

Other major changes have taken place in the individual's view of work. Three years ago it would have been very clear to me that a large portion of employees would (a) place great emphasis on variety in their work; (b) be eager for total career changes from time to time; (c) accept with equanimity the need to be geographically mobile; (d) be frequently dissatisfied with the value of what they were doing; (e) place a very high value on jobs that gave them personal control over their time (e.g., "flextime," long weekends, frequent vacations, and sabbaticals); and (f) expect rapid personal economic progress. Job security would, perhaps, have been at the bottom of the list.

But that list would have been made when employed persons had no real concern about job security; when, as one job for educated and skilled people disappeared, one or more would be created. Now we are in a period marked by vast increases in concern about job security and a shift in people's view toward more emphasis on family considerations and maintenance of community roots. The result is likely to be increased interest by employees in improving their skills or developing new ones so that they are more attractive to employers, some of whom feel in a position to be more demanding and less considerate of employees' needs. As the economy improves, the question is whether we will return to the values of the 1970s or maintain those of the early '80s.

The answer to that question is likely to be found, in part, in technological developments. The explosive growth in the availability of computer technology and the amazing reductions in its cost seem to have the potential of revolutionizing clerical employment. But if this happens, where will the displaced clerical worker go? Is there on the horizon some vast new supply of jobs for persons with lower skill levels?

There are four possible outcomes. (1) We may find that we cannot, in fact, create enough employment to absorb the labor force. In that case we will have to concentrate on a redistribution of available employment so that more people may share in its fruits. (2) We may find that the skill levels of large numbers of people must be substantially changed to meet the needs of the large new industries. (I am far less sanguine than many that the burgeoning information industry will generate vast new employment; I am particularly pessimistic that it will provide opportunities for those with low skill levels.) (3) We may see demands on government to create employment in public agencies or private non-profit organizations in areas of no interest to business. (4) Many people may have to adjust their economic expectations and standards of living to a new reality of their potential income. This may, in turn, generate pressures on government for more assistance in providing economic security.

Whatever the direction of change, there will be a great need for educators who can help people change their attitudes and skills with, or ahead of, the times and adjust to different life styles that stem from changing economics.

Family Management Problems

The American family has changed tremendously during the mid-century. Births out of wedlock rose from a 1950 low of 4 percent of all births to a 1979 peak of 17.1 percent. The proportion of marriages ending in divorce has increased; nearly one half of all marriages performed in 1973 are projected to end in divorce. One out of two children will spend some part of their lives in a one-parent home.

More than 54 percent of children now live in homes in which the mother is working. Even among mothers with preschoolers that proportion exceeds 45 percent. There is some debate as to whether this is a permanent phenomenon. It will be interesting to see whether the trend changes if high unemployment persists. There remains a strongly held and increasingly vocal view among some women and men that women with children do not belong in the labor force. My own judgment is that there will be a short-term decline in the proportion of women working during the child's preschool years, but no decline in the longer term.

In the last three decades the geographic dispersion of families continued to increase. The support systems of the large family were less available to families with young children or older parents. Consequently, married couples as well as single parents have increasingly had to rely on their own resources for family management and for coping with such problems as delinquency, abuse of drugs and alcohol, family conflicts, child abuse and neglect, and the isolation of the elderly, all of which are commonplace and probably increasing in frequency.

I believe there is a trend for families to regroup in support of their members. Certainly there is more resistance to moves related to employment. Some of this is due to the problems of dual careers, but I sense also a desire among the younger generation to be closer to their families. Nevertheless, there will be, for the forseeable future, very large numbers of people needing help in family management from individuals outside the family. A variety of public, voluntary, and even for-profit agencies and groups are trying to meet that need, but the prospect is for great shortages of funds for these agencies. The alternative lies in the development of supports within neighborhood, social, business, and religious organizations.

Implications for Community Education

The implications of the coming changes raise fundamental issues about the role community educators could or will want to play. President Reagan is asking Congress to abandon, over a 10-year period, virtually all federal responsibility for human services. If the President persuades Congress to do this, state and local governments, voluntary organizations, the churches, businesses, families, and individuals will be on their own in trying to cope with human problems. Nothing on the economic horizon indicates that any of these groups will have the financial resources to employ the staff necessary to serve people in need. Historically, even under the most ambitious publicly financed programs, we have never come anywhere close to meeting needs; the issue now is the extent to which we can create support systems that are not significantly dependent on public funding.

What we should be looking at is ways to maximize use of whatever resources exist. **That means using those resources to catalyze and support all types of volunteer, self-support, and mutual support systems.** Expressed in community education terms, it means using trained community educators to build skills and motivation in private organizations and individuals so they can do those things for which public funding is limited or unavailable. Only by mobilizing these private organizations and individuals can we achieve the critical mass in human services necessary to the future of American society.

Community education has a real potential for helping society cope with the future. But to realize that potential, community education will have to be freed from schools to work in a wide variety of organizations and environments. Many educators will have to move out of schools and become tutors, advisors, and supporting resources to organizations that have the capacity to work in environments outside the school system. Some educators may have to avoid direct identification with the schools because of the hostility some groups feel toward the schools.

What Could Be Achieved?

Sometimes it helps to postulate an ideal, not because it is necessarily achievable, but because it provides a target against which to test reality. I would state the ideal in three ways:

1. *Any group of reasonable size, whether ongoing or ad hoc, that is dealing with human service issues and needs to expand its knowledge and skills can find help in achieving that objective from a community educator who is acceptable to the group.*
2. *Whenever public or private officials see a human services need that requires expansion of knowledge and skills in a specific area or among specific groups, there are community educators available with the capacity to interest, motivate, and assist the public in organizing to meet society's needs.*
3. *When there are conflicts among groups and individuals, there are people to help in resolving those conflicts.*

A Modified Institutional Base

If community educators are to meet the objectives I have set forth, they must modify their institutional base. They must be able to work in a variety of organizations, using various sources of funding, while maintaining a home base within the education system. For purposes of salary equity, career advancement, retirement, and other benefits, the community educator needs an ongoing personnel system. Certainly there are individuals who can and would work as free agents, taking their chances on the future, but I think we learned in the War on Poverty that it is romantic to think there are enough dedicated people to achieve a critical mass of service.

Fortunately, there are models that show how an acceptable institutional base can be constructed. One is the U.S. Public Health Service (PHS). At the heart of PHS has been a corps of officers (physicians, dentists, nurses, epidemiologists, and many other specialists) who willingly accepted assignment to other federal agencies, to state and local agencies, and even to foreign countries. During those assignments they functioned as full members of the other organizations and were subject to their policies, but for personnel purposes remained part of the PHS.

A second model operated under the Inter-governmental Personnel Act (IPA), under which federal employees could be assigned to state or local governments or to educational institutions for periods varying from one hour to two years while legally remaining federal employees, retaining federal insurance and retirement coverage. IPA also brought state and local employees into federal agencies; these employees retained their status as employees of their parent agencies.

A third model, called the President's Executive Interchange Program, permitted federal employees to accept assignments in private companies and vice versa. Space prohibits a recounting here of all the complexities of this and the other models. The point is that when federal agencies used them well, they had very positive results.

The Local Community Educator Corps

How could such a model be applied to community education? There might be created, as an auxiliary to a local school system, a semi-autonomous Corps of Community Educators who have the talent and interest to work across institutional lines. These individuals would be available for assignment to any public or private organization involved in the provision of human services. Their functions would be educational in nature, but they would often deal with aspects of organizational development, group motivation, and conflict resolution. They might find themselves deeply involved as catalysts to problem analysis, policy development, and program implementation. The most important ingredient they would bring is an understanding of how the educational process can be used to make things happen, how individuals can become stronger through a group educational process.

Certain principles should be applied in developing a Corps:

1. *Service should be wholly voluntary; the educator should have an explicit right, without prejudice, to refuse an assignment.*
2. *An organization should request assistance and should have the right to refuse, without prejudice, the assignment of a particular educator.*
3. *Successful service in the Corps should be given significant credit in setting salaries and making promotions within the school system.*
4. *Boards of education should be willing to waive normal requirements to permit outsiders with special skills to serve temporarily as community educators within the school system.*

5. *State education agencies (SEAs) should consider serving as brokers for arranging assignments. The SEA might also consider assigning its own personnel through such a system.*

6. *The local education agency (LEA) or SEA should be alert to situations in which its educators might be helpful. To that end, the agency should be in close contact with local government officials and private planning organizations such as United Way. Community educators should be encouraged to seek out or stimulate opportunities in which their talents could be effectively used. A planning or advisory group of public and private agencies (including United Way planning organizations or their equivalents) would be highly desirable.*

7. *If possible, the LEA or SEA should have an appropriation with which to pay part of the Corps' expenses when it is in the public interest to do so. However, the receiving organization should make a meaningful financial contribution toward the costs involved.*

8. *Financial support for the Corps' activities could, and perhaps should, be shared by the school board, the local government, and private organizations. It will be greatly to the Corps' advantage to be thought of as a* **community** *resource rather than as as school program.*

9. *The school board should consciously limit its involvement in choosing projects and assigning people, but it should have the right to recall community educators to meet the needs of the school system and to approve any personnel changes.*

There are also some cautions to keep in mind:

1. *Assignments should be made carefully. A few bad assignments will convince both outsiders and insiders that the Corps is a dumping ground.*

2. *The parent organization should remain in close touch with the assignee, not for purposes of supervision, but to reassure the individual of his or her continuing ties to the education agency and of a real job to which to return.*

3. *The LEA or SEA should understand that it may permanently lose some educators to the organizations to which they are assigned.*

Examples of Use of Community Educators

Following are examples of situations in which a community educator might play a useful role:

1. *A state government has a policy of deinstitutionalizing people with mental health problems. Many of these people have no relatives or friends in the community. The community educator agrees to spend two days a week working with patients, one day at the institution working with patients about to be released, and the other day with a mutual support group of patients already in the community. Funding is provided through Title XX of the Social Security Act and/or through a service contract with the releasing institution.*

2. *The health department sees many expectant mothers who are having difficulty managing their older children. The department has no legal responsibility in this area but knows that the problems, left unattended, could become serious. It recommends that the Corps become involved. With funding from a local community foundation, the community educator works twice a month with a parent group, concentrating on issues related to managing older children. An objective is to make the group self-sustaining.*

3. *A group of senior citizens would like to work with preschool centers in their city, but both the seniors and the center directors feel that the seniors are out of touch with techniques for working with young children. The seniors decide to chip in enough money so that a community educator can organize a training program for them.*

4. *A great need for day care of handicapped children has developed in the community. County officials are concerned about safety and health issues as well as the quality of care offered to handicapped children in family day care homes. The county staff is small, and there are no funds to train family day care mothers in the specialized needs of handicapped children. They do have inspection funds, however. A community educator becomes a consultant to the inspectors, helping them redesign their inspection so it becomes more of a training tool. The day care mothers, feeling the need for more training, ask for a Corps member to help them form their own organization for staff development. The state government agrees to use Education Consolidation and Improvement Act funds to support the effort.*

5. *The Acme Corporation would like to employ minority youth with low levels of skills in jobs that have real potential. Government funds are available to prepare these youths for their first jobs, but advancement will depend on carefully tailored training programs. The employer and employees agree that the corporation will provide space, materials, and volunteer instructors if the employees will pay a community educator to organize and supervise the training program.*

6. *A housing project faces bankruptcy, and the Public Housing Authority agrees to turn it over to a tenant organization if the tenants will manage it. Because the tenants have limited skills, the authority agrees to pay a community educator to develop a training program in basic maintenance, minor repair, and security skills so that those services may be performed by volunteers, thereby reducing project costs.*

7. *A community of lower-income families find they no longer qualify for Medicaid. Several families must remove elderly parents or chronically ill children from hospitals and nursing homes. A family care committee of volunteers (including students) is formed to help the families provide care in their own homes. The community educator hired by the group arranges basic training and helps the group develop a quality control system.*

8. *Community residents think that citizen participation in decisions about spending human services funds is a sham, in large part because they do not understand the budgetary process and documents. The state provides a community educator to arrange training in an environment acceptable to the citizens.*

9. *The XYZ Corporation finds its competitive position eroding and decides to involve employees in management decisions. It contracts with community educators to work with employees and corporate officials in planning that involvement.*

Why Community Educators?

The roles described above are similar in some ways to those played by other types of workers, e.g., community organizers, trainers, and social workers, but I think community educators will be accepted in many situations in which other professionals would not be because community educators are policy-neutral, not identified with one faction or another, and dedicated to good process. They would not be enforcing the policies or regulations of a government agency, but responding to needs seen by the people involved. Over several years community educators have shown a capacity to work with many different types of people and to tailor the learning process to individual motivation and skill levels. They have successfully introduced flexibility and innovation into previously rigid school bureaucracies. Finally, many of them seem to have a highly developed sense of mission and an affinity for hard work.

Conclusion

The prospect is for massive changes in human services throughout the country. These changes, as well as newly emerging problems, will occur in an environment of severly reduced public resources. Formal and informal private services are likely to proliferate in the absence of government funded services. Public officials, voluntary agencies, and self-help and mutual support groups will all need help in using those private services to deliver effective human services under trying conditions.

The unique experiences and achievements of community educators create a presumption that they could play a highly useful role in facilitating necessary changes. This may, however, require adjustments in their relationships to school systems. Community education needs some freedom from the school system if community educators are to achieve critical mass in supporting the overall human service effort. Models exist as to how this can be done. Basically, community educators would remain part of the formal school personnel system but be permitted to work in many other types of organizations, both public and private, using a wide variety of public and private funds.

APPENDIX A

THE PRESIDENT'S PLAN

The President and his advisors have been forthright in saying that they hope to remove the Federal government entirely from authority over and financial responsibility for human services. A clear strategy to accomplish this objective is now emerging as reflected in the chart and timetable below.

Timetable	Block Grants	Income Maintenance	Funding	Other
FY 1982	57 programs consolidated into 9 block grants with authority transfered to states.	Eligibility narrowed; services diminished; tough administrative requirements.	25% reduction in dollars.	Deregulation of new and some existing programs. Abolition of some reporting and audit requirements. Staffing reductions in Federal agencies. Curtailment of research and professional development.
FY 1983	Several more programs consolidated into block grants.	Further reductions in eligibility and and services. Even tougher administrative requirements.	Further reduction in dollars.	Further deregulation. Further reductions in Federal staff. Further curtailment of research and professional development.
FY 1984	Trust Fund of $28 billion which states may use to buy Federal programs, take them over, or use for other purposes.	Federal government assumes Medicaid. States take over AFDC and Food Stamps.	Further reductions in dollars.	Close to total deregulation. Virtually no Federal staff help or monitoring.
FY 1987	Most federal administration of of service programs and block grants ends.		Begin phase out of trust funds.	
FY 1991			Federal funding of services ends.	
Speculative	Local education and handicapped programs end? Programs for the aged altered?	Social Security changes. Ending of Medicaid/Medicare?		Federal role in research further curtailed?

APPENDIX B

THE FEDERAL/STATE TRUST FUND

The President proposes to create a Trust Fund in support of 43 separate programs in FY 84. This total includes 19 grants for transportation, revenue sharing, and other purposes that are not human services. The trust fund would be available to the states in three phases. Between 1984 and 1987 a state may use the money to reimburse the Federal government for a continuation of programs operated under federal rules. It may also use the trust fund money to take over some or all of the presently federally funded programs. Or the state may treat the money as "super revenue sharing" and use it for any purpose the state chooses.

Beginning in FY 88 the Federal programs will disappear entirely and each state will have to decide what, if anything it wishes to continue.

Also in FY 87 the trust fund will be reduced 25%. Further reductions of 25% each year will bring the trust fund to an end at the close of FY 90.

Administration officials have promised that there will be close consultation in developing the needed legislation with state and local officials and such talks already have begun.

The transfer of these programs will eventually have the effect of destroying them because there will be few or no Federal rules on how the money is to be used.

If the transfer occurs on October 1, 1983 the Federal government will begin to provide $28 billion to the states out of a Special Federal/State Trust Fund. This fund would come from a portion of the excise and windfall profits (oil) taxes.

More than half of this money now comes from the windfall profits tax on oil. Currently the oil companies are reporting lower profits so that total revenues may actually drop in future years.

The Administration apparently does not plan to increase the fund in future years to compensate for inflation.

The *human services* programs which would be affected are listed below. Those which were block granted in FY 82 are shown with a plus symbol. Those proposed for further block granting in FY 83 have two plus symbols.

Vocational Rehabilitation++
State Block Grants (ECIA-Ch.2)+
Child Nutrition++
Adoption Assistance++
Runaway Youth
Social Services Block Grant++
Community Services Block Grant+
Alcohol, Drug Abuse and Mental Health Block Grant+
Maternal and Child Health++
Black Lung Clinics++
Migrant Health Clinics++
Women, Infants & Children++
Community Development Block
Vocational & Adult Education++

CETA++
Low Income Energy Assistance+
Child Welfare Services++
Foster Care++
Child Abuse
Legal Services
Health Prevention Block Grant
Primary Care Block Grant+
Primary Care, Research & Development
Family Planning++
Nutrition++
Urban Development Action Grants

Reaction Paper To: Jule Sugarman's
"Achieving Critical Mass in Community Education"

by
Jack Minzey

Jule Sugarman's premise is that the purpose of any institution is to serve the society for which it was created. Therefore, the personnel of an institution must know what the society is like, so they can carry out the responsibilities for which the institution was intended. Sugarman shares his view of coming changes in our society and its institutions, and describes a new role for the community educator in this new setting.

"New" roles for government in education are new only to those who were not around at the beginning of federal financial support to education in the 1950s. Before Sputnik, schools received little financial aid from the federal government. Education was perceived as a province of the state, and most educators wanted it that way. "States' rights" was an important concept, and federalism (as it was defined then) threatened to centralize things in a way that was unacceptable to many people. There was concern that federal aid would bring control by a non-responsive, non-accountable bureaucracy—and indeed many people today feel that the amount of current federal regulation is not justified in terms of the financial benefits received. President Reagan seems to be returning to where we were in the 1950s, and the problem may be more one of adjustment than prescription. What we are witnessing is the circular nature of change, and those who would like more federal support for education need simply wait a few years until such support is re-introduced as a "new" something or other.

For those of us in community education, the change will really not be all that great. We waited a long time for federal support, and the energy exerted in this cause has not had significant results. We currently have minimal recognition from the federal government, and the financial support has been little more than token. In short, the federal government's support of community education has been disappointing at best.

Community education seems to be more acceptable at the state and local levels, where the movement has received both program and financial support. And this is as it should be, since the community education concept accentuates the smaller community. The categorical nature of a federal grant may assure that money will find its way to a particular program, but there is something to be said for having decisions and guidelines made by those in the smaller community rather than by a bureaucrat who has no understanding of more localized concerns.

Some observations may be added to Sugarman's points about age distribution. The year 1969 was the last time that parents of school-aged children outnumbered non-parents (51 percent to 49 percent). The number of parents has declined regularly since then; the percentage of parents is 30 percent now and will be 20 percent by 1990. This change would seem to have great ramifications for our communities. Certainly one of the things that needs to be considered is how public schools might use their tremendous resources to address community issues they have not had time for or have not perceived as a part of their responsibility.

Sugarman notes the move from industry-related jobs to those related to services and the new concern for self-improvement (perhaps to enhance job security). I am heartened by his suggestion that one answer to unemployment may be new jobs in public agencies and private non-profit organizations. This would certainly offer increased attention to many formerly neglected human problems.

I would like to emphasize a point about unemployment only implied by Sugarman. Most futurists are predicting a massive transition from an industrial to a technological society. They also predict an impact that will be more profound than the 19th century shift from an agricultural to an industry society. In the new information society, the main strategic resource will be knowledge, rather than capital. If this prediction is accurate, and there is mounting evidence that it is, education will take on a new aura. Educational institutions will have not only increased responsibility for their traditional clients but also a mandatory obligation related to lifetime education, which heretofore has been a luxury of choice. Nations, states, communities, and individuals will recognize that quality of life is dependent on the level of education of the individual, and we might then move from an educational system based on limited schooling to a much broader interpretation of education and clients.

I hope that Sugarman is correct on the future of family life. His statement that "there is a trend for families to regroup in support of their members" is nostalgic; those of us who long for the return of the extended family hope it will come true. Many other futurists would disagree with Sugarman on this point, and only time will tell who is correct. I think I have seen the same signs that Sugarman has seen, although I must admit that my bias on this issue may be blurring my vision.

One possible change that Sugarman does not address should be mentioned. That change has to do with the move from a representative to a participatory democracy. Historically, we have identified ourselves as the greatest democracy in the world. In truth, we are probably an oligarchy; at best, we are a representative democracy. The old Jeffersonian principle of an elitist society has continued to permeate our system of government. We pay lip service to broader participation and grassroots involvement, but an actuality the operation of our political system is based on very limited participation by our citizens, a situation continually fostered by the system itself.

The past two decades have produced not only an awareness of the representative aspect of our political system but some overt moves in the direction of participation. More and more communities have recognized their role and responsibility in a participatory democracy and have begun to use those devices that make the system more accountable (election, protest, recall, economic sanction, initiative, referendum). This involvement is appearing not only in government but in the business sector as well. The move toward participatory democracy will have a great impact on our society and its institutions and may be the most important change predicted for the '80s.

Sugarman points out the close tie between community education and the public schools and suggests that this relationship may be "unnecessarily constraining" to community education. Community education and the public schools do have a close relationship, but it is not a relationship of exclusiveness. Community education is a concept, a philosophy. It implies that the entire community should be educated, with education defined as any input that helps an individual with other life experiences. Thus, education is a much broader term than schooling, and, in light of this definition, all members of the community are involved in education as both teachers and learners.

Community education has the same generic sense as any other concept such as democracy, socialism, or Christianity. The concept has a set of basic beliefs, and anyone who espouses those beliefs is a believer. The concept of community education has its own set of principles that describe the philosophy. Although the following beliefs are not universally accepted, they represent some principles of the community education concept on which there is general agreement:

1. Education is not synonymous with schooling and deals with an area much broader than technical training or vocational preparation.
2. Education is a lifetime process and an integral part of the environment in which we live.
3. Many groups and individuals are involved in the education process, and every community has an abundance of untapped educational resources.
4. Education is a very valuable resource.
5. We should seek to maximize the use of facilities and resources since they can accomplish collectively much more than they can individually.
6. Involvement of the community is a community right that results in better decisions and better community support.
7. Improvement of the smaller community is the best approach to improving the larger community.
8. Services should be delivered as close as possible to where people live.
9. Education should be based on the needs and problems of the people for whom it is planned.
10. The educative process (problem solving) is the most effective way to meet individual and community needs.

Any one who supports these principles believes in community education. The community school is simply one institution's attempt to respond to these beliefs. This does not make community education the province of the schools any more than democracy is a province of the schools simply because schools implement the principles of democracy in their operation.

Community school people are those who believe in community education and are attempting to change the role of the school to coincide with their beliefs. I hope there are persons from other disciplines who are community educators by belief and who will expend their energies to change their institutions (libraries, community colleges, universities, businesses, unions, social, and governmental agencies, etc.) in a similar way. The fact that school people have been the most active in responding to community education should not deter others nor leave the impression that only one agency can deliver the promises of community education. Sugarman's observation about community education's school-based identity is one many of us share. The answer, however, is not to get the schools to do less, but to get other agencies and institutions to do more in community education. Within the framework of this discussion, I accept his concern but also state that I am a community educator by belief who is a community schooler by practice.

The reason I have turned my energies to the public schools is that that is the only area in which I have expertise. While I have great concern for community education in other disciplines, it would be presumptuous of me to attempt to make changes in areas in which I have neither training nor experience. Because of this, I shall limit my comments to what the community school can do in connection with other community educators in order to deal with the problems identified by Sugarman.

I applaud this understanding and appreciation of the capacity of "trained community educators to build skills and motivation in private organizations and individuals so they can do those things for which public funding is limited or unavailable." The roles he describes for community educators in terms of education, community development, group motivation, and conflict resolution are roles most community educators would welcome. And Sugarman's reference to the educative process reinforces ideas given to us by Maurice Seay many years ago.

I would like to add some cautions to the very useful ones proposed by Sugarman and suggest a somewhat different community education model. I believe that he attributes to the community educator areas of expertise that are too diverse to be found in one individual. To serve as a facilitator is an attainable function, but to be involved in areas as different as senior citizen programs, mental health, parenting, day care for the handicapped, vocational training, and management of low-income housing would seem to require knowledge and time beyond the capacity of most individuals. We have already had community educators who tried to do things outside the realm of their training; the result was unsuccessful programs and negative relations with experts in whose fields the community educators tres-passed. These experiences also resulted in a perception that community educators are people who practice everything without a license.

I would therefore like to suggest a slight modification in the Sugarman proposal. I speak primarily as a community schooler with an interest only in the school's role in community education, and I believe firmly that the primary or gemeinschaft unit is critical to this plan.

There should be a trained community school person at every elementary building in the school district. This person would be assisted by appropriate staff, including professionals, paraprofessionals, volunteers, and secretarial staff. The main responsibility of this person would be to relate community needs to community resources, to function as a broker between those who have a need and those who can supply a service. The method of operation would fall into one of the following sequential categories:

Category 1: A straight brokerage function. Clients would be referred to existing services, and agencies would be informed of potential clients. Solutions would come from the simple matching of current services and those needing those services.

Category 2. Applies when there are needs and responsible services, but no appropriate programs to meet the needs. Community members would be made aware of the agencies responsible for a particular kind of service, and agencies would be informed of persons needing a particular kind of help. It would then become the responsibility of that agency to provide the service or to join with others to provide it. This procedure would restore a degree of accountability to our agency system, and would lead toward cooperation among organizations whenever a need exceeded the ability of any one group to deliver a service. The community school director would also have the role of helping the community find ways to get service if agencies were reluctant to supply it.

Category 3. To be implemented when no agency is able or available to deliver appropriate service. The community school director would initiate such community action as is needed to solve the problem with local resources. This might result in programs or activities beyond the expertise of the community school director or community members, but the action would be justified because the director would have already determined that there was no existing agency or program to respond.

These steps would emphasize a facilitating function for the community school director and would reduce duplication and interference in areas outside the realm of the community school director's training. It would also re-emphasize a basic community education belief that unnecessary competition or duplication should be avoided and that a good community educator will never create programs already operated effectively by other groups or agencies.

This model would seem to be compatible with Sugarman's orientation and suggestions. Certainly all of his goals and concerns and his justification for using school-based people to do such a job are applicable. The categories above are suggested as a refinement of, not as an alternate to, his plan. I see the Sugarman model as reflective of the way that Category 3 might work and suggest that two intermediate steps precede the activities he proposes.

Sugarman is a community educator, although his formal credentials are in the other fields. His paper attests to this, and I am certain that most community educators will respond to it with a loud "Amen."

Reaction Paper to: Jule Sugarman's

"Achieving Critical Mass in Community Education"

by
Susan Baillie

Introduction

Sugarman examines the potential of community education and human delivery from the broad perspective of future governmental, demographic, health, employment, and family trends. I agree with many of his speculations on the future, but I have serious reservations in some areas and a few additional suggestions.

Government

In his assessment of future trends in government, Sugarman raises but does not adequately address two central issues: the proper responsibilities of American government, and the distribution of these responsibilities among federal, state, and local governments. His analysis seems to assume that President Reagan's rather compassionless image of government is the wave of the future. He says that many people have reservations about what the federal government has been trying to do in recent years but does not make clear that the reservations seem to be limited to the government's efforts in the area of human services, a relatively small portion of the federal budget.[1] The current Administration apparently believes that the federal government's role should be limited principally to spending for defense of the country and revitalizing corporate involvement in the economy. But there are many who disagree with the Administration, who believe that the federal government has responsibility for the welfare and well-being of all citizens.

Although President Reagan has managed to cripple some of the federal human services effort, the Administration's programs are by no means necessarily the wave of the future. Just as FDR came after Hoover, there could be substantial revitalization of federal efforts in the human services area after Reagan. Programs may change in their **nature** and **delivery**, but the federal government may resume major responsibility for the welfare of its citizens. Public opinion polls consistently show support for the provision of services by the federal government (unless the word "welfare" is used). State and local governments and private organizations may become more involved, but it is important to note that one of the reasons federal responsibility increased was that other governments and groups lacked either resources or willingness to provide adequate services on an equal and just basis.

State and local governments and private groups vary considerably in their ability to provide for their citizens. One of the federal government's roles has been to equalize those differences. Another has been to address those human service needs that are national in scope, not specific to states.

Another issue that Sugarman fails to address adequately is **who** will be making future decisions about federal responsibility. Some Americans have shown an unwillingness in recent years to accept election results as the final indicator of what the government's role should be. Increasingly, people are questioning the advice of experts in deciding what is good for the country. Current movements to freeze nuclear weapons development and to protect the environment are good examples of citizen involvement in crucial issues—and we have yet to hear the final word from senior citizens about social security. In the current economy, in which high unemployment, declining production, inflation, and decreased funding for human services have been accompanied by increased tax incentives for corporations and tax cuts that primarily help the rich, it is unlikely that citizens will just sit back and watch what happens. There are already movements in some areas towards greater economic democracy. The May 16, 1982, **New York Times** reported:

> New coalitions and campaigns have been forming around both economic and international issues on the national state and local levels, many groups have been broadening their focus, and new organizations are springing up at the community level. . . .
> Leaders of these movements say that the Reagan Administration, by cutting social programs and building up the military, has stimulated the formulation of new coalitions of organizations with such disparate aims as lower interest rates and nuclear disarmament.

Whether these new coalitions represent a long-term trend of citizen activism is uncertain, but they do suggest both dissatisfacton and willingness to act on the part of many people.

Sugarman does not discuss the Administration's inconsistency in defining a federal role. At the same time as the Administration moves toward decentralization of human services programs, it has supported centralization through constitutional amendments on the issues of abortion and school prayer.

Health Care

Sugarman sees a trend toward preventive health care, but his suggestion that private employers and private organizations may hold the key to mounting preventive programs is not adequately discussed. He offers no evidence that private employers and private organizations would be willing to assume the burden of spiraling health care costs. Private health care insurance is not equally distributed; many individuals have none, while current and former government employees (such as veterans) have good health care insurance. The United States is the only advanced industrial national without some form of national health insurance for its citizens. Is this not a potential trend in health care?

Employment

Sugarman does not offer clear speculation on future economic trends, perhaps because the current Administration does not have a clear economic policy. It appears that full employment is not an immediate goal, so the costs of unemployment will continue to be a burden to the working public for the next few years.

Implications for Community Education and Human Services Delivery

Sugarman suggests that changes in the federal role in the delivery of human services could have a major effect on the role community educators could or will want to play. As is evident from his analysis, a crisis in human services is upon us. There is already a substantial unmet need for services not covered by federal programs; reductions in federal support will increase the demand for services from state and local governments, voluntary organizations, the schools, and others working in the human services area.

Sugarman's proposed strategies for community educators center primarily on helping organizations and individuals organize to deliver human services. He sees a need for community educators to work somewhat independently of the local school system while bringing to the delivery of services "an understanding of how the educational process can be used to make things happen." Sugarman does not suggest how the strategies he proposes would be funded, given the slashing of so many school, local, and state budgets, nor is he clear on the educational pedagogy he proposes. His examples of new roles for community educators include working with deinstitutionalized mental patients, child care providers, youth, tenants, families, etc. In the past, community educators have primarily played facilitating roles; this proposed shift suggests a need for new types of training for community educators.

One example Sugarman uses is in the current domain of community educators: facilitating citizen participation in decision-making. This is perhaps community education's most important and useful role, one with potential for considerable national impact in human services delivery. This role should be expanded. Community educators already have the training and ability to help people improve their own lives by providing them with equal access to information and a chance not just to cope, but to take action.

Another role in which community educators have a proven record is the coordination of human services programs at various service sites. Although these programs may not bring about major changes in the social structure that has created some of the human services needs, they do help individuals live better.

Building on currently successful community education models may be the strategy for greatest national impact. A number of these models already involve some independence from school systems; one model does not involve the schools at all. The successful models[2] include:

- The school-based community education center.
- The human resource center, a multi-agency center often connected with a school.

- Municipality-school district cooperative community education programs.
- Recreation department—school district cooperative community education programs.
- Community college—public school cooperative programs.
- Not-for-profit independent community education programs.

These models vary considerably. Some programs offer a wide range of human services in such areas as health, employment, education, housing, and welfare, and serve a range of citizens from infants to older adults, while other programs offer a smaller range of services. Community educators have shown considerable skill in facilitating the coordination of services to end duplication. They have found ways to meet many of the needs of children, families, and older adults in a coordinated human resource center, often increasing services while eliminating duplication. Their success is well documented.

Some existing programs may be able to absorb increased demand for human services, but community educators will have to be clear about the areas in which they are best able to meet needs. The major impediments to expansion appear to be:

1. **General lack of of knowledge** *about community education models for human services delivery. There is a need to let people know about existing successful program.*
2. **Agency turfism.** *Agencies may fear they will lose some power and authority by participating in cooperative efforts and be motivated by self-preservation in times of budget slashing.*
3. **Service boundary disputes.** *Agencies often do not have identical service areas. For example, a school district might serve two towns, each of which serves only its own residents for some needs, while the county government provides other services across town lines.*
4. **Bureaucratic immobility.** *It is not easy to change bureaucratic structures, nor do bureaucracies respond rapidly to external change.*
5. **Difficulties with community participation.** *There is sometimes concern that community participation takes too much time and that consensus is hard to reach. More commonly, the difficulties revolve around the issue of who will control what services. As many observers have pointed out, democracy takes a great deal of time and effort.*
6. **Legal and financial problems.** *Legal questions often arise on program jurisdiction, insurance liability, and financial issues. Financial problems seem to be related to the administrative organization proposed and the choice of a governing body. For example, some school districts are ineligible for some federal funds while city governments are eligible. Private groups are often ineligible for some types of government funds.*

Existing community education programs have demonstrated that these difficulties can be surmounted. If there is a dramatic national shift in the delivery of human services, more cooperative efforts will be required and some "turf" issues will be settled by government mandate or by a shortage of resources. Community educators should take the lead in trying to convince others that meeting human needs is more important than protecting turf.

Conclusion

The public must make difficult decisions in the 1980s about how the limited resources with which they support their governmental bodies are spent. Public officials and experts can help provide information and advice, but ultimately people must decide what is good and essential for themselves and others. The Reagan Administration has challenged some long-held assumptions about what the government should provide and who should benefit. People must be prepared to respond to these challenges.

Community educators can play a useful role in this process. They can help people get the information they need to make decisions. They can also continue to improve the coordination of human services. Perhaps the question for community educators in the 1980s is not how to bring together a critical mass of community educators, but rather what their precise role should be in assessing critical needs and determining how and by whom these needs can be addressed. Community educators have the potential (and in some areas a proven record) of being not only providers and coordinators of services in various community-based organizations but also key educators, helping the public decide in a rational manner what is in their best interest.

NOTES

[1]For more information on this issue, see "Poverty in the United States: Where Do We Start?" **IRP Focus**, vol. 5, no. 2 (Winter 1981-1982).

[2]Susan Baillie, **Community Education in the United States: A Review of Alternative Approaches** (prepared for U.S. Office of Education, Community Education Program, 1978).

Susan Baillie, Lawrence DeWitt, and Linda O'Leary, **The Potential Role of the School as a Site for Integrating Social Services** (Syracuse, NY: Educational Policy Research Center, 1972).

George Wood and Lanny Carmichael, **Its Name Is Community Education (A Variety of Options in Practice)** (Ball State University, 1981).

Also, the U.S. Department of Education produced a series, **Proven Practices in Community Education,** which is available to the public.

PART V

Social Issues

PART V: SOCIAL ISSUES

SUMMARY

V. M. Kerensky says that we are in the "midst of change that demands new terms and concepts." Educators must use creative new approaches because the monolithic school systems of the past run the risk of falling of their own dead weight. Kerensky advocates systems-age thinking and expansionist decision-making approaches for educational planners in the coming post-industrial society.

Applying the concepts of John Naisbitt, a social trend analyst, Kerensky presents a case for community educators as "high touch people." Naisbitt uses the term "high tech/high touch" to describe the way human beings respond to technology: when a new technology is introduced into society, there is a counterbalancing human response—"high touch"—or the technology is rejected. Kerensky presents several examples of this phenomenon in his paper and illustrates how community education programs and processes can help maintain equilibrium between high tech and high touch by providing "touch."

Amitai Etzioni characterizes the United States in the 1980s as an "underdeveloping nation" with low productivity, living off assets built up over a hundred years. But he believes that people are now willing to make sacrifices to revive the economy. Etzioni says we need more resources for education and proposes three major shifts in public educational policy.

First, we should put a larger proportion of our educational resources into educating preschool and elementary age students and a smaller proportion into higher education. This "downward shift" of educational resources, Etzioni believes, would be a more efficient use of limited resources because it is more efficient to teach things right the first time around, and because many college graduates work at jobs for which they are overqualified.

Second, Etzioni would have our educational system provide greater work-study opportunities for 16-18-year-olds. He stresses that these opportunities should be meaningful, supervised experiences.

Third, Etzioni recommends a year of mandatory national service following the senior year of high school. He argues that national service would address the youth unemployment problem, furnish young people with opportunities to try their hands at new skills, promote the values of societal usefulness, and serve as a "sociological mixer."

Everette E. Nance examines the social implications of current economic policies and conditions and suggests the need for a new social contract between the private and public sectors of our society. He identifies prejudice as the major impediment to social equity because it limits our capacity for community building. Public education has borne the heaviest responsibility for helping Americans deal with their prejudices.

Nance charges that Etzioni's recommendation for a "downward shift" of educational resources and emphasis on vocational skills reflects an elitist view that would broaden the gap between "haves" and "have nots." Pointing out that opportunities for a year of voluntary national service already exist, Nance opposes mandatory national service.

In an era of scarce resources, community education's advocacy of wise use of resources and establishment of organizational linkages between private, public, community, and voluntary sectors is absolutely necessary. Nance quotes Cunningham and Payzant in characterizing the shared leadership that will be necessary to implement community education philosophy.

William L. Smith and Helen R. Wiprud address two major social challenges: (1) how to assimilate large numbers of culturally diverse immigrants while preserving their cultural pride and heritage; and (2) how to influence the impact of advanced technology on public education.

They examine the concept of cultural diversity, which has replaced the old "melting pot" approach to minority groups. Some of the major problems facing immigrants and minorities are presented, with suggestions to community educators for possible responses.

Smith and Wiprud also examine the implications of advanced technology and the information explosion, providing examples of how computers and other electronic technology may drastically change approaches to learning, education in general, and society itself. Concerns addressed in this paper include how to avoid giving unfair educational advantage to children of the affluent; how to maintain writing and reading skills in a society that increasingly depends on communication by picture accompanied by the spoken word; how to maintain a common body of knowledge in an age of individualized learning; and how to counteract the effects of isolation in the "electronic cottage." Smith and Wiprud state that "the power of community education lies in its potential for gathering up the forces of individuals into a group small enough to interact meaningfully with each other and large enough to make a difference." They suggest ways in which community education could be the agent for linking advanced technology and cultural diversity and solving problems created by both of these social challenges.

Sandra T. Gray shares Smith and Wiprud's concern that advanced technology will increase the existing disparity between the "information rich" and the "information poor." To realize the goal of equal access, she outlines specific activities to be included in a plan of action for community educators. She gives examples of programs that have been successful in introducing school children to advanced technology, especially through the use of volunteers. Gray urges community educators to help the public gain control over the mass media to ensure "a human future."

David A. Santellanes and Larry L. Horyna expand the focus of the Smith-Wiprud paper by discussing technological advances other than the computer (i.e., diverse types of telecommunications) and social issues other than cultural diversity (i.e., mobility, loneliness, changing family structures, changing population patterns, and increased leisure time). They agree that we must be concerned with quality face-to-face interaction in an era of advancing technology and state that community education has the ability to personalize education and facilitate interaction. They give examples of constructive uses of technology for community educators.

The authors suggest that the process used to address community concerns may be more important than the solutions to specific problems. They present a formula for solving social problems: community + discussion + needs and resource assessment x people + action = community problem solving.

COMMUNITY EDUCATORS: THE HIGH TOUCH PEOPLE

by
V. M. Kerensky

When society requires to be rebuilt, there is no use in attempting to rebuild it on the old plan.
No great improvements in the lot of mankind are possible, until a great change takes place in the fundamental constitution of their modes of thought.

John Stuart Mill

The traditional world view is in trouble. We are in the midst of change that demands new terms and concepts. We hear a great deal about the Third Wave, high tech, and the post-industrial or information society. Some view these new ideas as building blocks that can be added to the existing structure of our society. Others believe that a new age is dawning, an age that will require a transformation in the way we view things, events, and institutions. Russell Ackoff calls it the **systems** age, which will incorporate a new networking of ideas, events, and institutions—a new way of solving problems.

The Pace of Change

Ten years ago Alvin Toffler snapped us out of some of our complacency about the new environment with **Future Shock.** He has done it again in **The Third Wave.**

In 1973, Daniel Bell, in **The Coming of Post-Industrial Society,** called our attention to the changing shape of the economy and of social development and class structure. Other writers use the terms "information society" or "knowledge society" to describe the changed social system of the post-industrial era.

Ackoff, Bell, Toffler, and others are trying to shock us out of a concept of our current environment that views change as simple, linear, and predictable. They are calling for a new realization that the social environment is becoming increasingly protean—that ours is a global society affected by rapid, explosive, non-linear, non-predictable change.

The idea of exponential curves—the acceleration of doubling rates of all kinds—has now become commonplace. We know that the time for circumnavigating the globe decreased exponentially every quarter of a century by a factor of two between Nelly Bly's voyage around the world in 1889 and the first transworld airplane flight in 1928, and by a factor of ten since then. Derek Price claims that the amount of scientific work since Newton has doubled every fifteen years, or presumably about three times in the course of the working life of a scientist.[1]

Change in Size and Scale

Our age is distinguished from the past not only by the unpredictability of change, but by its size and scale.

Consider, first, the matter of numbers. It is startling to recall that when the Constitution which still guides American society was ratified, there were less than four million persons in the thirteen states of the Union. Of these, 750,000 were Negro slaves, outside society. It was a young population— the median age was only sixteen—and at that time fewer than 800,000 males had reached voting age. When George Washington was inaugurated as First President of the United States, New York City, then the capital of the country, had a population of only 33,000.[2]

Our nation at its founding was an agricultural society. Few people lived in the cities, which were defined as having 2,500 or more inhabitants. Most of the population lived in sparsely populated areas. It was a First-Wave, pre-industrial, gemeinschaft society.[3]

A change in scale does not mean simply that institutions become larger. No biological organism or human institution that undergoes a change in size and consequent change in scale does so without changing its form or shape.

Bell discusses the concept and process of structural differentiation as applied to human institutions:

The concept of structural differentiation, as derived from Durkheim and Max Weber, and elaborated by Talcott Parsons and his students, is probably the key sociological concept today in the analysis of crescive social change. It points to the phenomenon that as institutions grow in size and in the functions they have to perform, specialized and distinct subsystems are created to deal with these functions. With the growth of specialized subsystems, one finds as well new, distinct problems of coordination, hierarchy, and social control.[4]

Our institutions may continue to grow larger and more specialized and become the "cultural drift" of modern society, evolving toward bigness with an accompanying specialization and rigidity that marked the demise of other civilizations. Living systems are in a constant state of renewal, reorganization, and restructuring as they struggle to maintain a dynamic equilibrium, but man-made systems can achieve size far beyond their optimum. Many large school systems have followed the path toward structured differentiation as they have grown larger and larger.

Policy-makers must address this question of size; our monolithic school systems run the risk of falling on their own dead weight. We continue to elect members to "school boards" that are not boards at all, but legislatures that establish policy and procedures for 100 schools or more. In many large urban districts, a school board member's constituency is larger than the constituencies of some U.S. senators and governors.

Addressing the Future

In the past, the problem of size has been addressed by decentralization, breaking the institution into smaller, often fragmented, parts. The assumption was that breaking a complex institution into simpler parts would solve the problems of size, scale, and complexity. It was further assumed that if each of the smaller units would solve its part of the problem, all the solutions from the different parts could be assembled into a solution of the whole.

But post-industrial societies may not work this way. System performance depends critically on how well the parts work together, not merely how well each performs separately.

In the Systems Age we tend to look at things as part of larger wholes rather than as wholes to be taken apart. This is the doctrine of expansionism.

Expansionism brings with it the synthetic mode of thought much as reductionism brought with it the analytic mode. In analysis an explanation of the whole is derived from explanations of its parts. In synthetic thinking something to be explained is viewed as a part of a larger system and is explained in terms of its role in that larger system. For example, universities are explained by their role in the educational system of which they are part rather than by the behavior of their parts, colleges and departments.

The Systems Age (expansionism) is more interested in putting things together than in taking them apart. Neither way of thinking negates the value of the other but by synthetic thinking we can gain understanding of individual and collective human behavior that cannot be obtained by analysis alone.[5]

Russell Ackoff gives a vivid illustration of the pitfalls that can result from reductionist problem-solving methods:

Suppose we collect one each of every available type of automobile and then ask some expert automotive engineers to determine which of these cars has the best carburetor. When they have done so we note the result. Then we ask them to do the same for transmissions, fuel pumps, distributors, and so on through every part required to make an automobile. When this is completed we ask them to remove the parts noted and assemble them into an automobile each of the parts of which would be best available. They would not be able to do so because the parts would not fit together. Even if the parts could be assembled, in all likelihood they would not work together well.[6]

An expansionist decision-making approach should be central to educational planners. Simply reducing the size of a school district may provide some relief to the myriad of problems, but the real goal should be optimal size, scale, and form. All organizations—public and private—are parts of a larger purposeful system.

Second Wave civilization placed an extremely heavy emphasis on our ability to dismantle problems into their components; it rewarded us less often for the ability to put the pieces back together again. Most people are culturally more skilled as analysts than synthesists. This is one reason why our images of the future (and of ourselves in that future) are so fragmentary, haphazard—and wrong.[7]

Accepting existing patterns and perceptions of schools and schooling and simply following the reductionist patterns of the industrial era will have little effect. Today's schools are modeled on factories and reflect Second Wave, industrial-age thinking. The curriculum is in large measure a series of discrete and disconnected parts, many of them a throwback to pre-industrial, or First Wave, thinking. They are atomistic rather than holistic.

Second Wave schools emphasize:

• *Teaching process*	*rather than*	*learning process*
• *Rigidly scheduled units*	*rather than*	*Quest for information*
• *A terminal process*	*rather than*	*Continuing process*
• *Rote memory*	*rather than*	*Creativity*
• *One right answer*	*rather than*	*Tolerance for ambiguity*
• *Molecular ideas*	*rather than*	**Molar concepts**
• *Product*	*rather than*	*Process*
• *Who is right*	*rather than*	*What is right*
• *Stability*	*rather than*	*Innovation*
• *Standardization*	*rather than*	*Flexibility*
• *Specialization*	*rather than*	*Synthesization*
• *Specific information*	*rather than*	*Appropriate content*
• *Bureaucratic accommodation*	*rather than*	*Entrepreneurship*
• *Hierarchies*	*rather than*	*Free flow of information*
• *Power over*	*rather than*	*Power with*

Even if systems-age thinking were somehow miraculously introduced into the existing school structure, we would still miss the essence of post-industrialism: a synthesis of schools and community in an educational system. Schools alone, no matter how good or how much in tempo with the times, are only one aspect of a community's educational system. A community's lifestyle, its economic, civic, communications, health, transportation, and safety systems are all tied together in a community system. it is the entire community that educates.

If the entire community system (both good and bad) is to be recognized as the educational system, a paradigm shift in thinking, planning, and problem-solving is needed. The term "paradigm shift" has been a key concept of futurists in the past few years. Marilyn Ferguson, author of **The Aquarian Conspiracy,** shared the idea with delegates to the First Global Conference on the Future in Toronto in 1980, crediting Thomas Kuhn, whose book, **The Structure of Scientific Revolutions,** introduced the concept. A paradigm is a framework for organizing perceptions; when anomalies, inconsistencies, and breakdowns in existing paradigms occur, new paradigms may develop.

Edmond Fuller, book reviewer for the **Wall Street Journal**, credits Marshall McLuhan with envisioning a paradigm shift, although Fuller does not use the term.

> Principally he (Marshall McLuhan) made me realize a truth about television based on an analogy to the automobile. When the motor car was invented, people first called it a 'horseless carriage', as if that defined and confined it. Not until it had outrun all the horses in the world and Pegasus together, cause much of the surface of the globe to be paved over with concrete or macadam, made us a neo-nomadic people and contributed to the start of the sexual revolution, did people realize that the automobile had not been a horseless carriage after all but a radical, irreversible alteration of the culture and environment.
>
> In the same way, McLuhan said, it was a mistake to think that television was just radio with pictures. Television, he asserted, also was a radical, irreversible alteration of the culture and environment and therefore of the lives of those who were adults when it first appeared but far more so for succeeding generations growing up with it.[8]

A paradigm shift is needed in education because, in Ackoff's words, "We fail more often because we solve the wrong problems than because we get the wrong solution to the right problem."[9]

Community Education in a High Tech, Post-Industrial Society

McLuhan's view of television as a new form has been confirmed. He envisioned a vast communications web of sight and sound that would function as a nervous system for the entire planet. When the power of the computer is added to this communications web, the resultant "electronic cottage" alters the human environment with unpredictable consequences.

In this scenario, schooling as we know it has a bleak future indeed. But if education is seen in holistic, expansionist terms, education is riding the crest of the Third Wave.

Will all educators be high technicians in the post-industrial society? John Naisbitt, chairman of the Naisbitt Group, a Washington, D.C., research firm that advises businesses on social trends and their impact, says no. Naisbitt analyzes the future optimistically.

> As we moved through the Seventies industrialization and its technology moved more and more from the workplace to the home. . . .Throughout these years, social visionaries were unanimously predicting that technology would breed only more technology, that progress would move only in a mechanized straight line, until every home in the U.S. became an 'electronic cottage'. they were operating under a fallacy.
>
> Something else was going on. Out of the alienation and evolving new values was growing a new self-help and personal-growth movement. Much has been written about these new values and directions, but no one has connected them with technological change. In fact, each feeds and shapes the other; and it is this interplay of high technology and our human response to it that I call high tech/high touch.

> High tech/high touch is a formula to describe the way we have responded to technology. What happens is that whenever new technology is introduced into society, there must be a counter-balancing human response—the 'hightouch'—or the technology is rejected. The more high tech, the more high touch.[10]

The dual directions of high tech/high touch reflect the tendency to maintain a dynamic equilibrium between technological development and human contact. Practicing community educators could add to the following examples by assessing the wants and needs of their communities.

EXAMPLES OF THE HIGH TECH/HIGH TOUCH PHENOMENON

HIGH TECH		HIGH TOUCH
Television	*accompanied by*	*Human potential movement*
		Revival of special interest groups
		Special-interest cable TV
High-tech medical diagnosis	*accompanied by*	*Return of family doctors*
		Neighborhood clinics
Jet planes	*accompanied by*	*More face-to-face national and international meetings*
High-tech kitchens	*accompanied by*	*Food boutiques, food specialty shops, re-emergence of ethnic foods*
Word processing and computer printouts	*accompanied by*	*Revival of handwritten and personal notes*
Robotics	*accompanied by*	*Revival of handmade personalized goods*
		Customized automobiles
		The rise of the "prosumer"
High-tech hospitals	*accompanied by*	*Hospice movement*
High-tech fast foods	*accompanied by*	*Revival of high-touch restaurants striving for ambiance and grace*
High-tech equipment	*accompanied by*	*Soft color design, coziness*
Designer-labeled goods	*accompanied by*	*One-of-a-Kind, personalized creativity*
Computer-printed statistics	*accompanied by*	*Quality circles*
Large, bureaucratic, impersonal public schools	*accompanied by*	*Small, private, personalized schools*
Electronic security and surveillance	*accompanied by*	*Rebirth of community action groups, foot patrols*
		Crime watch groups

Vivid illustrations of the high tech/high touch phenomenon are encountered by visitors to Tokyo. On a visit to study Japanese productivity, we were astonished by the number of people whose jobs would be classified as "surplus" in Western industrial societies. Elevator hostesses greeted us on high-tech automatic elevators. Two cashiers plus a host at most restaurants made sure that guests were pleased with the service. White-gloved taxi drivers operated new cars with white linen headrests and automatic door openers. We experienced high tech/high touch at every turn. We went to Japan to study high technology and productivity and came away understanding the high tech/high touch phenomenon.

Community education offers high touch experience to accompany the high tech of a post-industrial society because it provides for the networking of human resources while maintaining an equilibrium with technological networking. At its best, the community education process is both holistic and synergistic, involving an entire community in the educational enterprise.

Community educators have been criticized in the past for "thinking differently," but even critics would credit community education with some good ideas. For example:

- *cooperative agreements between recreation, social service, and other community agencies*
- *opening schools for community use*
- *day care centers and "latch key" programs*
- *development of human resource centers in schools affected by declining K-12 enrollment*
- *advisory councils*
- *volunteers in the schools*
- *community action groups*
- *an orientation to process rather than product*
- *enrichment classes taught by community members*
- *community involvement*
- *summer programs for youth*
- *public use of school libraries*
- *police liaison programs*
- *community surveys*

Unfortunately, these and other community education processes and programs are viewed as isolated illustrations or add-ons to the existing school paradigm. The current tendency is to accept the present form, function, and organization of schooling as an absolute. The result is that increasingly the present school structure and educational paradigm do not fit the society in which we live or in which we are likely to live in the future.

Many community educators are being forced into bureaucratic molds despite their objections. Often they are chastized for their expansionist outlook. Their conceptual paradigm **is** different. The community education concept was founded and developed through creativity. Its only chance for continuing as a social form is through more creativity.

New forces and trends are frightening to many of those who now control our educational structures and institutions. Letting go of old notions and moving on to new has never been easy. But the old paradigm is crashing down all around us. For those who look to the future with vision and creativity, this time of transition is an opportunity, not a crisis. Already, there is a growing awareness that the concept of community education and the creative community process it advocates are not aberrations that can be drawn into the old paradigm or ignored entirely.

This article is part of a book on Community Education and the Future to be published this fall.

It is the fourth in a series of Community Education Bulletins on the Future of Community Education published by the Center for Community Education and the Charles Stewart Mott Professorship, Florida Atantic University, Boca Raton, Florida.

NOTES

[1]Daniel Bell, **The Coming of Post-Industrial Sociey** (New York: Basic Books, Inc., 1973), pp. 169-170.

[2]Ibid., p. 171.

[3]V. M. Kerensky and E. O. Melby, **Education II Revisited, A Social Imperative** (Midland, Mich: Pendell Publishing Co., 1975), p. 11.

[4]Bell, **The Coming of Post-Industrial Society,** pp. 173-4.

[5]Russell L. Ackoff, **Redesigning the Future** (New York: John Wiley & Sons, 1974), p. 14.

[6]Ibid., p. 14.

[7]Alvin Toffler, **The Third Wave** (New York: William Morrow and Company, Inc., 1980), p. 145-6.

[8]Edmund Fuller, "Marshall McLuhan: Bright ideas From a Fast Mind," **Wall Street Journal,** January 21, 1982.

[9]Ackoff, **Redesigning the Future,** p. 8.

[10]John Naisbitt, "High Tech/High Touch," **Metropolitan Home,** October 1981, p. 23.

THREE KEY MEASURES TO HELP RECONSTRUCT EDUCATION IN AMERICA*
by
Amitai Etzioni

The United States is becoming a new kind of nation, an "underdeveloping nation." This is a nation whose economy is in reverse gear, by most measurements slipping backward a few notches each year. Potholes and inflation are just two symptoms of a weakening economic foundation.

The first sign of this weakening was a decline in productivity in the 1960s and '70s. There was a feeling then that it was all right to trade economic growth for social growth and social enrichment. But now, in the 1980s, the overwhelming majority of the public has decided it does not want to put up with the consequences of an economy that is in reverse gear. Most people are not satisfied with sunsets and rapping and other things that are free; they want the things a high-gear economy will buy. I'm not talking about gadgets and gimmicks, although we continue to be unfavorably inclined towards those; I'm talking about a high standard of living, social services, and defense.

We have lived for a while off the assets we built up over a hundred years, and we have simply run them down. Now we realize that putting the economy together again must have a relatively high priority. We are willing, in varying degrees, to give other things a lower priority for a time. The Reagan Administration received, in effect, that mandate, but things are not working out as planned. Economically speaking, we are in serious trouble. If inflation is defined simply as "too much money chasing too few goods," inflation can be reduced by increasing production. The most inflationary industry of all is the defense industry, because defense costs a lot of money and produces nothing for the marketplace. Because we are planning to put a trillion and a half dollars into an industry that will add nothing to the marketplace, we will face very severe inflation when we finally come out of the recession.

In that context, what is going to happen to education? In my judgment, we have always needed more resources for education. Our human resources need as much shoring up at the moment as our material resources. It is my purpose here to illustrate the approach to education suggested by the preceding analysis.

There are several major changes in public policy (not necessarily limited to governmental and certainly not to federal policy) that would help to reconstruct schools. Three of these changes are discussed in this paper: a "downward" shift in educational resources; more opportunities for students aged 16 to 18 to combine work and study; and a year of national service.

---

*This is based on a segment of the book **An Immodest Agenda**, to be published by McGraw-Hill in October 1982.

A major shift of educational resources from four-year colleges to elementary and secondary schools. American schooling as a whole is top-heavy. A very high proportion of the young population stays much longer in the educational sector, especially in colleges, than in other societies. As many as 50 percent of college-age Americans actually attend college, compared to about 10 percent in West Germany or France. This is not to suggest that the U.S. should have as few of its young in college as these countries, but that 50 percent may be too expansive.

This overeducation is slowly being recognized as college graduates find that a college degree is no longer a secure ticket to a job. Unemployment rates for college graduates under age 25, although nowhere near the rates for inner-city youth, are high (5 to 8.3 percent from 1974-1977); more important, an estimated one fourth to one half hold jobs that do not require college education. In the view of the Carnegie Commission on Higher Education, overeducation on the college level is both a misuse of scarce resources and a political time bomb.

One reason for overeducation is that colleges, especially junior and community colleges, are doing remedial education to compensate for work not done in the high schools. In New York's City College, for example, expensive professors of comparative literature are teaching remedial English to graduates of New York City high schools who are unable to write a simple statement correctly.

As concern for the scarcity of resources increases, the time is ripe to try again to complete more of the educational task at earlier age levels, when it is more cost effective. A downward shift of resources could be achieved by adding no new public resources to college, especially four-year colleges, except for research, and adding resources to primary, elementary, and high schools.

It is much more efficient to teach a subject effectively, the first time around than to allow pupils to waste time, acquire poor study habits, grow in alienation, and then try to correct for all these later. A study of low-income children who attended preschool in the 1960s suggests that, regardless of their background and intelligence, these children are far less likely to require special education, be retained in grade, or drop out of school than similar children without preschool experience. Irving Lazar and Richard Darlington of Cornell University, coordinators of the Consortium for Longitudinal Studies, report:

> We can safely conclude that low-income children benefit from preschool programs—in being more likely to meet the minimal requirements of later schooling—and that this finding is not due to initial treatment/control differences in sex, ethnicity, early intelligence level, or early family background.

Preschool graduates did markedly better in later schooling than their nonpreschool counterparts, scored higher on achievement tests, and were more likely to express pride in specific achievements.

Greater work-study opportunities for 16-18 year olds. A more radical reform would start schooling at age 4 and continue it until age 16, to be followed by two years of mixed work and study. Schools could either recognize certain kinds of work as providing educational experiences equivalent to classroom time (e.g., work as a carpenter's apprentice instead of in the school's carpentry shop) or provide internships in voluntary or government agencies on a part-time basis. This is one of the recommendations of the National Commission on Youth, whose report is aptly titled "The Transistion of Youth to Adulthood: A Bridge Too Long." The Commission also recommends lowering the age of mandatory school attendance to 14. Taking a different approach, a Carnegie study, "Giving Youth a Better Chance," suggests that school could be cut back to three days a week, in effect leaving half time for regular (as distinguished from "educational") employment, without necessarily any loss to education. The work-study years should be aimed at easing the transition from school to the work world and at addressing, in these last years of schooling, a variety of needs.

Current work-study programs have had mixed results. Ellen Greenberger and Laurence Steinberg, social psychologists at the University of California, found that young people in work-study programs received little on-the-job training. Few developed relationships with adults (potential role models) on the job, and the students who worked used more alcohol and marijuana than those who did not. On the other hand, when Northwestern High School of Baltimore sent 600 students to work one day a week as volunteers in hospitals, offices, and primary schools, the young people gained in maturity, insight, the reality of their expectations, and involvement.

A year of national service. This interruption of the lockstep march from grade to grade into and through college has been widely recommended. While the suggested programs vary in detail, many favor a year of voluntary service, with options that would include the armed forces, the Peace Corps, VISTA, and the Youth Conservation Corps. Some who recommend a year of national service would designate the senior year of high school. I prefer the year following high school, to replace the first year of college or work. There are both pragmatic and normative merits in a year of national service. Pragmatically, national service would address the youth unemployment problem. In an average month of 1979, while the unemployment rate for all workers was 5.8 percent, it was 9 percent for those aged 20 to 24 and 16.1 percent for those aged 16 to 19. Unemployment is demoralizing for the many individuals involved. It also harms the rest of society, because unemployed youth make up a sizable portion of the criminal population, particularly violent street criminals. A year of meaningful national service might help many youth avoid crime by assisting in positive psychic development, enhancing self-respect, and increasing optimism about the future.

A year of national service could also introduce young people to skills they may later wish to develop. For those planning to go to college, service after high school would provide a break in formal education and time out to consider goals in a setting that would be largely noncompetitive.

On the normative side, national service would provide an antidote to youthful egocentricity as young people became involved in providing vital services. Thus, an important criterion for including a particular kind of service in the program should be its societal usefulness. The possibilities are myraid, from improving and beautifiying the environment, to tutoring youngsters having difficulty in school, to visiting nursing homes and schools for the retarded to check on the quality of services. Safeguards would of course have to be in place to assure that national service jobs do not take away the jobs of others by providing a pool of cheap labor.

One of the most promising payoffs of a year of national service is that the program could serve as the great sociological mixer America needs if a stronger national consensus on fundamental values is to evolve. Americans have few structural opportunities for the shared experiences necessary for development of shared values, which are essential if the polity is to reach agreement on courses of action without undue delay and disruptive conflict.

One of the major reasons for America's low consensus-building capacity is the fact that our schools are locally run. There is no common national curriculum: our schools transmit regional, racial, and class values. A year of national service, especially if designed to bring people from different geographical, educational, religious, racial, and sociological backgrounds together, could be an effective way for boys and girls from a variety of backgrounds to get to know each other on an equal footing while working together at a common task. The "total" nature of the situation—being away from families, peers, and communities, and spending time together around the clock—is what promises sociological impact.

The cost of universal service would be formidable. There would be offsets or savings in other areas, of course: the expenditures for young people who would be serving in the armed forces anyway; government grants to college freshmen; unemployment and welfare payments to 18-19 year-olds; and the multiple costs of crime, which would almost certainly be reduced. Even with these offsets, and assuming that 10 percent of the age group would not participate because of mental or physical disability, the net cost of a year of national service would be billions of dollars. Obviously, the idea will receive serious consideration only if there is great public support for it, and a parallel commitment by political leaders.

Reaction Paper to: Amitai Etzioni's
"Three Key Measures to Help Reconstruct
Education in America

by
Everett E. Nance

Two major social indicators have influenced public policy and had a dramatic effect on the American way of life: a vacillating economy, and social problems. Many of the social problems that confront us now can be traced to economic pressures and concerns about equity during the latter part of the 20th century.

The Economic Environment

Mtangulizi Sanyika, writing in a recent issue of the **Economic Development and Law Center Report,** gives a good summary of how we came to our current economic situation.

> *Many of the federal programs that meet the needs of low- and moderate-income Americans were begun in the thirties, during the Administration of Franklin Roosevelt, e.g., welfare, unemployment compensation, aid to the disabled, food stamps and nutrition programs. The Truman Administration introduced the first urban renewal programs, and the Kennedy and Johnson Administrations, initiated many of today's social and human service programs as we have come to know them. In the 1960's the federal govenment implemented a wide range of entitlement programs in a major attempt to eliminate urban and rural poverty. The so-called 'war on poverty' gave us such legislation as Urban Renewal and Urban Redevelopment, the Economic Opportunity Act, Model Cities, and Neighborhood Revitalization. These programs were followed in 1974 by the Community Development Block Grant program, which consolidated several earlier programs, and most recently Urban Development Action Grants. In February 1981, the Reagan Administration unveiled a new economic recovery plan for the nation as the cornerstone of its domestic policy.*[1]

The Reagan plan is based on the premise that excessive federal spending is the chief cause of inflation. Reductions in federal contributions to social programs have been followed by proposals to transfer responsibility for most of these programs to states and localities. This represents a radical change in economic philosophy. For nearly 50 years, Keynesian economics was the dominant influence in the United States, beginning with the Presidency of Franklin Roosevelt. Keynesian economics, named for British economist John Maynard Keynes, assumes that underconsumption is the cause of unemployment, and that the government should therefore create jobs or make social welfare payments in order to stimulate demand for products. One side effect of Keynesian policies is inflation, because demand for goods keeps prices high. Inflation can be reduced by reducing demand, but this has the effect of creating unemployment. The problem for American economists has been to devise a policy that reduces inflation without causing unemployment.

The Reagan Administration has turned from Keynesian theory to "supply-side" theory, whose chief proponent has been Arthur Laffer, professor of finance and business economics in the School of Business Administration at the University of Southern California. Supply-side theorists believe that increasing the supply of goods is the best way to control inflation. The theory has three main elements:

1. An economic program emphasizing supply (production) of goods, rather than demand (the means to buy them).
2. The goals of reducing inflation while stimulating private-sector employment and individual initiative.
3. The realization of these goals through the implementation of four key programs:
   a. Business and personal tax cuts to encourage saving, investment, and productivity.
   b. A slow down in the rate of increase in government spending.
   c. Reduction of government intervention and greater reliance on the free-market system, including reduction of government-imposed barriers to investment, production, and employment such as regulations restricting business.
   d. Implementation of monetary restrictions to bring inflation in line with the growth of the economy.[2]

Supply-side theory seems to support what Robert F. Bundy calls the "super-industrial view" of the future,[3] in which continued economic growth is accompanied by rapid change. Opposed to this is the view of a post-industrial society, in which the industrial mode of production is no longer dominant, some limit to economic growth and change is assumed, and decentralization of larger institutions occurs. In this view of post-industrial society, reliance is on the self and the small group rather than on large institutions and elitist professions.

Public values currently seem to be somewhere between Keynesian and supply-side policies and between the super-industrial and post-industrial views of society. Some people are still living as if this were a time of abundance, while others are dealing with the hard realities of scarce resources. The central fact is that most people are not aware of the implications of the economic shifts of the Reagan Administration, whose policies suggest that a new social contract must be established between the private, public, and community sectors of our society. Galbraith has observed that cooperation between the technostructure and the people rests upon the consent of the people, who must agree — or must be taught to think — that economic growth and a constant rise in personal income are the national purpose.[4] But such a national purpose is inherently self-defeating, according to Galbraith, because people become more dissatisfied with the quality of life as they become more educated. Only a vast economic and political expansion of the public sector (which includes the community sector) holds promise of improving the quality of American life.

Implications for Education

Michael J. Bakalis, writing in **Phi Delta Kappan,** says that schools acted as a safety valve to relieve the pressures of social unrest that accompanied the growth of industrial America as the physical frontier disappeared.[5] Quoting Ray Allen Billington, the late American historian, Bakalis concludes that future historians will identify the 1970s as the decade in which American values, rooted in the frontier and based on abundance, began yielding to European values developed over time in an environment of scarcity. Bakalis believes that reduced abundance will affect the relationship of schools with the whole society.[6]

The current economic situation and the Administration's supply-side policies have already affected public and private education in America. The federal block grants to the states represent reduced federal contributions to local educational budgets. School officials are being forced to re-examine their priorities and thus redefine the role of public education.

The Social Environment

Many current social problems can be traced to concerns for equity among various ethnic minorities in America. Robert Bundy stated it thus:

> In the sixties America was embroiled in controversy and bloody confrontation in virtually every phase of our national life. Many long unattended social evils were thrown open to public scrutiny: racism, sexism, alienation, civil injustice, abuses of power and a terrible war. The social disorder of the sixties proved beyond any lingering doubt that older values and cultural forms had been seriously undermined in our society. We must penetrate to the very core of what makes and holds a culture together. The history of a culture is a history of its images of the future. These images reveal that vitality of a culture. In a sense the future is prologue to all history.[7]

We still face the social ills that "were thrown open to public scrutiny" in the '60s. They are merely symptoms of a much deeper problem lurking in the hearts of many Americans, the problem of prejudice. Prejudice is emotional and irrational; it is characterized by fear and despair that close off our social imagination and cripple our inventive capacity. Prejudice permeates all facets of American society. It dramatically affects our institutions and organizations and seriously limits our capacity for community building. We cannot solve our social problems until we can overcome our prejudices.

Implications for Education

No sphere of American society has been more dramatically affected by prejudice than public education. Major responsibility for helping America deal with its prejudices has fallen on the schools. The concern for equity, primarily of the black minority, resulted in court decisions during the '50s that plunged the public school systems of America into a prolonged chaos from which they may never recover. The same condition could have befallen housing, business, and employment, but the focus of the minority has been on education, probably because education was seen as the route to "the good life."

While public education has been dealing with desegregation in response to court decisions, an ongoing subconscious battle continues to be waged against prejudice — subconscious because the issue has not yet been laid openly on the table so that it can be dealt with effectively. Equity in education is a goal that is still miles distant; equity as the ethic of the majority community may never be achieved.

The Etzioni Solutions

Our current economics policies and the nature of our social environment have implications for Etzioni's proposed solutions to America's educational woes. Etzioni says that our educational system is top heavy, that too much money is allocated to higher education and too many Americans attend college. He recommends a "downward shift" of educational resources to the elementary and secondary levels and emphasis on vocational training to relieve society of an overeducated population. While it is true that our institutions of higher education need revamping to become more relevant to the world of work, Etzioni's proposals would have the effect of further widening the knowledge gap between the "haves" and "have nots." Similarly, his suggestion that the mandatory school attendance age be lowered to 14 would encourage more "have nots" to drop out of school. Etzioni points out that low-income children benefit from preschool programs; I would add that all children benefit from preschool programs. But support for preschool should not come at the expense of higher education. Etzioni's downward shift of resources would have the effect of giving further support for a society based on class; equity in such a society would never be realized.

The jobs of the future will require a highly educated citizenry. Etzioni cites the view of the Carnegie Commission on Higher Education that "overeducation on the college level is both a misuse of scarce resources and a political time bomb." But tracking young people into vocational programs with reduced academic emphasis would only serve to encourage illiteracy and reduce the likelihood of a highly educated citizenry.

I disagree with Etzioni's recommendation for a year of mandatory national service, especially as a device for keeping 18 year-olds out of the job market. National service should be voluntary, and the opportunity for voluntary service already exists.

Implications for Community Education

The community has undergone a series of changes over the past several years. One significant change is a growing awareness of the inadequacies of society. There is a thrust toward greater participation in decision-making on problems growing out of equity concerns. To be effective participants, citizens must have knowledge of the issues involved and suitable vehicles for channeling personal energy. Community education could be the vehicle by which citizens get involved in every aspect of community life.

Although most community education programs are housed in schools, the focus of the programs themselves has been much broader. So far, social programs have not been a priority, except in isolated instances. Recent national strategy sessions conducted by the Community Education Office of the U.S. Department of Education and the National Community Education Association may change that. While public schools will probably continue to be a priority, other social concerns will get attention. The shift will be in the direction of establishing linkages between the private, public, voluntary, and community sectors. In an era of scarce resources, organizational linkages will be absolutely necessary. This will require a new kind of leadership and community educators with a much broader background than education. Cunningham and Payzant offer crucial dimensions of the kind of leadership I believe will be necessary.

> One of the most obvious challenges to leaders of the future is the ability to comprehend and respond to ever intensifying complexity. Nothing is simple anymore. Nor is it likely to be so again. So leaders from this point forward will have to acquire the knowledge and skills that will allow them to understand and respond to problems (1) that are multi-dimensional; (2) that will permit them to incorporate data and information from diverse sources (many of which earlier appeared to be unimportant or unrelated) in their problem assessments and eventual decisions; (3) that will permit them to be rational and reflective in a setting that has few attributes or characteristics of a settled, reflective environment; and (4) that will allow leaders to sort through data that issue from diverse, heterogeneous (almost alien) sources and produce goals, objectives, courses of action that will generate support and confidence from their constituencies.[8]

Harland Cleveland also sees complexity as requiring a new executive style:

> Beyond the animal energy required to be a change agent in an environment of extreme complexity, the Public Executive of the future will, I think, be marked by a set of attitudes and aptitudes which seem to be necessary for the leadership of equals, which is the key to the administration of complexity. They will be more intellectual, more reflective, than the executives of the past; they will be 'low-key' people, with soft voices and high boiling points; they will show a tolerance for ambiguity; and they will find private joy in public responsibility.[9]

Our world is complex and becoming more so. Rosabeth Kanter says that:

> We need leaders that can manage decline and manage expectations in slower growth institutions. Leaders of the future need to manage in the face of a less controllable environment while holding fragmented constituencies together. Leaders will have to satisfy many stake holders while giving greater voice to followers. They will have to share leadership.[10]

Kanter could be describing the community educator of the future.

NOTES

[1]Mtangulizi K. Sanyika, "The New Block Grants and Community Alternatives," **Economic Development and Law Center Report,** vol. XII, no. 1 (Winter 1982), p. 3.

[2]Cornelia Wyatt, "Supply-Side," **Working Woman,** November 1981, p. 104.

[3]Robert F. Bundy, "Social Visions and Educational Future," **Phi Delta Kappan,** September 1976, pp. 84-90.

[4]Irving Kristol, "Professor Galbraith's New Industrial State," **Fortune,** July 1967.

[5]Michael J. Bakalis, "American Education and the Meaning of Scarcity," **Phi Delta Kappan,** September 1981, pp. 7-12.

[6]Michael J. Bakalis, "American Education and the Meaning of Scarcity, Part II," **Phi Delta Kappan,** October 1981, pp. 102-105.

[7]Robert F. Bundy, p. 84.

[8]Luvern L. Cunningham, and Thomas W. Payzant, "Skills, Understandings, and Attitudes Needed by Leaders in the Future," (paper presented at the UCEA Partnership Meeting and the American Association of School Administrators meeting, Atlanta, Georgia, February, 1981).

[9]Harland Cleveland, "The Future is Horizontal," in **The Future Executive** (New York: Harper and Row, 1972).

[10]Rosebeth Moss Kanter, "Power, Leadership, and Participatory Management," **Theory Into Practice,** vol. XX, no. 4, 1979, pp. 219-221.

CULTURAL DIVERSITY AND ADVANCED TECHNOLOGY: A POTENTIALLY SYMBIOTIC RELATIONSHIP IN THE CONTEXT OF THE COMMUNITY

by
William L. Smith and Helen R. Wiprud

Two major challenges we face as a society are the increased numbers of recent immigrants into our country and the revolutionary changes in our information technology. The question of how to assimilate large and culturally diverse populations, while preserving their cultural pride, has been brought forcefully to national attention by recent waves of immigration from Haiti, Cuba, Mexico, and Southeast Asia. And the information revolution resulting from recent technological advances has been justifiably compared to the information revolution that followed the invention of the Gutenberg press.

Most Americans are aware of the problems posed by the cultural diversity in our midst, and most have some sense that their lives will be drastically changed by computer technology. In contrast, how many have heard of community education, or could give a passable definition of it? Can community education really confront cultural diversity and computer technology and have a positive impact on either or both? This would seem to be a case of David taking on not one, but two, Goliaths.

It may well be that community education is a kind of David—a movement, that, although appearing insignificant, may quietly and steadily provide an answer here and an answer there to one problem after another, until many big problems of many kinds are solved first in the community, then in the state, and finally on the national level. How many people several thousand years ago thought that David, whoever he was, would have a lasting effect on Goliath?

Cultural Diversity—What Are the Problems?

There have been diverse cultures in what is now the United States since settlers from various parts of Europe began to arrive. Our approach to this cultural diversity has evolved over the two centuries of the nation's existence. At first, the aim of the immigrants seemed to be to become as Anglo-Saxon as the dominant nationalities in the young nation. As the country developed and the population spread, the goal became a "melting pot," involving both intermarriage and a blending of cultures into a distinctly "American" culture. The melting pot goal is now being replaced by the concept of "cultural pluralism," a term that means essentially that individuals ought to be able to maintain their cultural identity without sacrificing their right to participate as equals in all aspects of the common American culture. Donna M. Gollnick and Philip C. Chinn state it this way:

Cultural pluralism within the context of multicultural education refers to the right of individuals to choose how ethnic they wish to be. Within a multicultural society individuals are neither forced to conform to the dominant Anglo culture nor to maintain ethnic identity separate from the common culture. The nature and contributions of the many ethnic groups that compose our nation are recognized as a fundamental part of all education. Cultural diversity is accepted as a national strength rather than an obstacle to be overcome.[1]

The present cultural pattern in the United States is complex. Certain areas in Florida, the Southwestern states, and Minnesota have had heavy influxes of immigrants in recent years. Almost every city in this country has acquired over the years large populations of minorities, people who came to this country many years ago and have lived—sometimes by choice and sometimes by necessity—in communities separate from the majority. These include Asians, Africans, Puerto Ricans, Poles, and many, many others. The majority population has discriminated against the minority, a fact that should not be surprising even to a casual student of world history, since discrimination against minorities has occurred throughout the ages and throughout the world.

The problems faced by minorities in the U.S. occur in every aspect of their lives. Some problems are more pressing and severe for recent immigrants, although they may to some degree still affect immigrants who have been here for many years. Pressing problems include learning English, finding employment, adjusting to everyday life, finding affordable housing, and getting health care. More pervasive problems shared by all persons from a minority culture, no matter how long they have lived in this country, include the majority's lack of appreciation of minority cultures, often caused by a lack of information and personal contact; a resultant lack of cultural pride on the part of minorities; and the majority's fear of a distinguishable minority when jobs, housing, and government services are scarce.

The solutions offered have been multiple, ranging from community action through state initiatives to federal legislation, including the Ethnic Heritage Studies Act of 1972 (now Title IX of the Elementary and Secondary Education Act of 1965) and recent programs enacted to help in the settlement of newer refugees. Since the 1960s, educators have been working toward what is termed "multicultural education," a nationally focused form of the older international/intercultural education movement. Some states now require a multicultural component for teacher certification, and various national education organizations have been active in their support of multicultural/international education since the late 1940s. The steps that have been taken in communities to meet the problems faced by minority cultures will be described in a later section of this paper.

Advanced Technology—What Will the Problems Be?

Advanced technology in this context refers to the technology of storing, communicating, and using information in ways made possible by the development in recent years of the computer, television, and other electronic devices. The development of the capabilities of each of these separately and in combination is expected to change life dramatically by the beginning of the 21st century.

Predictions for future use of the new technologies are based on two well-founded assumptions: (1) that computers capable of sending as well as receiving information will be common in U.S. homes; and (2) that large information-communication centers will store immense quantities of information that can be called upon instantaneously by the home computer. There is, for example, wide agreement that:

- The site of learning may shift from the classroom to electronically operated centers and eventually to the home. This will be made possible by single videodiscs containing a complete multimedia teaching package—e.g., a video sequence presenting background material and information, a simulation of some phenomenon as in biology, an interactive execution of the simulation program, perhaps appropriate graphics or an audio sequence, and then a testing program, followed if necessary by another simulation as determined by the preceding test.[2]

- An in-home shopping system may develop. The consumer would receive product information on the home computer from an information-communications center and would be able to order directly from the manufacturer, processor, or major distributer, who would deliver directly to the consumer. This direct selling would save energy, intermediate handling costs, and time. The results might include: (1) a gradual decline in the number of retail establishments; (2) increased vertical integration among retailers and manufacturers; (3) take-over of the market by those organizations with enough capital to develop the communications technology; and (4) a consequent limitation of consumer choice.[3]

- "Paperless" newspapers may be delivered through home television. An individual could choose which news item to receive through the computer's link to an information-communication center.[4]

- Oral communication may become more important as the focus of learning shifts from the printed word to the picture accompanied by the spoken word.

These predictions are made for about the year 2000 or a little later. Obviously, actions taken between now and then may affect what actually does occur. The speed with which the telecommunications field has developed in the recent past may serve as an indicator of how quickly we must move.

The development of the microcomputer and the videodisc between 1975 and 1978 made available a relatively inexpensive computer of manageable size with a large storage capacity. The way was paved for distribution of computers to homes and schools.

Although computers have been used in U.S. schools for two decades, it is estimated that there are only 52,000 microcomputers and computer terminals in classrooms in the country's 16,000 school districts. About 50 percent of secondary schools, 14 percent of elementary schools, and 19 percent of other types of schools (e.g., vocational, special education) have at least one microcomputer or computer terminal. Many districts are considering buying or leasing computer equipment, but only about 18 percent actually plan to introduce computers within the next three years.[5] In contrast, a 1978 survey showed that more than 74 percent of children between the ages of 9 and 17 had a calculator or access to one.[6]

The original prohibitive factor in acquiring computers was the cost of the hardware. Now major inhibitive factors are lack of high-quality course ware and inadequate training of teachers and administrators. There is wide agreement on these points among educators and computer specialists.

According to one supplier of education software, "the figures that go around the industry are that only 3-4 percent of the educational programs that are available are worth looking at."[7] One of the first major studies on the quality of available courseware states that "programs currently available on the market do not make full use of the learning potential of classroom microcomputers."[8] Most of the programs reinforce prior learning by drill-and-practice methods; few try to develop such skills as critical thinking, problem solving, and synthesis of concepts. Furthermore, 95 percent of the large computer-managed programs are in the field of mathematics, and few packages on any subjects are for use in secondary schools.[9] Ludwig Braun, who has been exploring the use of computers in education for more than 15 years, explains the situation this way:

> The essential problem here is that the private sector (publishers and computer manufacturers) is unwilling to commit resources at the level required because the market hasn't developed sufficiently to ensure profitability in courseware production; but until courseware is developed in sufficient quantities, school people are unwilling to commit **their** resources to the provision of computer power for their students—thus establishing a 'vicious cycle' which will dissipate very slowly unless there is substantial intervention. Because of the magnitude of funding required to develop a market of sufficient size that the private sector will take over, such funds must come from the Federal Government.[10]

Or perhaps the funds may come from communities because of widespread local demand for the effective use of technology in education. The cost of courseware and electronic devices remains high.

Other factors inhibit classroom use of computers: (1) the parts and programs of some hardware systems cannot be used in the hardware of another system; (2) computers break down frequently, and technicians may not be readily available, particularly in small schools. Ludwig Braun, while noting that microcomputers are less subject to breakdown than larger computers (because there are fewer points of interconnection), observes:

It does not require many failures to discourage a teacher from using a device or system. Once a teacher rejects such a system, it may be years before she/he will consider trying it again. For this reason, system reliability is one of the most critical issues in applications of computers in education.[11]

Current computer use in schools only scratches the surface of the possible, perhaps reflecting the lack of sophisticated courseware. There is considerable computer-assisted instruction in which the computer presents instruction and quizzes and records a student's progress, but this kind of instruction is auxiliary to the teacher and usually occurs in conventional subject areas. The computer is also used for drill and practice, simulation, and gaming. At the secondary level, it is beginning to be used to develop problem-solving skills through teaching programming, an area in which there is apparently a good deal of teacher enthusiasm.[12] Although it has not yet been shown that the computer produces higher educational achievement, there is broad evidence that it increases student interest and motivation.

The importance of computer-related technology in the job market is already great. An estimated 25 percent of all jobs now require interaction with a computer;[13] that figure is predicted to be 65 percent in the near future.[14] Jobs that concern information now account for more than 55 percent of all jobs, up from about 17 percent in 1950.[15] These are startling figures in light of the estimate that only 1 percent of people in the United States really feel comfortable using a computer.[16]

Public interest in computer technology is increasing rapidly, however. Publications aimed at computer amateurs and educators have appeared; retail computer stores have proliferated; hundreds of computer clubs have been founded; computer shows aimed at the amateur are being held;[17] about 300,000 microcomputers are being used in homes, schools, and businesses;[18] Community Thinkers' Tournaments have been held for several years in Ann Arbor, Michigan, and in Los Angeles, using communication and instructional gaming technology;[19] and Harvard University has made computer literacy a requirement for graduation, with other universities expected to follow.[20]

Clearly, the technology is available for computers to invade and radically change our society, and the advance force is already here. We know enough to speculate on the nature of the changes and foresee possible educational and social problems. Some of the problems are short-range, having to do with the next few years; others are related to the year 2000 scenario of a computer in every home and tremendous information transmitting centers. The potential difficulties pointed out by futurists, computer specialists, and educators include:

● How to influence the development and spread of information technology in a way that is beneficial to society. This is an immediate problem.

- How to avoid giving an unfair educational advantage to the children of the affluent, who will be able to afford computers before the less advantaged. This problem ranges from the present until there is a computer in every home, if indeed that does occur.
- How to maintain writing skills and the desire to read in a society that increasingly will depend upon communication by picture accompanied by the spoken word. The problem is both short- and long-range, because the present ubiquity of television has already greatly reduced the amount of reading done by children, and this in turn has adversely affected their writing ability.
- How to counteract the various effects of isolation if the setting for both work and learning changes from the marketplace and the school to the home. One effect would be a decrease in the ability to communicate successfully face-to-face; another would be loss of the intellectual stimulation of sharing ideas with peers and teachers. This problem is obviously long-range.
- How to maintain the existence of a common body of knowledge among people who are able to select the information they will receive. Lack of a common body of knowledge might decrease a sense of community among people, and a lessening of knowledge about other people might lead to a lack of concern for them. This is also a long-range problem.

Robert J. Harman, Executive Editor of the **St. Petersburg Times**, says:

> I see the move to any kind of system where there is no longer a **common agenda of new information** as sinister. I see it as a further invitation to drop out, to disengage from the process. Carry that tendency to its extreme and each of us can become an island away from the mainland unconnected to and unconcerned with each other.[21]

Community Education—Where Does Its Power Lie?

The Community Education Advisory Council to the U.S. Department of Education describes community education as "a process of people in the community coming together in a public facility to discuss their needs, interests, and problems."[22] The council lists the following elements as common to most community education programs:

- Use of a public facility, such as the school.
- Involvement of people of all ages, income levels, and ethnic groups.
- Identification by the people of their needs and problems.
- Development of a variety of programs to meet these needs.
- Coordination of services among diverse agencies and institutions in the community.
- Multiple funding sources, both public and private, at the local, state, and federal levels.

The particular strengths of community education, and those most relevant to the subject at hand, include:

- The programs are diverse in that they are responsive to the needs of individual communities.

- The programs can adapt to changing needs, since the decision-making mechanism is relatively small and programs are subject to change without major dislocations of people.
- Existing resources are used, including programs already in operation in various agencies, buildings previously used only part time, and expertise of people already working in the community. In a time of financial constraints, such cooperation and avoidance of duplication are particularly important.
- Participating individuals feel an identification with the community and are more committed to improving it.
- Participating in community efforts and programs expands the horizons of individuals, increases their concern for the needs of others, and makes them more understanding of people different from themselves.
- The integration of all community elements recognizes that most children and adults receive a major share of their education from the community, rather than just from the school. As Henry Steele Commager said:

> For it is, after all, the community which performs the major job of education, not the schools; performs them through a hundred miscellaneous instructions from family to farm, from government to playing field, from churches to labor unions, from newspapers and journals to comics and radio and, above all television.[23]

- All elements of the community are involved in the community education process, including people from minority cultures. (Such involvement has been encouraged by the requirements of various federal courts.)

Not all community education efforts live up to the ideal or to their potential. And although the movement has grown steadily since it came to national prominence in the 1930s, it is far from ubiquitous. An estimated 5,600 programs were active in 1980.[24] That means that, an average, 6.5 percent of the estimated 86,000 schools in the U.S. are centers for community education activities.

Ultimately, the power of community education lies in its potential for gathering up the forces of individuals into a group small enough to interact meaningfully with each other and large enough to make a difference. John Naisbitt, a professional analyzer of societal trends, believes that groups such as the community ultimately possess tremendous power. He writes of "a profound conviction that this is a bottom-up society. Despite the conceits of some of us who live in Washington or New York, things don't start there. Things that restructure the society start out in the society, not in the largest metropolises in the country."[25] He notes that currently "we are participating in the political process in this country at more and more a local level. While vote totals for national office are going down, the totals for local consideration, local initiatives and local referenda, are going up—to as high as 75 percent turnout, and in some cases bumping up against 80 percent."[26] If Naisbitt is correct, the time for community education to spread and become most effective is now! That community education centers and schools, reflecting the diversity of communities in the United States, should successfully address the cultural diversity of this country seems quite natural.

Cultural Diversity and the Impact of Community Education

Alvin Toffler noted that we are coming into a "de-massified age in which we see increasing diversity at every level of the society and social structure," and adds: "I wonder whether basics don't include toleration for diversity if we're going to live in a world of diverse groups."[27]

The U.S. Conference of Mayors gathered information from more than 20 cities throughout the country on the ways in which community education is being used to address the social concerns of cities. One of the topics addressed in 1981 was **Community Education and Multiculturalism: Immigrant Refugee Needs and Cultural Awareness.**[28] Effective programs were identified in Boston, Massachusetts; Chula Vista, California; Duluth, Minneapolis, and St. Louis Park, Minnesota; Elizabeth, New Jersey; Hialeah, Florida; and Houston, Texas.

The adaptability of the community education process to changing needs has made it particularly useful in dealing with the varied problems caused by the heavy influx of immigrants and refugees to urban centers over the last few years. The services provided have included language training, employment, acculturation, easing community tensions and heightening cultural awareness, health services, and housing. The success of community education in helping recent refugees and immigrants indicates it can have an impact on the development of cultural pluralism in this country. Community education has the potential to provide accurate assessments of needs, contact between people of diverse cultures, and the information and knowledge required to solve multicultural problems.

The potential of the community education center or school to provide the information and training required by a minority population is greatly increased by computer technology. Here is a notable example of the symbiotic relationship of cultural diversity and advanced technology in the context of community education. The computer is an effective tool for teaching English, for example. Aided by a computer, the community education center can serve as a clearinghouse for job and housing information, and go far beyond that by providing training for specific jobs through videodiscs, as the software becomes available. The ability of computer systems to take the user on a trip through a city—turning left or right, stopping, reversing, and interacting with the user depending upon his or her choices of various options—will lead to the development of computer programs that will help teach the immigrants how to use public transportation, go to the grocery store, handle money, open a bank account, become familiar with the local laws and government agencies, learn about health opportunities, and cope with other aspects of everyday life. The possibilities for developing cultural awareness in both the minority and the majority populations are multiple, and in fact require no more technology than is now available. What is needed is that video programs on the various aspects of the cultures in a particular community be widely available and that their use be encouraged in as many ways as possible.

Advanced Technology and the Potential Impact of Community Education

Community education links and shares all sources of information and education in a community. Information-communication technology acquires and shares information, making it readily available to all computers linked to it. Advanced information-communication technology seems made to serve community education. How it may do so is not the subject of this paper, but how community education may affect the technology is. And part of the answer to that question may simply be, "by using it."

The extent to which computer technology is currently being used in community education centers and schools seems to be so far unexplored. We do not know how many computers are available for community education use in homes, cooperating agencies, organizations, and businesses, or how those computers are being used. A survey of computer technology use by community education centers and schools would perhaps be helpful. We do know that some interesting experiments are under way in communities, whether they are officially part of a community education program or not. For instance, a project in Menlo Park, California, called "Computer Town USA!" is seeking to make the town the first completely computer-literate community in the world by:

(1) placing microcomputers in the public library so that access is easy;

(2) running courses on programming in the library;

(3) convincing local merchants (e.g., the pizza parlour and the book shop) to place microcomputers in their establishments and make them available to the public;

(4) establishing a Rent-a-Computer program so that local residents may have access to computers in their homes at a nominal cost;

(5) offering a Rent-a-Kid service so that people who do not wish to do their own programming can hire some of the fine young programmers whom they have trained; and

(6) visiting senior citizens' homes to introduce computing to the elderly.[29]

This concept is being shared with other communities through a newsletter; and help is provided to those who express an interest.

In other cooperative relationships involving community education and computer technology, parents with technology experience serve as resources to the schools; hardware companies donate or lend computers or arrange for hook-ups into a mainframe computer; and computer companies share their personnel with the school to provide computer instruction. New Jersey Public Television is establishing a national network to develop programming ideas and delivery systems and is attempting to assess the interest of community education in using television.

Addressing the Problem

How to assure beneficial development. Perhaps the most immediate impact that community education might have on advanced technology would be in helping to solve the first problem listed earlier, how to influence the development and spread of information technology in a way that is beneficial to society. Community education deals directly with local needs, ideally reflecting all elements of the community. Community educators are particularly well equipped to: (1) determine what the members of the community need to know; (2) learn from a computer specialist in a cooperating business or agency how computer technology could help fill that need; (3) present a specific request to courseware developers for particular courseware; and (4) greatly influence the production of courseware by banding together with other community education centers with similar courseware needs, thus assuring purchase on a wide scale. Since the voices of the various community education centers are as various as the many communities of which they are the representatives, the development would also be diverse, and properly so.

Community education centers could also greatly influence the future development of technology and its use in education by arousing public interest through discussions, seminars, classes, etc. Guy Dosher, a consultant working with management information systems in San Diego, writes:

> *Perhaps the most important lesson learned in attempting to design an information system for human service organizations is that considerable negotiation among individuals involved in agency work must occur to reach a consensus on what information is needed and how it is to be used. The particular design of a system proves to be not as important an issue as the process followed in reaching agreement as to its nature, and the education process needed to insure adoption.*[30]

A deliberate and thoughtful approach to educational technology by a large number of people would eventually lead to consensus and influence industry's direction. Widespread public interest could also limit the possibility that direction would be in the hands of a few persons heading the two or three corporations with enough capital to control the direction of the development. Sociologist Arthur B. Shostak writes:

> *Given the enormous costs of preparing new software for telematique school systems, fewer and fewer giant suppliers may survive a competitive struggle for business, the winners increasingly holding sway over the content, selection, character, and a real worth of telematique subject matters.*[31]

How to assure fair access. Another benefit of widespread public discussion of information technology is the likelihood that familiarity with the technology will increase the demand for hardware, electronic devices, and courseware, and that increased demand will bring a decrease in cost.

Lower costs have obvious implications for addressing the second problem listed above, how to avoid giving unfair advantage to the affluent. Lower costs will help to spread information technology to those who might be last to come into contact with it—older people, minorities, and the poor.

The availability of computer technology in community education centers would help offset the educational advantage now held by the children of affluent families, but the degree of advantage may not be very large in view of the limited quality of courseware now available, except in the important area of computer literacy and programming.

How to maintain reading and writing skills. Community education can address the third problem listed, how to maintain reading and writing skills in an age of pictures and spoken words, by discussion and consideration of the problem, perhaps in conjunction with a general discussion of the development of educational technology. While the usefulness of the computer in teaching and writing has been demonstrated, a technology that is heavily dependent on pictures is not likely to incorporate much of either. Saving the written word, with the accuracy of thought it demands of the writer and the access it gives to literature and history, may be a difficult challenge. Whether it is worth doing and, if so, how to do it, are worthy subjects for consideration by as many people as possible and as soon as possible, before the issue is determined without anyone's having made a decision pro or con.

How to counteract isolation. Concerning the fourth problem, isolation in the home, if the home does indeed become the setting for all work and learning through the ubiquity of the computer and large information storage centers, there would obviously be no need to go to a community center to learn. Jack D. Minzey and Clyde LeTarte write:

> It seems probable that the greatest problem that man will face will not be in creating technological devices but in being able to function as a human being within the technical maze that will be created.[32]

On the other hand, a strong community center could serve to counteract isolation by offering opportunities for discussion with peers and teachers, providing the human warmth and contact that no electronic device can give. It would help keep alive the skills of face-to-face communication that could become dulled if the family were the only source of human contact.

John Naisbitt has an interesting theory about the trend toward isolation:

> ...we are moving in the dual direction of what I call High Tech/High Touch. What I mean by that is that the introduction of any high technology into a society, particularly this society, must be accompanied by a compensatory human response—a balancing—or the technology will be rejected.[33]

In support of his theory, Naisbitt cites the flourishing of the movie theatre after the introduction of television, the poor response to electronic banking systems, and the interest in the quality of death following the development of life-sustaining technologies. Naisbitt writes: "People want to go to the office, to be with people. And, the more technology we have, the more they are going to want to be with people."[34] Alvin Toffler basically agrees:

I believe as people work more at home their social ties with coworkers in the office factory will attenuate somewhat. But conversely, their ties with other family members and with the local community will be deepened. I believe people who spend some time working at home are going to find they want to get out at the end of a day's work.... I believe to the degree that we do transfer work into the home it becomes unnecessary for people to move from one community to another when they change jobs....

Now that suggests we may have a higher degree of local stability. It means people will have a greater incentive for participating in community life, an incentive that is greatly reduced if one thinks they'll be moving out in a few months.[35]

How to maintain a common body of knowledge. Perhaps the instinctive desire and need to be with other people will solve the last problem posed, how to maintain a common body of knowledge among people who are able to select the information coming into their homes. If it does not, a system for recognizing degrees of learning similar to the system used today in our schools and universities is likely to survive in one institution or another, perhaps in community education centers if the school ceases to be the focus of learning. A system of recognition responds both to the human desire to compete and excel and to the need of employers to determine the extent and quality of the knowledge of a potential job-holder. In any case, our curiosity about our fellow human beings would tend to make us want to find out about the doings of others. The community education center could facilitate the satisfaction of all these instinctive needs and desires by bringing people together to solve common problems and address common needs.

Recommendations

Community education centers and schools could use advanced technology to address the problems that arise from cultural diversity by:
- Preparing audiovisual and computer-based materials on successful and innovative multicultural programs for distribution to other schools and centers with similar problems.
- Encouraging development of computer courseware on the cultures and concerns of recent immigrants and other minority populations.
- Providing training in computer skills, particularly to minority populations. The computer's predominant use of visual rather than oral and written communication makes computer training more accessible than training in other fields to persons for whom English is a second language. The possibility for higher salaries should provide motivation:

*The demand for people with computer skills is far in excess of the
supply, and their average income is significantly higher than that
of others lacking computer skills. A school that gives a student 50
hours of hands-on experience in computer use is also giving that
student a first-year income advantage of $1,000, which is
compounded* **annually.**[36]

● Encouraging persons who are actively participating in the community
education process (including some from minority cultures) to become
informed on the ways in which that process operates in other
countries and to consider whether techniques used elsewhere might
be adapted for use in the United States. A sophisticated awareness of
the effects of very different political systems would be necessary.
Peter Hackett, associate professor of comparative and international
education at the University of Virginia, points out:

> *To varying degrees. . . third world countries are trying a number of
> innovations to reform their formal educational systems, marked
> by an emphasis on local needs, involvement of ethnic and family
> ties, and local management of technology.*[37]

Community education can and should influence the direction of
technological development by taking the following steps:

● Organizing community discussions, seminars, and workshops on the
possibilities, both positive and negative, inherent in the developing
information-communication technology in order to increase public
understanding, encourage the expression of thoughtful conclusions,
and work toward the emergence of national leadership to influence
developments. This recommendation is consistent with a basic belief
expressed by Minzey and LeTarte:

> *Democracy requires involvement—it cannot survive without it.
> We must turn our attention back to local human involvement in
> very basic issues and problems if we are to survive.*[38]

● Forming a special team of computer specialists and educators from
community businesses, schools, and other agencies to study specific
ways in which information-communication technology might be used
in education and in sharing information with other communities.
Special attention should be paid to developing effective courseware
compatible with existing hardware, especially in the areas of
multicultural education and computer training. The ways that other
nations have provided computer training for large numbers of their
population should be examined for applicable ideas. Community
purchase of a minicomputer should also be discussed because of the
advantages of having a central group of videodiscs available to all
outlets.

● Employing youth who have had computer training to help instruct
adults and other youth in computer literacy at the community center.

This would encourage young people to acquire training in order to get summer or after-school employment, and would bring young and older people together in a relationship that could be revealing and stimulating for both.

● Stengthening the national network of community education centers and schools and their mutual interrelationships in order to increase diffusion of effective practices, cooperation in use of materials, and influence over the development of information-communication technology in the nation. As Carolyn O'Donnell noted:

> When communities are assisting each other, exchanging information, they are also developing friendship, a sense of responsibility, and an expanded sense of community. And what a great way to help people understand and welcome a new technology that is frightening to some and disliked by many.[39]

The network should consider preparing a survey of the amount, kinds, and location of computer hardware, devices, and courseware currently available in community education centers and developing a system of sharing useful computer information. The network might materially effect the development of effective, usable courseware by pooling the conclusions reached through discussions carried on in each community and decisions arrived at by special study teams. This joining of forces might result in enough demand for particular items or types of courseware to make development of the course profitable to individual companies. A network could also become a successful advocate for preservice and inservice training of teachers in computer education, multicultural education, and community education.

Strengthening the national network of community education centers and schools is not without risk. There is no doubt of the power of a large group of people organized effectively. The danger is that such a community education group might lose its most valuable asset, the participation of all elements of each community, and become a top-down rather than a bottom-up organization. Such a group might also lose its adaptability, diversity, human warmth, and accurate reflection of local need. Don Davis expressed a similar concern in 1977:

> One of the problems of community education is that it is highly professionalized, highly controlled by professionals . . . and that the role for advisory and for community people . . . ranges from nothing at all to a very modest kind of token mass participation. . . .[40]

The challenge to community education is to achieve balance, neither leaning toward tiny, amateurish, disorganized, and ineffective units nor coming down so far on the side of professionalism and organization that it loses its precious participatory nature, from which all its strength derives.

In other words, the David can only conquer the Goliaths if it remains a David. As a David, it can have an impact far belying its size.

NOTES

[1]Donna M. Gollnick and Philip C. Chinn, "Multiculturalism in Contemporary Education," **Journal of the School of Education/Indiana University**, vol. 56, no. 1, (Winter 1980), p. 6.

[2]Ludwig Braun, "Microcomputers and Video Disc Systems: Magic Lamps for Educators?" (State University of New York at Stony Brook, April 1978; mimeo), p. 48.

[3]Don W. Schultz, "How Will Consumers React to a Pushbutton Marketplace?" **Phi Kappa Phi Journal** vol. 60, 1980, pp. 12-16.

[4]Ibid., p. 16.

[5]**Education USA**, vol. 24, no. 19, (January 4, 1982), p. 143.

[6]Ibid., p. 155.

[7]Quoted in **Education USA**, vol. 24, no. 19, p. 152.

[8]Alex Heard, "Educational Software Flawed, Study Concludes," **Education Week**, March 31, 1982, p. 18.

[9]Ibid.

[10]Ludwig Braun, "Computers in Learning Environments—An Imperative for the 1980s." (State University of New York at Stony Brook, April 1980; mimeo), p. 11.

[11]Ludwig Braun, "Computer-Aided Learning and the Microcomputer Revolution," **PLET,** vol. 18 no. 4, (November 1981), p. 228.

[12]Fred M. Hechinger, "New Tools Present Teaching Challenge," **The New York Times** (August 12, 1980) and Arthur Luehrmann, "Planning for Computer Education—Problems and Opportunities for Administrators," **NAASP Bulletin,** vol. 65 no. 444, (April 1981), pp. 65-66.

[13]Arthur Luehrmann, p. 63.

[14]"Experts to Ponder Future of Literacy," **The Baltimore Sun** (March 28, 1982).

[15]John Naisbitt, "The Restructuring of America—High Tech/High Touch" (reprinted from **Concepts**, Spring 1981), p. 1.

[16]John Love, "Search for Tomorrow," (reprinted from **TWA Ambassador,** November 1980), p. 4.

[17]Ludwig Braun, "Microcomputers and Video Disc System," pp. 9-13.

[18]Ludwig Braun, "Computer-Aided Learning," p. 224.

[19]Laymen E. Allen, "Community Thinkers' Tournaments for Coordinating Other Community Resources To Complement the Educational Function of Schools," **J. Educational Technology Systems,** vol. 6, no. 4, (1977-78), p. 271.

[20]Ludwig Braun, **"Computer-Aided Learning,"** p. 227.

[21]Don W. Schultz, **"How Will Consumers React,"** p. 7

[22]**Community Education: The Federal Role** (National Community Education Advisory Council, undated).

[23]As quoted in Walter D. Talbot, "The Role of State Departments of Education in International Community Education," **Community Education Journal**, vol. 5, no. 4 (July/August 1975), p. 14.

[24]**The Federal Experience Under the Community Schools Act** (U.S. Department of Education, 1980), p. ii.

[25]John Naisbitt, "The Restructuring of America," p. 1.

[26]Ibid., p. 2.

[27]Alvin Toffler, as quoted in **The School Administrator**, April 1981, p. 29.

[28]**Community Education and Multiculturalism: Immigrant/Refugee Needs and Cultural Awareness** (United States Conference of Mayors, 1981), pp. 7-23.

[29]Ludwig Braun, "Computer-Aided Learning," p. 226.

[30]Guy Dosher, "The Management Information System," **Journal of Alternative Human Services,** vol. 4 no. 3, (Autumn 1978), p. 31.

[31]Arnold B. Shostak, "The Coming Systems Break: Technology and Schools of the Future." **Phi Delta Kappa,** 62 (January 1981), p. 358.

[32]Jack D. Minzey and Clyde LeTarte, **Community Education: From Program to Process** (Midland, MI: Pendell Publishing Co., 1972), pp. 267-68.

[33]John Naisbitt, p. 3.

[34]John Naisbitt, p. 5.

[35]Alvin Toffler, p. 28.

[36]Arthur Luehrmann, p. 63.

[37]Peter Hackett, "Comparative Perspectives on a Sense of Community and the Challenges for International Community Education," **Community Education Journal**, vol. 5 no. 4, (July/August, 1975), p. 33.

[38]Jack D. Minzey and Clyde LeTarte, p. 273.

[39]Carolyn A. O'Donnell, "Applications of Telecommunications," **Community Education Journal**, vol. 9 no. 2, (January 1982), p. 27.

[40]Don Davis (transcript of a presentation at a workshop on "Visions for the Future," sponsored by the Western Centers for Community Education Development, May 1977), **Workshop Summary Report**, p. 9.

Reaction Paper to: Smith and Wiprud's

"Cultural Diversity and Advanced Technology: A Potentially Symbiotic Relationship in the Context of the Community"
by
Sandra T. Gray

Smith and Wiprud recognize that the great power of the community must be harnessed and used constructively to address the dual challenges of rapid technological change and growing cultural diversity. As a society, we must devise ways to use our new technologies to transmit and share our cultural riches. And we must take immediate steps to ensure that all people—including those who have been historically by-passed—have equal access to advanced technology.

Before the invention of the printing press, only the rich and powerful enjoyed the benefits of the printed word. Bibles were chained to tables in the churches so that throngs of worshippers could share the few copies that were available. Once pages could be mass produced, the elite no longer had a monopoly over the printed word. A book that took months for an apprentice to copy in calligraphy could now be produced by the thousands in the same period of time.

With the proliferation of the printed word, former tasks became obsolete. Education focused on getting information, and citizens were expected to learn to read, to be literate. Old systems of messengers gave way to new institutions like the post office. By 1837 the British Post Office was carrying more than 88 million pieces of mail each year.[1] By 1960, the United States Post Office was distributing 355 pieces of mail each year for every man, woman, and child in the country.[2] Even the greatest futurist present at the first demonstration of the printing press could not have forecast the revolution this invention brought about in three centuries.

Today, we are part of an information revolution unprecedented in history. Computers are only one sign of the change. The rate of change is frightening to observe. We now have a chip the size of a book of matches that stores all the information a person needs to know in a lifetime. As educators and citizens, we must ask what this means for education.

Lack of access to information is creating a new stratification in our society. It is already apparent that we have a disparity between the "information rich" and the "information poor."[3] A recent **Time** magazine article described the amazing feats of a new generation of "microkids" who are spearheading an electronic revolution. One thing about the microkids is clear: they are from families with money to spend on information and education. The article estimates that there are about 100,000 computers now in use in U.S. schools (roughly one for every 400 students) and observes that many of them are in affluent suburbs. The author predicts that there will be 300,00-650,000 microcomputers in the schools by 1985.[4] Testimony before a U.S. House of Representatives subcommittee in

1980 warned that "the electronic school plugged into the electronic home will push suburbia into the 21st century long before the urban or rural schools achieve a readiness for such a move."[5]

Lack of knowledge about computers is causing a separation between generations of people as well as between culturally diverse groups in various geographical regions and economic circumstances. Ignorance of computers will render persons as functionally illiterate as ignorance of reading, writing, and arithmetic. To achieve educational equity in our learning society, we simply must provide access to computing for all students; for community educators, this means all members of the community.

How can we achieve a national consensus that will support an adequate technological education for every student, whatever his or her economic, social, cultural, or geographic background? To realize the goal of equal access, all community educators should incorporate the following considerations into an immediate plan of action:

1. Immediate establishment of a community education technology task force to:
   ● survey the training programs being conducted in community education centers;
   ● identify collaborative programs between community education and local business and training programs that use volunteers with special skills; and
   ● compile and analyze the data and disseminate it to all decision-makers.
2. Establishment of "think tanks" or "think consortia" to organize discussions, seminars, and workshops for the community in all aspects of the information revolution. The consortia can draw on the highly trained personnel of corporations, especially in the high-tech industries. Volunteers could be invited to participate in the plans and act as consultants for the sessions. In Massachusetts, in a model of the National School Volunteer Program, a coalition of school volunteers, corporate executives, community representatives, and school personnel planned and implemented a successful Tecnology Fair.
3. Collaboration between community educators and other leaders in public school systems and the publishers of computer software to develop curricular approaches for which the computer is uniquely suited. At the present time, few K-12 computer packages are truly innovative.

   A model in this area is Project C.O.F.F.E.E. (Cooperative Federation for Educational Experiences), a program spearheaded by the Superintendent of the Oxford, Massachusetts, Schools; the French River Teacher Center; and Digital Corporation. Recently validated by the National Diffusion Network, the program has helped adolescents with histories of academic failure and truancy make significant gains in achievement through an instructional program based on specially designed computer software.

4. Proliferation of community education centers to every major school district in the U.S. A major national policy for the funding of these centers must be a topic for consideration by the technology task force. In Japan, and Germany, a

national policy has been delineated and funds allocated to support a national effort.

5. Identification of one volunteer in each community education program to receive training in technology. This person could act as liaison to other community education programs as well as to the local public school systems for long-range planning and coordination. High-tech industries have training programs at their regional and national training centers that could be used for this program.

These trained volunteers should assume the role of advocates for technological change within their communities and assume a leadership role with executives and high-tech corporate managers in short- and long-range planning. Community educators and the public must gain control over the mass media to insure survival and a human future.

New challengers require new initiatives. My criticism is that we are too timid. We need to examine more creative approaches for moving education beyond the chalkboard and the eraser. Our children and young adults already suffer from Pac-Man mania, which will have lasting consequences. The problem we must address immediately is how we can collaborate to bring the computers from the arcades into the community education centers and the schools.

NOTES

[1] Alvin Toffler, **The Third Wave** (New York: Morrow & Co., Inc., 1980), p. 3.

[2] Ibid, p. 50.

[3] Craig Ritter, "The Endpaper," **The Executive Educators,** March, 1981, p. 44.

[4] Frederic golden, "Here Comes the Microkids," **Time,** May 3, 1982, p. 53.

[5] Donald G. Hayes, "Education in the Suburbs—So Goes the Nation" in **Needs of Elementary and Secondary Education in the 1980's** (Washington, D.C.: Government Printing Office, 1980), p. 350.

Reaction Paper to: Smith and Wiprud's

"Cultural Diversity and Advanced Technology: A Potentially Symbiotic Relationship in the Context of the Community"

by
David A. Santellanes
Larry L. Horyna

William L. Smith and Helen R. Wiprud have addressed two issues of critical concern in our society. They have provided good examples in support of their major contentions, and their references to contemporary events and literature provide the reader with up-to-date information.

The manuscript has shortcomings: its examples of computer use are almost all instruction-oriented; its view of multiculturalism is limited; and it overemphasizes computers and neglects telecommunications, community access television and immediate feedback cable television. Moreover, the authors offer no examples of how program administrators and managers could use advanced technology to become more effective and efficient.

Advanced Technology

Smith and Wiprud have done a commendable job of delineating the advantages of computer technology in an educational setting, but they have failed to provide useful examples of how professional community educators can use computers to increase the quantity and quality of community education services to their constituents. If a community school coordinator has access to a computer, he or she could, for example, use it to improve operations in the following ways:

Record keeping. Records of the demographic characteristics of persons involved in community education activities could easily be programmed into a computer according to specific classes and locations. Other variables that could be included are: reasons for enrolling in the class or activity; participants' other interests; and skills or information participants would be willing to share with others. This list is obviously illustrative, not inclusive.

Needs assessment. Needs assessment data could be stored in a computer for use and updating throughout the year. The data variables could be isolated to assist coordinators in providing more effective services to certain target populations. Relevant data could be shared with other agencies, or if a central terminal was available, the same data could be used by all interested agencies. The needs assessment data would be helpful to proposal writers trying to secure funds for a community as well as to program planners.

Evaluation. Data related to the community education program's impact could be stored in a computer and analyzed for evaluation purposes. A minicomputer could actually analyze the data and organize tables to present the results graphically. The analysis could be simple or complex, depending on information needs.

The computer will undoubtedly continue to influence our lives and will, of course, have an impact on community education. However, the humanist in us worries about the potential for overapplication of computer uses by local community education practitioners. Smith and Wiprud express a similar concern: that we will become so preoccupied with expendiency through computers, we will neglect the importance of high quality face-to-face interaction. One of the beautiful things about community education has been its ability to personalize education and encourage people to interact with each other; development of a sense of community is frequently identified as a major goal of community education. The overuse of computer technology could make it easy for coordinators and community residents to avoid extensive human contact, thereby making community education just another program with little emphasis on the process of human interaction.

The future use of computers in community education may be constrained by lack of funds. In these times of financial famine, it may be difficult to justify acquiring a computer when the immediate task of most public agencies is to reduce the work force. And if it is true, as Smith and Wiprud contend, that educators, who are in many cases the supervisors of community education practitioners, have been resistant to using computers, the potential for obtaining them could be minimal. A solution might be joint purchase or shared time by several cooperating human service agencies. Perhaps demonstrating the computer's multiple uses through a cooperative project could pave the way for the purchase of additional computers and other technology.

Finally, if culturally distinct persons are to take advantage of modern technology, they must be oriented to its use in a non-threatening way. The fact that only about 1 percent of the general population feels comfortable with technology further complicates its use by minorities, who may already be skeptical about receiving assistance from majority members even without the introduction of complicated equipment. It will take a personalized approach to convince them that the new technology will help them learn new skills and provide them with the basis for more informed decisions.

Other Technology

Smith and Wiprud take a narrow view of advanced technology, focusing almost exclusively on the computer. This is unfortunate in that new technology includes a host of other advances that have, perhaps, a more immediate and direct application to education generally and to community education specifically. Computer development should not overshadow advances in several other areas: interactive television; dedicated television channels and programming; community access television; teleconferencing networks; video cartridges, discs, and recorders.

Multiculturalism

Although Smith and Wiprud emphasize services to newly migrated culturally distinct groups, the services they describe are also applicable to long-term U.S. residents from various cultural backgrounds. Obviously, the community education process can be applied in any cultural setting, with sensitivity to the unique history, needs, and resources of particular groups.

Some Perplexing Questions

Smith and Wiprud, like other thoughtful writers, raise more questions than they answer. Some unanswered questions are:

1. *To what degree will Americans ever fully accept the concept of "cultural pluralism," moving away from the long-held "melting pot" concept?*
2. *To what degree is "cultural pluralism" an urban phenomenon that is neither understood nor accepted in rural America?*
3. *To what degree can, or will, the concept of "cultural pluralism" become a viable part of the curricular of elementary and secondary schools?*
4. *To what degree will technology, particularly expanded satellite and cable television systems, help improve Americans' knowledge and understanding of minority cultures within our society?*
5. *To what extent will lack of access to technological advances broaden the gap between the majority culture and the poor and minority groups in our society?*
6. *Will the use of advanced technology in education and other human services free up resources that can then be directed toward the provision of new or expanded programs and services?*
7. *Will advanced technology, particularly computers, be used to identify, track, and further isolate culturally different people?*
8. *Will many of the technological advances achieve the same level of non-use as the video tape recorder, audio tape recorder, and overhead projector as a regular part of the instructional process?*
9. *Will rural areas of America continue to have less access to, and less acceptance of, both technological advanced and cultural diversity?*
10. *Will administrators and policy-making bodies ever truly accept the use of advanced technology as a tool to gain rapid public feedback on their decisions?*

Perhaps the answers to these questions will be less important than the process used to address them. The dynamics of a group that comes together to engage in purposeful dialogue could produce relationships that either resolve the questions or rephrase them.

Other Social Issues

A number of important social issues that could be addressed by community education are beyond the scope of the Smith-Wiprud paper. Some of those issues are discussed briefly below.

Mobility

It is estimated that the average American family relocates every three to five years. Many families relocate even more frequently. Temporary residents tend to avoid extensive community involvement because they do not expect their efforts to bear fruit during their tenure in the community. The knowledge of an imminent move may even preclude significant interaction with other community residents. Community education can have an impact on this problem by being aware of new community residents and using a "welcome wagon" approach to introduce them to the community and the community education program. This welcome could be an excellent opportunity to assess the needs and interests of new residents and informally inventory any skills they might be willing to share with others. People need to feel that they are an important part of the community during their residence, however brief. We must make it worthwhile for them to invest their time, ideas, and efforts in the community. Community education, with its flexibility and sensitivity to community needs, can do this.

Loneliness

Our society has many lonely people who seek social interaction but, apart from casual encounters in grocery stores or shoppng centers, find little. Perhaps it is time for use to realize that the activities we offer in community education may not be as important as the fact that we are offering people an opportunity to be together and to interact. Bill Kerensky, director of the center for Community Education at Florida Atlantic University, describes the community school as an "ordinary person's country club." He observes that people join country clubs for at least three reasons: (1) a need to be part of something bigger than themselves; (2) a need to have some control over their environment; and (3) a need to be recognized by others. Couldn't we capitalize on these identity needs through community education?

Changing Family Structures

The Census Bureau estimated in 1979 that "if current conditions persist, children born in the mid-1970s have 45 chances in 100 of living in a one-parent family for a period of at least several months before they reach the age of 18 years." The special needs of single parents are only beginning to be recognized on a wide scale. Working parents, whether they are in one- or two-parent families, are increasingly dependent on the school for support services such as child care and hot meals for their children. Ironically, while these parents increasingly depend on the school, they are less directly involved in the school and the community as a result of their employment. Community education can assist parents with special needs through programs such as "latch key" after-school child care, but we should also be developing reciprocal agreements under which these parents would be encouraged to become involved in support groups for people in similar situations. Perhaps working parents could develop cooperative child care programs to meet their needs at a low cost, with community education facilitating self-help groups to address issues of common concern.

Changing Population Patterns

The 1980 Census reveals a variety of trends that have major direct and indirect implications for both community education and public schools. While the continued North-to-South and East-to-West migration of Americans is significant, there are even greater educational implications in the "greying of America." Improved medical care and a reduction in the birth rate are increasing the average age of the total population. This trend will profoundly affect the political, economic, and social directions of our society. One effect already in evidence is a conservative political shift at all levels. This conservatism is likely to continue to be reflected in a lowered public commitment to human services, including education, with increased responsibility for these efforts being transferred to local communities. A particular concern is the fact that as many as 72 percent of the adults in America do not have children in the public schools. This percentage has changed dramatically in recent decades and is widely viewed as a major factor in the decline of public confidence and support for public schools. The ultimate outcome of these changing demographic patterns is likely to be either major reforms in both school programs and school finance or an increased willingness on the part of school officials to greatly expand the involvement of older people and non-parents in all facets of school operations. The latter approach seems to be gaining momentum already, as it is one immediate thing that can be done to help patch the rapidly eroding support base for public education in most American communities. Community education is providing both example and direction in this area.

Increased Leisure Time

Technological advances, shorter work weeks, job sharing, unemployment, underemployment, earlier retirements, increased life expectancy, and a variety of other factors have greatly expanded the amount of leisure time available to Americans. Whether leisure time is voluntary, or involuntary, the result is that an increasing number of Americans, particularly youth and older citizens, are faced with increasing amounts of unobligated time. This time can be used in ways that are constructive or destructive to individuals and to the larger society. The physical and mental well-being of millions of people is at stake. Providing opportunities for growth-facilitating, satisfying, productive leisure-time activities for people of all ages is an increasing challenge for all communities.

Without concern and constructive action on this issue, the potential for negative social impact is enormous. If leisure time is viewed as a resource for community improvement, it could be directed to fulfilling a myriad of individual and societal needs. Volunteerism in schools and other human service agencies, community action projects, and expanded recreational pursuits are just a few possibilities. Community education can and should address the leisure-time in far more aggressive ways than it has so far.

Summary

Harnessing local resources to address local needs is the key to solving social problems. Community education offers communities a formula for addressing problems. The ingredients in the formula change from community to community, but the formula remains the same: **community + discussion + needs and resource assessment x people + action = community problem solving.**

This formula is the heart of community education. Any social issue confronting a community can be resolved or at least better understood through the process of community education.

PART VI

Cost Effectiveness

and Efficiency

PART VI: COST EFFECTIVENESS AND EFFICIENCY

SUMMARY

Philip Doughty reporting on a review of existing literature focuses on the problem area most evident in economic analysis: the conceptualization, design, and planning of the study. He provides a set of guidelines designed to assist in the planning of cost-effectiveness studies. These guidelines are organized into three major sections: (1) rationale (purpose, audiences, and designers); (2) planning considerations (goals, means, sources, comparisons, emphasis, etc.); and (3) technical considerations (criteria selection, analytical approach, measure, analysis methods, decision-making models, etc.).

Doughty emphasizes the importance of critical decision-making before implementation of a cost-effectiveness study. He includes a checklist of decisions to be made in each of the three areas discussed.

Susan C. Paddock emphasizes that cost studies require time, training, and practice. She provides definitions of terms used in cost studies. She agrees with Doughty on the importance of front-end decisions but cautions that problems can arise in the conducting of even well planned studies. She points out that a disadvantage of the cost study is that a program may be abolished on the basis of its expense regardless of its social or political value. She emphasizes the importance of community involvement in cost-benefit even if some efficiency or some details may have to be sacrificed to get that involvement. Paddock also points out the potential for erroneous conclusions based on cost data and unanticipated results.

Barry F. Semple praises Doughty's guidelines as timely and valuable, and expresses concern that most community educators still do not preceive cost studies as being important. As evidence, he points to the void in the literature and the absence of the topic at community education workshops and conferences. Semple addresses cost effectiveness from the perspective of the questions being asked by policy and decision-makers regarding program costs in a time of curtailed budgets. He stresses the importance of identifying the audiences for cost studies and recommends that policymakers be the primary audience and taxpayers the secondary audience.

He believes that cost studies will strengthen community education's overall process mission. He acknowledges that it will be time consuming, but expects that the collection and compliation of data will pay significant dividends. Because he believes that the technical aspects, as outlined by Doughty, will intimidate many community education practioners, he urges that help be made available through consultants, inservice workshops, and the National Community Education Clearinghouses.

GUIDELINES FOR PLANNING COST EFFECTIVENESS STUDIES IN COMMUNITY EDUCATION

by
Philip Doughty

OVERVIEW

Reviews of benefit-cost or cost-effectiveness studies consistently reveal two problem areas: flawed conceptualization, design, and planning; and confusion and misuse of procedures. The guidelines that follow address the first of these two problem areas.

The guidelines are intended.for use by planners, managers, directors, and evaluators. Selected references have been identified to provide access to examples and further discussion.

The guidelines are organized into three sections, each corresponding to major, sequential sets of decisions. The first section (Figure I) addresses the rationale for doing a cost-effectiveness study. Most models and examples reported in the literature do not adequately address such issues as purpose, audience, and perspective. The second section addresses study plans and basic design decisions (Figure II). Ignoring these issues guarantees that the results of a study will be confused, confusing, and probably misleading. The third section (Figure III) lists options related to methods. This section deals with technical concerns: the selection of descriptive and evaluative criteria, the analytical approach, decision models, and cost analysis methods.

Cost-Effectiveness Planning Guidelines
Section I: INITIAL CONSIDERATIONS

Why?   I.   What are the **purposes** of the study?
- Planning
- Reporting/describing
- Evaluating
- Comparing/analyzing
- Research

Who?   II. What is the nature of the **audience(s)** of the study?
- Internal-external
- Political-social
- Professional-technical

Who?   III. Who will design and conduct the study?
- Evaluators
- Accountants/auditors
- Program planners and managers

FIGURE I

SECTION I: INITIAL CONSIDERATIONS

I. What are the purposes of the study?

There are at least five separate but not mutually exclusive purposes for conducting cost-effectiveness studies. It is likely that a final rationale statement will incorporate several of these purposes.

● **Planning.** Discussions about community education abound with references to proactive and reactive postures, the search for excellence, collaboration, and the sharing of resources. All suggest a planning emphasis with concern for the future.

● **Reporting/describing.** Annual reports, final reports, progress reports, and perhaps a dozen additional labels have been attached to descriptions of current, proposed, and completed projects. Included in many of these is a section that describes how and for what purpose resources were used.

● **Evaluating.** Many documents that report and describe the events, activities, progress, and results of a program also include assessments and judgments of the program's worth, value, and utility.

● **Comparing/analyzing.** Studies that include comparisons and contrasts between and within programs require special consideration during the initial stages. Requests to identify programs or program components that are better or worse, more or less efficient, or that have the optimum mix of resources require more complex analyses than are typically employed in education and other human service contexts.

● **Research.** Individuals desiring information from which generalizations can be drawn, perhaps with wider utility for community education, must consider the requirements and options presented for experimental or quasi-experimental studies.

It is likely that most community education studies will address several of these purposes. The challenge is to determine which purposes are essential and how or if multiple agendas can be served.

II. What is the nature of the audience(s) of the study?

Guidelines for the conduct of evaluation studies[1] typically include sections devoted to audience considerations. Most reports of cost-effectiveness studies do not. One inference that can be drawn is that the authors believe that a single cost-effectiveness study and a single report are appropriate for all audiences. But careful consideration of audience characteristics is important and should influence other planning components.

● **Internal-external.** Internal recipients, including evaluators and analysts, are concerned about formative review of progress, non-threatening recommendations for program improvement, and in-depth knowledge about a particular community. Audiences external to a program are likely to be more interested in a study's credibility, objectivity, and accuracy. Attempting to address both internal and external concerns is always a challenge.

● **Political-social.** Persuasive arguments about resource allocation, ownership of geographic and human service "turf," and access to funding sources all have political, social, and economic implications. Access to clients, students, facilities, and volunteers is also influenced by these factors.

● **Professional-technical.** A professional, technically oriented audience is interested in such details as implementation strategies, linkages between agencies, and the impact of alternative delivery systems. The concerns of this group are potentially different from those of the city council, the school board, or other decision-makers.

III. Who will design and conduct the study?

Another kind of audience is the individual or individuals who are selected or appointed or who volunteer to plan and conduct a study. The authors of most current cost-effectiveness studies have one of the following primary roles:

● **Evaluators.** Conventional evaluators usually emphasize the clarification and measurement of results. Occasionally, evaluation studies include comprehensive perspectives involving descriptions of goals, procedures, and resources, along with assessments of learners and long-term impact. Although few academic programs and evaluation articles include methods and designs oriented to cost-effectiveness, the shift to a broader perspective is easy and comfortable for many evaluators.

● **Accountants/auditors.** Internal and external auditors have a financial or economic perspective. Emphasis on budgets, funding sources, expenditures, and balance sheets obviously helps an agency or institution maintain control over expenditures and financial records. The procedures and reports of accountants and auditors will be of limited use to community educators, however, unless the auditors can be convinced to adopt a broader perspective of costs, purposes of resource allocation records, and relationships to program goals. An evolving literature from the business community on operations auditing appears to have promise in this regard.

● **Program planners and managers.** Individuals interested in leadership, direction, and program control often are also interested in the contributions of cost-effectiveness studies. Although program managers rarely conduct cost-effectiveness studies, they typically commission them so that informed decisions can be made about both new and continuing programs.

SECTION II: PLANNING CONSIDERATIONS

IV. What are the essential design elements?

Figure II displays a set of requirements and decisions that are rarely explicitly reflected in cost-effectiveness study reports. Some studies have used one or even several of these design elements, but not one has addressed all of them.

Section II: PLANNING CONSIDERATIONS

What?   IV.   **What are the essential design elements?**
A. Determine **goals** of the study.
B. Determine goals of the program(s) to be studied.
C. Determine if the study is to be of the:
___1) **absolute nature** of one community education program,
___2) **relative properties** of several alternative programs.
D. Determine if the study is to be of:
___1) **alternative ends** (goals),
___2) **alternative means** to a relatively common goal.
E. Determine source(s) of alternatives to be considered:
___1) **existing alternatives** (ends and means),
___2) **decisions to be made** (thus implying alternatives),
___3) **newly created alternatives** (futures invention).
F. Determine nature of the comparisons to be made:
___1) **a priori** (before implementation),
___2) **ongoing** (program is operational),
___3) **ex post facto** (program is completed).
G. Determine whether the study is to emphasize:
___1) program accomplishments (justification/evaluation),
___2) program costs (justification/accounting),
___3) combination (cost effectiveness).
H. Determine if it is possible to fix one component of the cost-effectiveness equation:
___1) fix costs with variable effectiveness,
___2) fix effectiveness with variable costs,
___3) determine that it is impossible or inadvisable to fix either costs or effectiveness.

FIGURE II

● **Determine goals of the study.** The purposes and prospective audiences are the major elements to be considered in constructing the goals for a study. These elements will drive the rest of the design process. They will impact heavily on all design decisions as well as on subsequent decisions about methods and procedures.

● **Determine goals of the program(s) to be studied.** It may come as a surprise that this step comes after consideration of the study's objectives. In fact, final specification of the program goals is not likely to occur until all the rest of the guidelines in this section have been considered. This is particularly true if the study is oriented toward the future and includes new alternatives. Determining the program goals will help establish the parameters of the programs being considered and eventually clarify such issues as means vs. ends and fixing cost or fixing effectiveness.

● **Determine if the study is to be of the absolute nature of one program or the relative properties of several programs.** The principal issue to address in making this choice is whether a single program or several programs are to be studied. If it is to be just one, the absolute, internal properties of the program are assessed in an attempt to determine if the program is cost effective; the comparison is conducted (explicitly or implicity) between the program's costs and its effectiveness. A typical judgment to be made in this case is whether resources were wisely allocated in order to accomplish specified goals.

A study of the relative properties of several programs usually requires a more complex design. Comparisons across programs using multiple criteria lead to discussions of relative strengths and weaknesses, and relative costs and effectiveness.

● **Determine if the study is to be of alternative ends or alternative means.** Probably the single most pervasive flaw in reported cost-effectiveness studies is the confusion of means and ends in defining the alternatives to be compared. This is particularly true in studies of alternative instructional delivery systems with markedly different ends (goals). It is difficult enough to compare programs with common goals and different means (approaches), or common means and different goals; confusing the ends and means probably guarantees invalid results.

● **Determine the sources of alternatives to be considered.** Several standard sources of alternatives can be compared and contrasted in a cost-effectiveness study. One obvious choice is an existing program with a documented history of development and performance. This could include a local option or one that has been sufficiently reported in the literature. A second, not quite so obvious, source is the decisions that are to be informed, recommended, or made by the study. These decisions often imply alternatives (real or simulated) that can be created and defined.

A third and challenging source of alternatives is to engage in futures invention with the goal of designing new alternatives. These may include alternative ends (new program goals) or alternative means (new instructional strategies, materials development, assessment schemes, or delivery systems). The more data that exist on an option, either from actual records or extrapolations from the literature, the more comprehensive and detailed the analysis can be.

● **Determine the nature of the comparisons to be made.** Planning for future program alternatives requires data different from those required to evaluate existing programs. Most studies consider both existing and proposed programs.

● **Determine whether the study is to emphasize the program accomplishments or costs, or both.** At this point in the planning process, it should be fairly easy to determine whether stronger emphasis should be placed on resource allocation issues or program results (impact, benefits, etc.). Technical expertise or methodological bias often plays a stronger role in this decision than careful consideration of purpose, audience, and other design factors. In general, a balanced cost and effectiveness viewpoint should be emphasized.

● **Determine if it is possible to fix one component of the cost effectiveness equation.** Given the many variables involved in a typical cost-effectiveness analysis (e.g., alternatives, time, cost-effectiveness), consideration is typically given to fixing some set or subset of these variables in order to simplify the comparisons and control for certain types of errors. The two principal conceptual approaches are the fixed-effectiveness and fixed-budget (cost) approaches.[2] A study may be structured so that the alternatives to be compared are all assumed to reach some specified level of effectiveness; in this case, the emphasis is on determining which alternative is least costly. The fixed-budget approach compares alternatives on an equal-cost basis to determine which alternative is most likely to yield the highest effectiveness (or greatest benefit or utility). Multiple analyses are sometimes conducted on the same problem; both the fixed-effectiveness and fixed-budget approaches are used so that comparisons can be made at several different levels of both effectiveness and cost.

The Office of Education (DHEW) sponsored and disseminated a handbook for evaluation practitioners entitled **The Resource Approach to the Analysis of Educational Project Cost**[3], which recommends an approach in which neither cost nor effectiveness is fixed. The handbook suggests a "pair-wise comparison" similar to that used by Doughty and Stakenas[4] and Lent.[5] In this approach, the value judgments of the decision-maker(s) are specifically incorporated into the decision of "whether or not the better outcome is worth the additional cost."

Section III: TECHNICAL CONSIDERATIONS

How?   V. **Methods**
- A. **Review and selection criteria:**
  - 1) Criteria selection
    - Who decides on what criteria?
    - How are selection decisions to be made?
    - Are political and/or social criteria to be included?
    - What decisions are to be informed by these criteria?
    - Are criteria separated from decisions about standards and measures?
  - 2) Types of Criteria
    - Efficiency
    - Impact
    - Utility
    - Value
    - Cost
- B. Determine appropriate **analytical approach:**
  - 1a) Aggregation of benefits,
  - or 1b) Disaggregation of benefits.
  - 2a) Qualifications and monetary valuing of benefits,
  - or 2b) Multiple measures and indicators.
- C. Select appropriate decision model:
  - Clarify relationships between resources (costs) and outcomes (effectiveness) by matching analytical approach decisions to decision model alternatives:
  - 1) **Aggregation and qualification**
    - ___ a) Benefit-cost ratios
    - ___ b) Net benefit
  - or
  - 2) **Disaggregation and multiple measures**
    - ___ c) Unit costs
    - ___ d) Effectiveness-cost comparison matrix
- D. Determine **cost analysis methods**
  - 1a) Use agency/institutional budget records,
  - or 1b) Use functional resource cost analysis.
  - 2a) Use single-cycle costing,
  - or 2b) Life cycle costing.
  - 3a) Aggregate all costs from various sources (including donated and "in-kind"),
  - or 3b) Clarify various sources of resources.
- E. Define appropriate **cost analysis components**
  - 1) Relevant and irrelevant costs
  - 2) Fixed and variable costs
  - 3) Recurring and nonrecurring costs
  - 4) Direct and indirect costs
  - 5) Internal and external costs

VI. **Link to implementation**
- A. Prepare final specifications for a study that most closely matches perspective, purpose, audience, model, and methods that will then inform the selection of procedures.

Figure III

SECTION III: TECHNICAL CONSIDERATIONS

V. Methods

This section does not specify procedures; rather, it identifies important components in cost analysis, possibly the area least familiar to community educators

● **Criteria selection.** There is a temptation to jump from design specifications to the selection of measures and measuring instruments, bypassing a potentially important set of decisions. Judgments about which variables to include and which to exclude can easily determine a study's utility and validity. Several authors argue that the decisions about the relationship between a program's goals, the dimensions of its performance (criteria), and measures of those criteria are perhaps the most important of all the decisions made in designing a cost-effectiveness study.[6] It is certainly easy to bias, intentionally or not, an otherwise well designed and well conducted study by selecting a criterion that subsequently portrays one alternative in a more favorable light than another. Differences in levels of performance between alternatives on most of these dimensions are to be expected, but without judicious and objective selection of the proper criteria, these differences can be either important or unimportant, and few decision-makers will be able to make the distinction once the study is completed.

The set of questions included in this section do not suggest either/or decisions but identify important issues that must be addressed at this stage in planning. **Who** and **how** are important for both political and technical reasons. Separation of criteria decisions from equally important, but different, decisions about levels of performance or standards for those criteria is critical. It is only after these decisions have been made that the issue of measures and measurement of those parameters of performance can be addressed.

● **Types of criteria.** There is a wide range of possible choices that can be selected for inclusion in almost any cost-effectiveness study. However, many authors argue for inclusion of a relatively specific set of types of criteria.[7] The criteria reflected in these guidelines are general in nature but sufficient to guide deliberations about which, how many, how much, and with what approach.

Efficiency.   Concerns about the use of resources are frequently important by themselves. For example, such time-related indicators as time on task, time to learn, and expenditures over time all reflect in some way the allocations of various resources.

Impact. For community educators, the ultimate goal is primarily large-scale systemic influence or impact. Other reflections of program performance such as benefit, effectiveness, and results can be included in this category.

Utility. In addition to considerations of efficiency and effectiveness, community educators are interested in services and programs that are useful. Combinations of these criteria may be appropriate if a program is efficient but not useful, or feasible and useful but not effective.

Value. Although little has been said thus far about the importance of ethics, worth, equity, and justice in considering community education alternatives, even a cursory inspection of the literature reminds the reader that these are in fact foundational criteria for all alternatives. Personal, professional, and societal perceptions of worth and value often are reflected only after a study has been designed and the evidence collected. This is particularly true in benefit-cost models that require analysts to quantify and value benefits in monetary terms. The concern here is that value (and values) be addressed early in the planning stage so that subsequent discussions about impact can be placed in proper perspective.

Cost. Placing the criterion of cost last on the list is appropriate for several reasons. It is often wise to address issues of quality, importance, value, and effectiveness before considering costs. Financial concerns drive so many of our major and minor decisions these days that we tend to forget that, at least in education, finances are means to our ends and not ends. The range and types of cost criteria that could be included in a study are extensive. Short- and long-term costs, societal and personal costs, opportunity and imputed costs are all possible areas of concern.

● **Determine appropriate analytical approach.** How to portray and array the results of a study is typically faced near its completion. In cost-effectiveness studies, however, the way in which the results will be arrayed must be decided long before data are collected. One alternative is to combine or aggregate the results using some standard measurement or unit of output. A related approach is to select one best indicator of impact or results as a single measure of effectiveness; this approach makes analysis of the results relatively simple (and easy to explain) and usually does not require separating benefits according to different beneficiaries (e.g., individuals, groups, communities).

A more appropriate approach (note author's bias in Doughty, 1979[8]) is to use multiple measures and multiple recipients of benefits as the basis for analyses. This approach permits the use of different kinds of evidence but also makes comparisons and contrasts a real challenge.

Another major analytical issue to be decided early in the planning is whether or not to quantify. This decision is often influenced by the professional and technical training of the study planners. At times, either the decision to be made (e.g., whether to allocate resources to human services agencies or to accelerate debt retirement) or the needs of the decision-makers will require that the results of a study be transformed into single, omnibus, quantified measures of benefit that can also be assigned a monetary value. The more typical study in education and other human services programs culminates in a range of measures, some quantified and others in narrative form. This approach lets decision-makers use their own values to judge the worth of the reported outcomes. This is obviously easier when a relatively restricted range of alternatives is being considered to accomplish one goal.

● **Select appropriate decision model.** One of the primary justifications for spending time and energy on cost-effectiveness studies is to have an impact on decisions. This is accomplished by informing and educating, recommending among alternatives, or actually deciding.

Four models or approaches to the decision issue are suggested by various authors.[9] Although different in form and analytical approach, they can be grouped under two primary models, one using aggregation and quantification of all criteria, and the other using data in a variety of formats. In the first model, benefit-cost ratios are constructed by determining the monetary value of an alternative's benefits and dividing the monetary value by the monetary costs of that alternative. The presumption is that a ratio greater than one $(B/C > 1)$ implies that the results were greater (worth more) than the costs. A similar approach uses the same monetary values but simply subtracts the financial costs from the monetary value of the benefits to determine the net benefit, if any. Both approaches rely on careful and objective decisions about the worth of outcomes. These decisions should reflect the values of the various audiences of the study, since these values are not explicit in the ratios or net benefits.

The second general model assumes that multiple measures and perspectives are appropriate and that study audiences are capable of considering several types and forms of evidence at the same time. Unit-cost models provide data that reflect the cost of accomplishing various goals or of engaging in various activities. If the unit in question is process-oriented, the unit-cost data are used as measures of efficiency or cost efficiency. If the unit is result-oriented, the unit costs are used as cost-effectiveness indicators.

Matrix models[9] are typically complex in terms of the types and variety of information included. No attempt is made to report data in a condensed or converted form nor to place monetary values on outcomes. A single data matrix can include one or several alternatives on one axis and several types of cost, process, efficiency, and effectiveness data on the other axis. Data within the cells of the matrix can be quantitative (e.g., gains in learning scores and dollars costs) as well as qualitative (e.g., narrative summaries of client satisfaction). Decisions made on the basis of either unit-cost or matrix models must be carefully guided by the concerns of correlation and causality, short- and long-term perspectives, and report recipients.

● **Determine cost analysis methods.** An area in cost-effectiveness studies that presents initial planning and conceptualization problems for educators is cost analysis methodology.[10] Several authors have provided useful guidance for educators embarking on a first venture.[11] Three particularly important decisions merit inclusion in these planning guidelines.

The first set of cost analysis decisions relates to the source of cost data and the methods used to categorize and report those data. One source of cost data is the conventional budget records of agencies and institutions, but these are usually not organized so that resources expended for a project or program can be attributed directly to that program. A better option is to conduct a separate analysis of the resources used or planned for use in a project. Conducting this kind of separate inventory of resources[12] usually requires more time and effort but will provide better estimates of the resources actually used or required for an alternative.

The second set of decisions requires careful consideration of the time frame for each alternative being considered. If the only issue is the cost of conducting a program for one cycle (year, semester, month), an analysis of resources consumed during that cycle is all that is necessary. Typically, the issues of concern are much broader so the life-cycle costs of programs must be considered. Start-up costs, multi-cycle operating costs, as well as termination costs must be documented or estimated, or existing programs will have an unfair advantage when program costs are compared.

The last set of decisions is related to the decision model. Aggregation of costs, particularly dollar costs, is an appropriate method if the purpose of the study is to describe the varieties and amounts of in-kind or donated resources. Donated, opportunity, or other non-monetary costs can be reported according to source but not added together.

● **Define appropriate cost analysis components.** Five different but related cost analysis perspectives are included in these guidelines as a stimulus for the procedures phase of a cost-effectiveness study. Each perspective has its own set of procedures and rationale. Most are relevant for most cost-effectiveness studies in community education. Several cost-related studies of community education[13], a series of international education studies sponsored by UNESCO[14], and doctoral studies[15] have used some of these perspectives.

VI.   Link to implementation

The options, requirements, and concerns suggested in these guidelines will not guarantee a successful (i.e., useful and powerful) study, but attention to them will help eliminate many of the major conceptual and methodological blunders evident in every reported cost-effectiveness study in community education to date—including studies conducted by this author!

NOTES

[1]A. Grotelueschen, D. Gooler, and A. Knox, **Evaluation in Adult Basic Education: How and Why** (Danville, IL: Interstate, 1976).

M.B. Young, et al., **Doing Your Community Education Evaluation: A Guide** (U.S. Office of Education, 1980), p. 66.

[2]G. H. Fisher, **Cost Considerations in Systems Analysis** (New York: American Elseview, 1971).

[3]**The Resource Approach to the Analysis of Educational Project Cost** (U.S. Office of Education, 1980), p. 86.

[4]P. L. Doughty and R. Stakenas, "An Analysis of Costs and Effectiveness of an Individualized Subject Offering," in C.D. Sabine, ed., **Accountability: Systems Planning in Education** (Homewood, IL: ETC, 1973).

[5]R. M. Lent, **Planning for Future University College Programs: A Cost-Effectiveness Evaluation of Alternative Instructional Delivery Systems** (Syracuse, NY: University College of Syracuse University, 1976), p. 120.

[6]A. D. Kazanowski, "A Standardized Approach to Cost-Effectiveness Evaluations," in J. M. English, ed., **Cost-Effectiveness: The Economic Evaluation of Engineered Systems** (New York: Wiley, 1968).

R. M. Lent, **An Examination of the Methods of Cost Effectiveness Analysis as Applied to Instructional Technology** (doctoral dissertation, Syracuse University, 1980).

H. M. Levin, "Cost-Effectiveness Analysis in Evaluation Research," in M. Guttentag and E. L. Struening, eds., **Handbook of Evaluation Research**, vol. II (Beverly Hills, CA: Sage, 1975).

[7]P. L. Doughty, **Effectiveness, Cost, and Feasibility Analysis of a Course in College Level Geology** (doctoral dissertation, Florida State University, 1972).

E. S. Quade, **Analysis for Public Decisions** (New York: American Elseview, 1975).

S. Temkin, **A Cost-Effectiveness Evaluation Approach to Improving Allocations for School Systems** (Philadelphia, PA: Research for Better Schools, 1969), p. 220.

[8]P. L. Doughty, "Cost Effectiveness Analysis Tradeoffs and Pitfalls for Planning and Evaluating Instructional Programs," **Journal of Instructional Development**, vol. 2, no. 4, 1979.

[9]P. L. Doughty, R. Lent, and A. Beilby, **Cost-Effectiveness, Analysis and Instructional Technology** (Syracuse, NY: ERIC Information Analysis Product, 1978).

[10]A. Herr, **Cost Analysis of a Community School: The West Side Complex, Atlantic City** (project report, New Jersey State Department of Education, 1979).

C. Lawton, M. Wilson, and D. Fearon, **Applying a Cost Benefit Analysis Approach to Determining Community Education Projects** (project report, University of Maine at Farmington, 1980).

[11]A. Beilby, "Determining Instructional Costs Through Functional Cost Analysis," **Journal of Instructional Development**, 1979, vol. 3, no. 2, pp. 29-34.

M. D. Carpenter and S. A. Harrart, "Cost-Effectiveness Analysis for Educational Planning, in S. A. Haggart, ed., **Program Budgeting for School District Planning** (Englewood Cliffs, NJ: Educational Technology, 1972).

S. A. Haggart, **The Resource Approach to the Analysis of Educational Project Cost** (U.S. Department of Health, Education and Welfare, 1978).

[12]Harrart, **Resource Approach.**

[13]Herr, **Cost Analysis.**

Lawton, et al., **Applying a Cost Benefit Analysis Approach.**

W. Stenning and R. Berridge, **Community Education in Texas: A Technical Report of Participants, Programs and Costs** (Texas Education Agency, 1978).

[14]P. H. Coombs and J. Hallak, **Educational Cost Analysis in Action: Case Studies for Planners — I, II** (Paris: UNESCO, International Institute for Educational Planning, 1972).

[15]Doughty, **Effectiveness, Cost and Feasibility Analysis.**

Lent, **Examination of the Methods.**

Reaction Paper to: Philip L. Doughty's

"GUIDELINES FOR PLANNING COST EFFECTIVENESS STUDIES IN COMMUNITY EDUCATION"

by
Susan C. Paddock

"Cost-effectiveness" seems to be the catchword of the times. The pressure for quantification and fiscal restraint has made the potential dollar savings suggested by cost-effectiveness analysis very appealing. We must be wary of that appeal, however, because poor use or misuse of cost-effectiveness analysis may be discouraging or even dangerous.

This is not to suggest that we shy away from cost-effectiveness studies. Instead we must, as Doughty does, consider them an important part of a comprehensive research, evaluation, and planning process for community education. We must know where and how we will use cost studies, and Doughty's paper is a critical element in helping us do just that. The paper is only a beginning, however, properly titled "Guidelines." Learning to do valid cost studies requires time and practice.

Doughty focuses our attention on an integrated research-evaluation-planning process, and, more specifically, on the "front end" of the analysis process. His emphasis may keep some community educators from asking first, "How can we measure...?" rather than the more appropriate, "What do we want to measure and why do we want to measure it?"

Since Doughty has bypassed a discussion of terminology, choosing instead to discuss cost analysis processes directly, it may be useful here to define some terms in a relatively simple way.

Cost analyses are either accounting or evaluation studies; evaluation studies are either research or planning studies. **Accounting studies** (e.g., auditing or cost justification) imply the presentation of quantifiable data without value judgments. An auditing study, for example, may show that a community education program costs $100,000 at a per-participant rate of $11.49; it will not show how this cost compares to the cost of other programs, or whether the cost is an effective use of public monies.

Evaluative cost studies, on the other hand, imply value judgments. These studies are more varied, based on their focus and intended outcomes. **Cost-benefit studies** compare the inputs and outcomes of a program and draw conclusions about the worth of those ratios. **Cost-efficiency studies** try to determine appropriate economies of scale—that is, at what point or in what way programs reach the optimum mix of resources, strategies, and results.

Cost-effectiveness studies seek answers to such questions as, what outcomes have accrued as a result of identified costs? Have selected strategies at specified costs led to the "best" programs? What strategies and resource allocations will lead to desired outcomes?

Cost analysis can tie together past, present, and future programs in a way that informs and assists decision-making. Cost-analysis studies are ultimately decision-making studies that assign value to inputs and, sometimes, to outcomes. Further, most of these studies are not simply cost-determination studies, but cost-choicing studies. That is, in the planning, conducting, and reviewing of cost analysis, choices are made that explicitly or implicitly define values. This valuing, central to cost analysis, is critical for community education. Do we choose power and control, for example, at the expense of compromise and community peace? Do we value efficiency and productivity more highly than equity and justice? Or, to put it another way, is the cost of equity—whether altered facilities or increased opportunities or new policies—one a community is willing and able to bear?

The community education philosophy of participation should affect all front-end decisions about a cost study. Doughty alludes to this, but the point needs emphasis. It may be impossible and should certainly be philosophically unacceptable to undertake a highly-sophisticated (and professionally sound) cost analysis whose purpose, procedures, and results are beyond the ken of the community. In order to assure participation, it may be necessary to sacrifice some information that a complex analysis could yield, but a more limited cost analysis is not necessarily inferior—just less comprehensive.

Community participation in cost analysis involves the risk that the community may choose an alternative other than the one the program leaders want. A council, examining cost information on day care programs, might decide the program is too costly, regardless of the social implications of abolishing it. The problem of being a professional community educator in a participative environment is highlighted by such a situation. Clearly, the use of cost analysis by communities requires that the front-end decisions described by Doughty reflect the full range of community values. The bottom line, however, is that we must also be willing to allow a community to abolish a program whose cost information so dictates.

In an earlier paper,[1] Doughty describes some of the tradeoffs and pitfalls in planning and conducting cost studies; his discussion in that paper is important enough to be summarized here. Doughty suggests that we err in three areas: in selecting evaluative criteria to guide the study; in collecting and reporting cost data; and in reaching conclusions based on available data. If we select the wrong criteria by which to collect or judge data; if we fail to use enough criteria; or if we use poorly-defined criteria, our cost studies will provide erroneous or inadequate information. Similarly, if we overlook important outcome variables; if we confuse throughput and output indicators; if we fail to recognize unanticipated effects of programs and processes; if we over-generalize results; or if we (and this seems almost endemic to cost studies) overquantify, ignoring qualitative data, we will have an incomplete cost study. Counting participant hours and participant costs, for example, falls far short of an effective cost analysis.

In the collection of cost data, it is important not to rely on previously collected data unless they are well documented. Doughty also warns against focusing only on dollar expenditures, using data and ratios improperly, and assuming causal relationships where none exists.

Competence is the ultimate aim of Doughty's paper. I hope that his guidelines will encourage many in the community education field to begin cost studies.

NOTES

[1]P. L. Doughty, "Cost-Effectiveness Analysis Tradeoffs and Pitfalls for Planning and Evaluating Instructional Programs," **Journal of Instructional Development**, vol. 2, no. 4 (1979).

Reaction Paper To: Philip L. Doughty's

"Cost Effectiveness Procedures and Practices for Community Education"

by
Barry F. Semple

Assuming that lack of access to a workable accountability procedure is one of the major barriers to measuring the effectiveness and efficiency of community education, the guidelines proposed by Doughty should be very valuable. My major concern centers around acceptance of this effort by community educators. I hope that these practical guidelines will reduce the natural fears many practitioners have about documenting outcomes and cost benefits.

A primary mission of community educators is to facilitate a planning and operations process that targets available resources on needs identified by the community. This usually involves both extensive involvement by groups representative of the community and a practical planning process that involves identifying community needs, setting goals, weighing alternative strategies, and marshaling available resources. This process could be significantly improved by the incorporation of a cost-effectiveness design.

It is striking that in this period of major reductions in both educational and human services budgets so few studies are available about outcomes and efficiency. Cost-effectiveness studies are seldom included in community education workshops and conferences; only one such study has been completed in my state, which has had many years of extensive community education activity.

Policy-makers and taxpayers have always been interested in solving community problems, but now many are asking how we can solve them more effectively and efficiently. Boards of education are asking, how many schools should we close? Which schools? Should closed schools be sold or used as community centers? What are appropriate thermostat settings for schools? How can we improve reading scores with less staff? Municipal governments are asking, how can we reduce welfare and unemployment costs? How can we reduce crime when we have shrinking budgets? How can we provide vital services without raising taxes?

These questions are good indicators of the need for better data on which to base tough budget decisions. Both policy-makers and taxpayers are demanding clear evidence of program benefits, but many reports by educational and social service administrators are still focusing on the need for their programs, and success stories about the participants. This information may be valuable, but it seldom provides the data needed to make the hard decisions about budget cuts.

Doughty's emphasis on identification of the purposes of a study should be a strong message to all community education practitioners. Measureable indicators of success must be clearly stated before the total design of a cost-effectiveness study can be addressed.

The community education process attempts to focus all available resources on identified community problems using various strategies involving the community, policy-makers, and program deliverers. Although this process is functioning well in many communities, too few community educators build into the planning process, or the final reports, tangible evidence to show that the most effective delivery will cost the fewest dollars.

If and when community educators become much more serious about developing cost-effectiveness studies, I would strongly urge attention to the first two purposes suggested by Doughty: planning, and reporting/describing. The other purposes—evaluating, research, and comparing/analyzing—will naturally follow the first two.

The use of Doughty's guidelines to improve community education planning makes a great deal of sense. Cost considerations are too seldom the initial planning focus. Some municipal governments, school boards, and community agencies are already reducing rental costs by relocating into available school space, and a number of joint agreements by governmental agencies have resulted in shared computer use, joint insurance coverage, bulk purchasing, etc. The savings from these joint efforts are logical and tangible outcomes of the community education process, but we often fail to look at cost savings **at the very outset**. We must make this a **major component**, not just a sometime by-product, of our planning process.

The reporting/describing purpose of cost-effectiveness studies is also extremely important. Many business people and concerned taxpayers who sit on policy-making boards wonder why we give so little attention to this area. We do not have to exclude out heart warming success stories, or our excellent involvement procedures, but we must begin to emphasize measurement of our efficiency in terms of effectiveness.

Most public administrators are now struggling with the conflict between meeting their primary goals and cutting costs. Educators are especially vulnerable to critics preoccupied with taxes, the economy, and educational productivity. We must learn to better document and report the benefits as well as the costs of our programs. I am firmly convinced that we can continue to develop an ongoing process for individual and community improvement. At the same time, we can incorporate planning and reporting procedures that will impress only those concerned with the bottom line.

As Doughty points out, identification of the prospective audience of a study is extremely important because it will influence all design aspects of the study. I strongly urge that policy-makers (especially at the local level) be given primary consideration, since they have responsibility for allocating increasingly scarce resources. They are also struggling with the difficult tasks of developing community consensus and gathering hard data as the basis for spending decisions. We cannot bemoan budget cuts on the one hand and on the other do little to assist the policy-makers who must make these decisions. This is especially true for community educators, since they are frequently facilitating the most viable, and sometimes the only, community-based planning process in town.

The secondary audience, and perhaps in the long run the most important, is the taxpayer. How well have we told him what he is getting for his tax dollars?

A study design that focuses on gathering practical and immediately usable data could strengthen community education's overall process mission, but we must be clear that the data are not an end, but valuable tools. Their inclusion in the community education process should result in better planning, clearer goals, better information about outcomes, and greater community support.

Those sections of the Doughty paper that deal with analytical approaches and decision models are fairly technical. I doubt that many practicing community educators will have either the background or the time to use this information effectively. This problem could be addressed in several ways. Cost-effectiveness studies could be topics for state and national community education programs. Some specific examples could be written and made available through the National Community Education Clearing-house. Consultant help may also be needed and appropriate.

Afterword

The Impact of Community Education
on National Educational and Community Social Issues:
A Brief Glance Back with an Eye on the Future

by
Sam F. Drew, Jr.

Community education has experienced enormous growth since its birth in Flint, Michigan, in the 1930s. Although some trace its philosophical roots to the teachings of John Dewey, most agree that community education became a tangile component of public schools through the resolve of Charles Stewart Mott and Frank Manley to keep five school playgrounds in Flint open after school hours in response to a community problem of deliquent youth.

The essence of community education is the **process** that launched that first program, but the process went virtually unnoticed as the program flourished. Largely through Mott's efforts and fortune, the program concept was extended beyond the boundaries of Flint to communities across the country. During the 1960s some practitioners of the program concept began to describe community education as a process. Some attribute this change to a process of evolution, but perhaps it was just an evolving recognition of what the program really was. It was as though the process that created the first program in Flint had just been discovered.

Defining "process" proved difficult, however. A program is tangible, and most practitioners settled into the comfort and security of "program." When, in 1974, the federal government adopted a role in community education, it was to develop programs. Community educators cheered this relatively small new source of funds and a new national credibility for their movement, but federal involvement did little to advance the notion of community education as process. In fact, the placement of community education in the federal bureaucracy and its subsequent placement in state educational bureacracies through federal funding probably retarded advancement of the idea of community education as process.

Through the years, many advocates have praised the potential of community education as process, but most would agree that it is a potential largely unrealized. Community education is generally thought of today as an "add on" program in the schools.

What **is** the potential of community education? What must occur for community education to realize that potential? It was to address these questions that this project, *The Impact of Community Education on National Educational and Community Social Issues,* was conceived. The goal was to assess the actual and potential impact of community education on various societal issues. Diverse viewpoints were sought from authorities outside the field. These authorities, together with a group of reactors who are primarily community education practitioners, met in Washington, D.C., for two days in the summer of 1982 to discuss and refine their ideas and presentations for publication in this volume. I observed the proceedings at that conference.

Generally Speaking. . .

The papers accomplished their respective purposes with varying degrees of success. Frankly, several of them seem misdirected in the context of the goal of this project. Thus, a paper such as Phil Doughty's although well conceived and written, would be more appropriate in a collection of writings on strategies for the survival of community education within the school system. In assessing the actual and potential impact of community education on major educational and social issues, cost effectiveness is a secondary consideraion to the viability of the process for improving the present system.

Several of the authors write primarily about the implications of their own research, with strained reference to its applicability to community education. Thus, Iannaccone's "Community Education and Turning Point Election Periods" makes interesting reading but is dependent on the reaction papers of Parson and Halperin to target its relationship to community education. Etzioni, whose paper also falls within this categorization, apparently decided not to draw a relationship between community education and his "Three Measures To Help Reconstruct Education in America." Either he sees no relationship or chooses not to address it. This paper, too, depends on its reactors to draw relationships for community education.

Despite the lack of specificity of these authors in defining the relationship and potential impact of community education to their respective theses, there is, vicariously, a lesson for community education practitoners. Each of us strives for a certain degree of authority in a practicular field of study; it is within our respective fields that we find security, challenge, and some measure of satisfaction. Community education theory promotes an interdisciplinary approach to solving problems, yet most community educators are no more familiar with turning point election periods than Iannaccone is with community education. Indeed, to paraphrase Mosher, who writes about community education's relationship to the political process in this volume, many community education practitioners are naive about the political nature of community problem solving. An interdisciplinary approach requires that we go beyond the boundaries of school-based community education, not just establishing a relationship between community education and other disciplines but integrating community education philosophy into these fields. The result is a brand new way of looking at things and a whole new cast of community education practitioners. We will not ingrain community education principles in others by working as a separate, school-based bureaucracy; only when the Iannaccones and the Etzioni's of the world hold dear the community education philosophy will true relationships be realized. Our role as "pushers of process" is not to find comfort in our own bureaucracy, but to establish our principles in other bureaucracies and systems. There certainly is unrealized potential in the application of the community education process to education, and community education's relationship to education should remain a primary focus. But the potential impact of the community education process outside the field of education will not be realized in the school-based model.

In other papers written for this project, DeJong and Gardner credibly relate the role of community education in promoting more efficient use of public facilities. Their best points relate to the democratic planning process inherent in community education.

Fantini equates community education with community-based education. The school reform he envisions—an educative community—**is** community education. Of the primary writers, Sugarman most accurately addresses the task set forth for the project. He discusses the relationship of community education to reform in the delivery of social services; his creative ideas deserve careful study because they truly focus on community education as process, and the application of that process to other disciplines.

Recurrent Issues

Taken collectively, these papers offer community educators much food for thought. We will have to sift through, glean out, analyze, and synthesize many thoughts and ideas, but the reward will be the discovery of some new directions for community education and fresh perspectives on some old directions.

A multitude of issues and ideas were advanced and discussed in the papers and during the conference, but several themes of particular relevance recurred frequently. Specifically, the following ideas garnered considerable attention:

● **Community Education as Process**

Almost all of the writers make reference to community education as process, but there is substantial variation as to what that process is or should be. Perhaps the most important ideas on this issue come from those who write of community education as a political process. Mosher's paper calls for better understanding by community educators of the process of power as a problem-solving technique. Both Mosher and Halperin write of the need for community educators to join that small percentage of the population that participates regularly in the shaping of public policy. The dominant theme here seems to be that community educators, if they are to be true brokers of resources, must come to grips with the exercise of power as it relates to the process of problem solving. There is more to matching needs with resources than meets the eye. Community educators must overcome their naivete about the implications of defining community education as a problem-solving process and gain better understanding of the process of power and its use in the arena in which they work.

● **The Reality and Potential of Commuity Education**

Beginning with the survey conducted by this project and running through the papers and the ensuing discussions is a consensus that community education has great but unrealized potential for improving schools and society. Fantini predicts a more relevant system of public education through community education. Halperin sees a strengthening of participatory democracy. DeJong and Gardner cite community education's potential for promoting the participatory planning that would result in more efficient use of public facilities. Smith and Wiprud write of community education's potential to remedy some of the problems associated with cultural diversity and technological change.

Many reasons are suggested for the failure of community education to realize its potential, among them a lack of consensus on a conceptual framework, a lack of understanding of the political process and its application to community education, a failure to communicate the concept accurately and persuasively to other educators, the emphasis on program rather than process, a failure to embrace the times in which we live, and the loss of federal leadership.

● **Community Education — The Great Communicator**

Although the context varies among the papers, a consistent theme of the writers is that the community education process is primarily the facilitation of two-way communication, linking school with community, agency with agency, and government with governed. McKenzie writes of community education as a link between school and community. DeJong and Gardner say that the erosion of public confidence in the "top down" method of policy planning grew out of lack of trust; they write of the need for new planning systems that include two-way communication, cooperation between the public and elected officials, and institutional collaboration. Kliminski, in his reaction, says that two-way communication must be formalized, with clear distinction between the roles of communicator and programmer. Sugarman cautions that two-way communication on a large scale is not a realistic goal but is appropriate and feasible in dealing with small issues at the local level. All agree that two-way communication is a necessary ingredient of a community education process that purports to match needs with resources.

● **Community Education as Educational/Social Reformer**

Many of the papers refer to the role of community education in educational and social change. Fantini and Kerensky write in the vernacular of futurism about changes in the educational system. Fantini equates community education with the community-based educational system he foresees. Kerensky says that community education has, in essence, been calling for a paradigm shift in education and that its failures are attributable to the schools' lack of recognition and understanding of paradigm shifts, and the persistent mislabeling of community education as a program rather than a process for addressing change. Etzioni states an opposite view; he says that the expanded world of the futurist has been suspended and that we are in an era of decline. Radig sees promise for community education as a community development agent; he believes that the ideas of Saul Alinski have as much relevance for community educators as do those of John Dewey.

● **Community Education and Public Policy**

If community educators are ever to actualize the definition of community education as process, they must develop an understanding of how the political system works in the making of public policy. Mosher's paper is intended to help the community educator "accept the legitimacy of political activity" in the role as bridge builder between the "world of the government official and that of the citizen."

Halperin alone expresses an opinion about an appropriate role for the federal government in community education. He chides community educators for energy wasted over the past few years to maintain the federal community education program and counsels a future strategy of "treating community education as a process rather than a program." He says that community education should be ingrained in public policy, "a set of powerful principles about the educational process that would infuse all of education in much the same way the Civil Rights Act of 1964 and Section 504 of the Vocational Rehabilitation Act Amendments of 1972 seek to leverage **all** educational delivery programs."

Questions To Be Addressed

Kerensky makes the point that community educators are better analyzers than synthesizers. Yet synthesize we must if we are to make use of the products of this project. As we go about the task of synthesizing, we might seek answers to three central questions:

1. What is community education?

The definition of community education is crystal clear to some practitioners, but less clear to others. If we define community education as a process, does that process derive solely from an educational philosophy? Is community education synonymous with community development? Is community-based education the same as community education? What is the appropriate base for community education? Should community education be a part of public policy?

2. What can community education do?

Can community education improve upon the delivery of social services? Can it be a communications link in public planning? Can it improve schools? Can it be a set of principles for guiding public policy for education and other social institutions?

Only when we have consensus on the preceeding questions can the third be answered.

3. How can all this be accomplished?

Do we seek a new federal role in community education? Do we move beyond the bureaucracy of the schools or act from that base? Do we link our future to new paradigms?

The answers to these questions cannot, perhaps, be found solely in this collection of papers, but synthesis of the ideas presented here should give us a start.

About the Editors

The Principal Investigator for the National Impact Project was Larry E. Decker. He has had more than 15 years of professional experience directly related to the field of community education. In 1967, as director of the Center for Leisure Studies and Community Services at the University of Oregon, he initiated the development of the University of Oregon's Northwest Community Education Center proposal funded by the C. S. Mott Foundation. In 1970-71 he was a community education doctoral fellow with the National Center for Community Education and Michigan State University. He served as the first system-wide director for the award-winning community education program in St. Louis Park, Minnesota, and was the first president of the Minnesota Community Education Association. He is currently an associate professor in the Department of Administration and Supervision of the University of Virginia and director of the Mid-Atlantic Center for Community Education. He is also the executive secretary of the Virginia Community Education Association.

Dr. Decker is a charter member of the National Community Education Association. He has served on the Board of Directors (1974-76); as chairman of the Federal Community Education Legislative Committee (1976-78), and as chairman of the National Training Task Force (1982-83). He was the recipient of the NCEA's Outstanding Service Award in 1977. Dr. Decker has published 25 articles and 10 books and monographs on community education and community services.

Donna Hager Schoeny, the Project Director, has had extensive experience in community education at the local, state, and national levels. She has published many articles and monographs on a variety of topics related to community education. She was responsible for a contract that was part of the United States Office of Education Commissioner's Initiative on Home-School-Community, which was designed to identify the agencies within the Department of Education that had the potential for linkage with community education, and to develop a plan for those linkages. She also served as liaison between the National Teacher Corps and the Department of Education Community Education Program. She was responsible for developing the U.S. Department of Education's first intra-agency agreement, which has since served as a model for other agreements.

Dr. Schoeny was editor-in-chief of the prototype issue of the **Community Education Journal** and has served as a consultant to the National Community Education Association on various other projects, and to the Department of Education Community Education Program and Teacher Corps. She was director of community education at the State University of New York at Potsdam; evaluator of special education projects at the University of Virginia; a Mott Fellow at the University of Virginia (1978-79); and a teacher, librarian, a school board member, and community education coordinator.